All in a Lifetime
An Autobiography

by
Inez Marks Lowdermilk

Recently a video tape entitled "An American Prophet" on the lives of Walter C. and Inez M. Lowdermilk is in process of completion, and will be available to TV and the public by the Lowdermilk Trust.

This edition of <u>All in a Lifetime</u> has been published for the Lowdermilk Trust by Westher Lowdermilk Hess as a gift to her mother, Inez Marks Lowdermilk, for her 95th birthday.

ISBN 0-9617461-1-4

Published by
The Lowdermilk Trust
Adaire Harris, Winifred Lowdermilk Hess, and
Mary Rose Black Ryan

DEDICATED TO YOUNG PEOPLE

IN APPRECIATION

"My cup runneth over" with gratitude for the wonderful life I have had and the 52 happy, active years I shared with my beloved husband. Special thanks go to Mary Rose Black Ryan who convinced and assisted me to put my memories down on paper; to my granddaughter Alison Hess for bringing these pages to completion; to my daughter Westher Hess for her tireless work coordinating the manuscript and to my friend June Elliot Brott who shared her literary talent. All those who have volunteered time and energy in typing the manuscript have my appreciation and a special thank you.

ELEVENTH COMMANDMENT

THOU SHALT INHERIT THY HOLY EARTH AS A FAITHFUL STEWARD, CONSERVING ITS RESOURCES AND PRODUCTIVITY FROM GENERATION TO GENERATION. THOU SHALT SAFEGUARD THY FIELDS FROM SOIL EROSION, THY LIVING WATERS FROM DRYING UP, THY FORESTS FROM DESOLATION AND PROTECT THE HILLS FROM OVERGRAZING BY THY HERDS, THAT THY DESCENDANTS MAY HAVE ABUNDANCE FOREVER. IF ANY SHALL FAIL IN THIS GOOD STEWARDSHIP OF THE EARTH, THY FRUITFUL FIELDS SHALL BECOME STERILE, STONY GROUND OR WASTING GULLIES, AND THY DESCENDANTS SHALL DECREASE AND LIVE IN POVERTY OR PERISH FROM OFF THE FACE OF THE EARTH.

WALTER C. LOWDERMILK

TABLE OF CONTENTS

TABLE OF CONTENTS

(continued)

PROLOGUE
1890 - 1985
THE WAY IT WAS AND IS

January 26, 1984 marked ninety-five years of living on this planet. I picked up a tiny computer lying on the table, pressed a few buttons, and was informed that my heart had beaten more than three billion times since I entered this world. I felt to see whether my pulse was weak and tired. Its beat was still strong and regular--as are my memories.

I sat down in a comfortable chair before my picture windows which look out on the Golden Gate Bridge and the San Francisco Bay from the Berkeley Hills, and allowed myself the luxury of reminiscing. I came to the conclusion that I have lived in the most remarkable period of history, that the technical advancement and the social changes during my lifetime exceed all those periods that went before.

Toward the end of the last century, my family drove by horse and wagon from southern California to the new State of Washington. There was not a mile of paved road anywhere. We covered thirty to thirty-five miles a day, putting up a tent each night. Recently, I made the same trip by automobile in less than three days on paved freeways and slept in deluxe motels. By plane the trip is less than three hours.

I remember the first automobiles and the great excitement they caused. They were so noisy we could hear one for some distance, so I had time to run down to the corner to watch it "whiz" by in a cloud of dust at ten miles an hour. My father got out of our buggy each time a horseless carriage was about to overtake us to hold the terrified horse's head until the noisy monster passed by. Later, when cars went fifteen miles per hour, my father said that was as fast as any human being should travel. Now we travel at fifty-five miles an hour with ease--and faster when the law allows--on marvelous highways.

As a child, one of my jobs was to fill the oil lamps in our house and clean their glass chimneys. Now I just press a button for electric light. Another daily childhood chore was to keep the woodbox filled for Mother's cooking stove and also for the potbellied stove we used to heat a room or two. Today I just touch the thermostat for central heating and press buttons for electric cooking.

Our first telephone was an amazing innovation, and our first radio was a marvel. I could not imagine how words and music could come through the air, through our walls and into our living room. I remember how our first record player had to be cranked by hand to make the music come out the large metal horn--powered by "elbow grease." Now we have not only radio and television, but are served by space satellites circling above us, transmitting moving pictures in full color.

In 1932 when my mother was 72, I gave her a special birthday present--a flight over the San Francisco Bay area in a Ford tri-motor. In the 1950s we sat on the roof deck of our house in the southern California desert and were thrilled to watch the first satellite, "Sputnik," tumble over and over across the sky. Later, in the 1970s, we watched men walk on the moon and actually heard their voices talking to each other and to us back on this earth! From horse and buggies to automobiles, to airplanes, to flights to the moon and beyond--what startling progress!

But in my opinion the most significant happening of all, one which affects more than half the world's population, is the changing position of women. In my youth there was an absolute double standard for men and women in morals, in work, in pay and in privileges, even in a progressive country as is the United States. Today most countries give women the franchise. I was thirty years old when American women were granted the vote, but in those days it was undreamed of in countries such as China where women were traditionally crippled by foot-binding and illiteracy.

In many countries women were treated like cattle-- purchasable, productive beasts of burden. They had virtually no medical care for themselves and their children, and were denied schooling. When I was a young girl, I remember a returned missionary telling our church congregation how the first schools for girls in Japan were ridiculed. When I was in West China, I suggested to a man that he send his daughter to school. His answer reflected the same sentiment. He said, "Why, the idea! You couldn't anymore teach my daughter to read than you could teach my cow."

When politics sent the western nations' guns to open the doors of various countries to trade, American women learned of tragic living conditions of women in those countries and desired to help them toward a better life. They could do so only through their churches, practically all of which had women's missionary societies. The Home Missionary Society worked locally for the poor, sick and handicapped, and the Foreign Missionary Society sent workers abroad to build hospitals, schools, universities and churches.

After centuries of suffering under the masculine conspiracy against them, the rise of women and girls to a freedom then undreamed of has been phenomenal. There is a force mightier than that of a marching army; it is the force of a great idea when its time has come to move. Women have indeed moved and continue to strive forward in the face of all challenges.

Note: In this book the spelling of foreign phrases and proper names is sometimes from memories of sixty and more years ago. In many cases the accepted spelling has been changed; in others, there are several recognized spellings differing between time periods and regions. I have picked those in use at the times and places of my story.

Yet my own life has shown me that, even with all the rewards of the new liberties for women, some of the greatest satisfactions can still be found through family loyalty and prayer. I hope these are not sacrificed for the new freedoms. While I pride myself on keeping up with the times, I frankly attribute the important decisions of my life to my faith in God, the divine guidance I received through prayer, and my faith in my husband, whose life became mine.

CHAPTER 1
FACING INTO THE WIND

The wind was brisk, the Pacific was steel blue, and a cool mist grazed the surface as our ship pushed into open sea west of Vancouver. The curve of the earth had long since hidden the North American continent from view. It was 1916 and I was 26--leaving my youth, my family and friends and my country to work for the next five years, perhaps forever, among a foreign people in a strange land. It sounded like the uttermost part of the world--interior West China. But thoughts of that were hidden behind the excitement of my first liner trip across a boundless ocean.

In those days, dining aboard ocean liners was a social event, and I had bought a new long evening dress especially for the formal dinners on the voyage. It would be like a party every evening. My hopes were in vain. Shortly after we reached the high seas, a frightening November storm arose near the Aleutian Islands. The tossing of the ship made me desperately seasick. My gown swung unworn in the tiny closet.

Lying inert in my berth, I could hear through the walls the little boy in the next cabin crying over and over, "Please, Mommy, make the captain stop the ship!" Oh, how I wished he could.

My cabinmates were a nurse and a teacher, also going to China. We were all in our twenties and looking forward to the excitement of the voyage. They adjusted to the ship's rocking and plunging and, except for occasionally coming to see that I was all right (which I never was), they left me quite alone.

To cover my disappointment at not being able to enjoy the voyage with the others, I forced my attention away from my misery by singing hymns or reciting to myself some of the long poems we were required to memorize in those days, such as "The Vision of Sir Launfal." I knew many hymns, and the poems had many lines, but they couldn't fill all the lonely hours.

I fell to reflecting on the years of my growing up. The more I thought of them the more I realized that everything about my background and training had steered me toward China. Nothing could have induced me not to go.

Some of my determination, I'm sure, was inherited. Both sides of my family were pioneer stock who came across the Great Plains and over the Oregon Trail. My paternal grand-father, Alexander Kesterson Mark, and his family settled in the Willamette Valley and donated land for one of Oregon's earliest schoolhouses. My mother's parents settled in West Union, about fifteen miles from where Portland is today. My mother's father, Henry Victor, helped build the first Baptist church west of the Mississippi. Today, both buildings are Oregon State Monuments.

Grandmother Victor died young and my mother, at age twelve, shouldered the responsibility for her three younger sisters and a brother. May cooked, washed, mended, and made beds in a crowded lean-to--just a roof of sod attached to a cave dug into the side of a hill--until the family could build a cabin on the homestead they had taken up in eastern Oregon. She gave such devotion and training to the little ones that all four became educated and she herself went to Normal school and became a teacher.

When Mother heard a returned missionary speak of the sad conditions of women in West Africa, she longed to help them. But 100 years ago it was virtually impossible for a pioneer woman to leave her family. So, when her siblings were old enough to manage the home and a promising young minister, William Henry Marks, proposed, she accepted this as her opportunity to do the Lord's work, and they were married.

I was the third of three children and a "P.K."--a preacher's kid--born in a Methodist parsonage in Oregon in 1890. My sisters were Winifred, six years older than I, and Beatrice, two years older. Being a P.K. meant that I went to Sunday School, church, and any other meeting day or night where Mother was expected to be, from the age of six weeks. I was well adjusted to sleeping on church pews, but for some reason became a far from well-behaved child when awake.

Methodist ministers were often transferred, so we lived in a number of towns when we moved to California. First in San Fernando, when I was six months old, then in Burbank, and later in Highland, a beautiful little community surrounded by citrus groves in the foothills east of San Bernardino.

In Highland we had a two-story house for the first time, which made me very proud. When the presiding elder of the Methodist Conference was expected to call, the whole family was ready to receive him exactly at three o'clock. He and my father went into the parlor for their meeting. I wanted to be sure that the elder realized that Daddy was a man of importance and lived in a two-story house, so I loudly climbed the stairs and stomped around in the room over the parlor until the commanding voice of my father brought the demonstration to an end.

My father ruled his family as a Victorian autocrat. Meals had to on the table on time, punishments were immediate, and his authority in the family absolute. His own mother had died when he was an infant and his own childhood had not been happy. He had become a hardworking, ambitious, young minister, finishing seminary work after he had a family. He was tall for his time, capable, handsome and meticulous.

My father believed in the Biblical injunction, "Spare the rod and spoil the child," and he did not want a spoiled child. He once was so exasperated with my naughty ways that he said to my mother, "I do not think that Inez will ever amount to a hill of beans."

But Mother's faith was a thing of wonder. Others might say her youngest was impossible, but to her, prayer could accomplish all things. She was petite--dainty and gentle--and never raised her voice nor punished any of us. Still, I remember the times she knelt with me, beside my bed, to help me tell the Heavenly Father I was sorry for what I had done and ask Him to help me not to do wrong again.

Aside from our rag dolls, my sisters and I had no toys. We were expected to use our own ingenuity to entertain ourselves. We invented games--like going from London to Paris (across our irrigation ditch) to buy new hats, which we made from pumpkin leaves and wild flowers. Pretense was fun for a while, but when I was bored I was naughty. My sisters had milder dispositions than I, and even after they became teenagers they were often my victims. I teased them constantly and pestered their boyfriends until they bribed me with nickels to make me stay away.

Nevertheless, I adored Beatrice and was especially devoted to Winifred in those early years. She was beautiful but frail and subject to frequent illness. She found it difficult to withstand a rigorous youth and life, so she devoted her life to our family. She was six years older than I and spent many hours teaching me.

We lived for a time in Arroyo Grande, an unprepossessing town, but one whose surroundings had royal beauty in the springtime when the wildflowers bloomed along the roadsides and carpeted the hills. As little girls we ran with our friends delightedly collecting them. We also enjoyed frequent trips to Pismo Beach on the Ocean to fill our gunny sacks with clams for our chickens to eat. We thought clams were limitless then, and the beaches and skies of the Pacific were open and clean.

Paso Robles, an agricultural center named for the magnificent oaks which dotted the broad valley, became our next home. Here we acquired our remarkable dog, Scotch, who became my devoted friend for years to come. Father often complained, "I wish Inez would mind as well as the dog. Scotch never has to be corrected twice for the same thing!"

Scotch always joined us in the regular few minutes of family devotion after breakfast. Mother would sing a hymn and Scotch would walk to his place in the corner and lie down. One day a neighbor gave Winifred an adorable miniature white poodle, Fuzzy. It soon became evident that Fuzzy had never been exposed to religion, for when we all dropped to our knees for my father's prayer, she ran from one person to another whimpering to be taken up into somebody's arms. Scotch could not stand this irreverent performance. He stalked over and deliberately bit her, then retired to his corner and lay down. His discipline of Fuzzy turned the family prayers into a few minutes of mirth. Even my father could not fully suppress his amusement.

The saloon was a force to be reckoned with in every town and city in America. Parents constantly warned their daughters of the drunken men commonly seen in the street. Nevertheless, most of the social and religious life of the community revolved around the church.

The church was an important source of education and character building. Besides inspiration for the soul, it gave one a sense of responsibility toward family and fellow man. It fostered respect for the written word and love of scholarship. Ideally, the church congregation was like an extended family, and this closeness was a constant challenge for people to relate to each other in a personal, creative way.

One of the nice things that people did to supplement the low salary of their minister and family was called a "pound social." Church members would organize a party to which each brought a pound or more of beans, sugar, flour, or maybe a chicken, fruit or vegetables--whatever they could contribute. We also were accustomed to wearing second-hand clothing, because these came from the "barrel" of things collected in city churches for the families of clergy in small towns.

My father had some homestead farmland in eastern Washington he wished to sell. So, in 1897, we made the entire 1600-mile trip from Paso Robles north by wagon and two horses on dirt roads, putting up a tent each night. At many places virgin timber grew down to the seashore. The rivers were wild and free. It was not unusual in the evenings to see deer or elk come down to the streams or coyote or fox come cautiously near our camp in the moonlight.

I remember the remains of the '49 Gold Rush that we saw along the way north--piles of rock debris from the river dredgings, rusting mine implements, deserted shacks and lonely gravestones. It was a long distance between towns, but we encountered people who were friendly and generous. For instance, one evening on the Klamath River in Oregon, my father was trying unsuccessfully to catch a salmon. A man watching him walked over to his traps, picked out a big salmon and made us a present of it. I'll always remember these kindnesses to strangers and, later in life, tried to return them.

We journeyed about thirty miles a day and rested on Sundays, when Mother would hunt up a church in which to worship. I never heard her complain of the hardship of the trip, though it took over ten weeks to reach our destination.

My father became ill with nervous exhaustion shortly after we returned to California. Although Mother tried to shield him from stress in every way she could, he was unable to continue the ministry. He bought a run-down orange grove in Highland hoping it would support us and Highland became our home once more.

Despite the additional demands placed on her by family illness, Mother managed to continue her church work. She always found time to do kind and compassionate things for neighbors or even strangers. I can still hear her singing as she worked. If ever things seemed to be at odds, she simply began singing and the clear tones of her voice would calm us and bring order to the room.

We had almost no income, but Mother managed to see that we were clothed, fed and inspired. She taught us to be thankful and useful, to always put our best effort forward.

She also taught us the value of earning our own money and encouraged me at the age of nine to begin cutting fruit at a neighbor's apricot and peach drying plant. That first summer I earned $25, which I proudly presented to my father as was customary for children to do in those days.

At the turn of the century, a P.K. lived under certain handicaps. A preacher's child was supposed to be a bright and shining light, a good example to other children in the community. Somehow I was an outstanding failure in this respect. Soon after I entered school in Highland I became known as the leader of mischief. I could always think up naughty things to do. I recall once, when a Salvation Army unit came to town, I incited the other children to march around the school yard beating on tin pans and singing gospel songs at the top of our voices in imitation. Every few minutes we would kneel, and in deep, exaggerated tones I would call upon Brother or Sister So-and-So to lead in prayer. This was followed by loud Amens and Hallelujahs. The religious townfolk were outraged. We children were having a hilarious time and couldn't understand why the adults insisted that we stop.

In school I couldn't seem to stay out of trouble and, when I received an "F" in deportment, my father laid down the law: "Unless you bring home an 'excellent', Inez," he said, "you may not go to a party or have company come over. You will hurry home from school every day for a month, crawl under each orange tree with a gunny sack and pull up devil's grass." This enforced discipline had a sobering effect on me. My next report card showed "excellent" in everything. After that, I made sure my grades were kept above the point of my father's wrath.

But Father wasn't always stern. Sometimes he surprised us with unexpected understanding and even humor. On one April Fool's Day, our maiden lady principal glanced up at the school's belfry as she was returning from lunch. There, dangling and waving out of the windows she saw eight pairs of girl's legs, skirts pushed high up. I had talked seven other girls into the stunt. What a sight it must have been, even with our thick stockings! The principal cut a handful of tree switches, stomped upstairs in her floor-length skirts and broke one on each pair of legs. Father always said that I'd receive a whipping at home if I ever got one at school, but when I confessed this latest transgression, he just laughed.

After eighth grade at Highland I began traveling by horse-drawn streetcar to the high school in San Bernardino and was made captain of the girls' basketball team. I could play almost anything by ear on our piano, so my family decided I should study music. Alas, my training ended with the fourth lesson, because I preferred to play ragtime rather than scales, and then run off to play ball with the neighbor boys instead of practicing.

I have only two photographs of my childhood and I am glad there are no more, for my sisters' beauty made my lack of good looks more noticeable. Photos embarrassed me because they always made my freckles look like a bad case of smallpox. I was so skinny that when the boy craze swept over my soul, I wanted to wear two pairs of thick stockings to make my spindly legs appear rounder.

This boy-crazy period was a trial for my parents, for there had been Harrison, Homer, Willie, Lyle, Lloyd, Bob, Charlie and Fred. "Puppy love" was "nauseating," my father said. No wonder he thought it would be good for his health if we moved. He could sell the orange grove at a good profit in 1905 and we moved to Pasadena.

Pasadena was a beautiful town at the base of Mt. Wilson and not far from the fast-growing little city of Los Angeles. It was surrounded by citrus groves and more were being planted eastward toward San Bernardino for almost fifty miles.

I was anxious to be independent, and to help my family financially, so I dropped out of my third year of high school and went to work at Cawston's Ostrich Farm. The great popularity of the plumes in the fashions of the day made ostrich raising profitable. Many plumes had to be willowed, a process of adding length to each of the feathery barbs by tying on another in a series of tiny knots. My long nimble hands soon earned me the reputation as the fastest willower west of Chicago, and I made good pay.

At age seventeen I had my first real beau, George. He was from a rich family, but he had no desire to study and dropped out of school to drive an ice wagon. When summer ended he drove a meat wagon and, finally, a garbage wagon. My parents feared that this friendship was getting out of hand! So, one evening my father announced at dinner: "We are going to Arizona for a change of climate and to take up some government land."

CHAPTER 2
CHANGING DIRECTION

Yes, these were some of the memories that came flooding back to me as I lay in my bunk on the ship to China. Because I was young, curious and usually energetic, several times I put on my lovely new gown and attempted to go up on deck and enjoy the voyage with the others. It was no use. I was too sick to move. Ships had no stabilizers to stop the rolling motion then, and we had no Dramamine for travel sickness. I fell back into bed realizing I would just have to wait out the storm. My mind began to drift again, this time to Arizona, to the adventures I had had there, and to a thrilling meeting that changed my life.

Father had gone to Wilcox, Arizona, ahead of the family in 1910 to find 160 acres of government land to homestead. Since Winifred was over 21, she, too, was able to file a land claim. Father wrote that he was able to purchase a "relinquishment" for her. "This is a piece that someone else gave up. It already has a cabin on it, so she can 'prove up' and get ownership quickly."

Winifred's cabin was in a lonely area, so when she had to stay there the required number of days to meet homestead requirements, I stayed with her. There were terrifying storms that season. One night we were sure her little wooden cabin would catch fire and burn to the ground. Lightning flashed all around us and the thunder which followed each

strike sounded like freight trains colliding. Winifred was
developing what were probably ulcers, and one night I was
awakened by her dry sobs of pain.

With the first ray of dawn I grabbed the nose bag of our
horse, Fanny, filled it with grain, and went out to the five-
acre corral to bring her in. Running here and there among
the mesquite clumps, sobbing and praying, I tried to locate
Fanny without success. Again I made the circuit, mindless of
the danger.

Rattlesnakes had been the previous lords of our land.
Sometimes we found them curled up on our doorstep or in our
kitchen garden, nearly invisible until one got too close. We
tried to keep always on the alert to see one sticking out its
tongue at us or rattling a warning by shaking its tail. But this
night I didn't care.

As it became lighter, I finally saw Fanny hiding in a big
clump of bushes down in the far corner. This time I caught
her and hurriedly harnessed her to our buggy, then drove
Winifred across the prairie to our house. Mother was already
up praying. She told us she had had a premonition we were in
trouble--She had seen Winifred's face etched with pain in her
mind's eye.

In the wide open spaces of Arizona I began to feel a great
sense of freedom. I was eighteen, maturing, and a long-
buried desire to do something worthwhile began to emerge.
The idea of doing good for its own sake was deeply ingrained
in the family tradition and I realized I had no goal in life. I
was suddenly and urgently aware of pressures to accomplish
something. This awakening may have been partly the
influence of a young man I met in the little white church in
Wilcox.

Walter Lowdermilk was staying with his parents in
Wilcox. He had been Student Body President of the University of Arizona and the first editor of its paper, The Wildcat.
A Rhodes Scholar, he was waiting to go to Oxford, England,
when the colleges were to open. He was twenty-two, intelligent, with the build of an athlete.

I was fascinated by his smile and the way laughter made wrinkles around his eyes. He would come and sit beside me during church service because, he said, he liked to hear me sing. Twice he followed our carriage home on horseback, had Sunday dinner with us and spent the afternoon at our ranch.

I looked up to Walter and probably put him on a pedestal. But I never dreamed that he really could be interested in me, a high school dropout. However, his energy and accomplishments fanned my own growing desire to make something of myself. I wondered, how could I ever measure up to this wonderful, gallant man? If I did have any romantic feelings for him then, I buried them deep and permitted myself only admiration for his achievements.

When my family returned to Pasadena, I was a very troubled young woman. Walter would be studying and working abroad for years, Beatrice was going into teaching, while I had no plan for myself at all. I was tormented by a sense of failure. One day I hid under our huge pepper tree, with its branches that swept the ground. I felt so wretched--confused and desperate--that I did as my parents had taught me: I asked God's help.

"I've made such a mess of my life, Lord," I earnestly prayed. "If only You will help me, I will do whatever and go wherever You wish. Please take and guide me." I listened with all my soul.

After a moment I felt suddenly a warm, soothing sense of peace. I knew then, for certain, that the Lord wanted me to prepare for some kind of service. I had only to find what that was to be.

I remembered the reports brought back by missionaries and travelers on the conditions in China. I had been appalled to hear that girls were given no schooling and that they were crippled from childhood by the cruel custom of footbinding. A passionate desire flooded through me to help the Chinese.

That day, under the pepper tree, I knew that I had to go to China. To work in China, I knew, would require extensive training and a college education. The challenge was exhilarating. I had a goal.

As soon as our minister's wife realized I was serious, she arranged a full scholarship for me at our Methodist Training School in Chicago. Our course emphasized social service work and trained us in connection with Jane Adams' famous Hull House near the stockyards. At the training school I volunteered for the tasks no one else wanted in order to prove to myself that I could do a job whether I liked it or not.

One Sunday evening I was scheduled to speak to a youth group at a small Methodist church there in the slums. City streets in 1910 were scarcely lighted, so I searched for the place in the darkness. There were only two lights, one in a building at the top of some steep stairs, and the other inside a saloon. No respectable woman ever entered a saloon, but where would the stairway lead? I was a scared, unsophisticated girl from a small town in the West. I found myself wishing I had not worn my best hat with its big white plume from Cawston's Ostrich Farm.

I pushed open the door of the saloon. Men sitting at the tables and standing at the bar immediately fastened leering eyes on me. With all the dignity and personality I could muster, I said in a clear voice, "I am to speak at a young people's meeting at the church in this area. Could you please tell me where it is?"

Their attitude changed at once, and they were helpful in directing me.

I returned to California with an inner strength that enabled me to secure scholarships and part-time jobs to get me through the University of Southern California, and to become president of my senior class and of the honor society, Torch and Tassel. I was far from a high school dropout now, and in 1916, with my B.A. and M.A. degrees, I sent in my application to the Methodist Board for Overseas Work. Before long a letter came from Bishop Lewis who was in charge of our church work in the Orient.

"My assignment to China has come!" I excitedly told my family. "They are sending me to Szechuan Province, way up by the border of Tibet. I'll be there for five years!"

We dashed to the atlas and found that Szechuan was truly the "uttermost part of the world." To reach it I would have to travel 1,500 miles up the Yangtze River to Chungking, then overland 250 miles by sedan chair to the Methodist headquarters at Chengtu, the capital. And I would have to learn Chinese, so I could open girls' schools southeast of there and help do away with the custom of footbinding.

Our Pasadena church congregation sent me off to China with their best wishes, prayers and love-gifts. My mother's expression of pride in me for fulfilling her own dream of serving overseas was the last thing I saw as my train pulled away from the Los Angeles depot taking me to Vancouver and the ship to China. How I looked forward to meeting my travel companions and Bishop Lewis, head of our overseas work in Asia, who was to escort us to our assignments in China!

In Vancouver we met the Bishop. He was a big, hearty man who helped us as we boarded the S.S. Empress of Asia for Shanghai for what we hoped would be a happy congenial voyage across the Pacific.

Now, after eighteen days of ghastly rough weather, I could see the quiet waters of Japan's Inland Sea through the porthole. Though weak from lack of food, I suddenly felt over my seasickness. I anxiously dressed and went to join the others going ashore for a tour. We had scarcely docked when thousands of Japanese laborers scrambled like ants up the sides of the big ship carrying baskets of coal to refuel the ship's engines. It was my introduction to the almost overwhelming masses of people in the Orient. Ashore, the beauty of Japan surpassed my imagination--the kimono-clad women, the children plump in their padded winter garments, the temples and pagodas, the mountain peaks.

Once more aboard ship, we enjoyed a calm sea and I was able to be on deck. Seventy-five miles from the China coast, we were met by a golden streak in the water, a pathway which we followed all the way to Shanghai--silt from the lands of interior China being carried out to sea by the great Yangtze River.

Our ship prepared to dock and Bishop Lewis herded our group together amidst the confusion of unloading luggage, last-minute farewells or greetings to anxious friends waving their welcomes onshore. China at last--my home for the next five years! We got into rickshaws and the coolies took us to our Mission Board hostel at a running trot. The wonderful sights, sounds and smells of China rushed in upon us. The noises of a Chinese commercial port--ducks cackling, roosters crowing, coolies shouting, horns blowing, high-pitched music coming from the windows--mingled in an unforgettable cacaphony. Laundry hanging along the streets and from balconies deadened none of the sound.

The many Western-style buildings and signs in English on business houses showed obvious attempts to cater to the foreigners. In front of one furrier shop, gold letters proclaimed: "Fur coats made out of your skin and ours." A tailoring shop had the sign: "Ladies' dressmaking establishment. Respectable ladies have fits upstairs." And at a railway junction I saw: "Leave your luggage with us; we will send it in all directions."

This made us chuckle, but Bishop Lewis said, "Just think of how the Chinese must be laughing at the ridiculous mistakes made by foreigners trying to speak Chinese!"

After a few days we boarded a large Yangtze steamer which took us through the delta and on through some hilly country to the city of Hankow. Here our boat anchored offshore, and a sampan transferred us to a smaller, less comfortable river steamer headed for Ichang, gateway to the Yangtze Gorges. This section of the river had always been navigated by junks. When going upstream, these were hauled forward by men who strained on ropes made of stiff bamboo fibers as they made their way along the dangerous, shelf-like paths cut into the cliffs high above the water line.

Bishop Lewis had arranged for us to be the first Americans to use a new steamboat introduced on the upper river. We would make the trip up to Chungking with special coal-burning engines made for forging against the strong current and mounting the dangerous rapids of the gorges. But when we arrived at Ichang, we learned to our dismay that Mr. Brant, the American captain, refused to make the trip because the river level was so low. He said he would not risk trying to navigate among the treacherous boulders. Our only alternative would be weeks of cold discomfort aboard a junk. Resigned to this disappointment, Bishop Lewis began making arrangements for a habitable junk to be readied quickly so we could be on our way, and he even paid a big deposit.

In spite of these preparations, I kept telling Bishop Lewis, "I have a feeling in my bones that we will definitely go by steamer." The same kind of premonition Mother had when Winifred was ill in Wilcox.

Then, just as we were ready to leave by junk, the water rose suddenly from heavy overnight rains upstream and Captain Brant changed his mind. He agreed to make one last trip of the season up to Chungking. As we all stood at the steamer's railing, Bishop Lewis said with his broad smile, "Inez Marks, henceforth I shall make no more travel plans without first consulting your bones!"

Soon our boat lay low in the water, crowded with passengers and heavily loaded with the merchandise and satchels of silver dollars belonging to those returning upriver after selling their goods in Shanghai. With a great deal of shouting, bells ringing and whistles blowing, the captain steered us on our way.

Oh, those fascinating gorges of the upper Yangtze, where the wild water rushes between towering cliffs! As our steamer climbed the rushing rapids between huge, rounded boulders, I watched Captain Brant running back and forth on deck, swearing and yelling orders to the crew. Perspiration ran down his face despite the cold. Flames leaped high above the funnels as the engines were forced to their utmost. We feared a boiler would burst!

At one section of the river the current was so strong that our boat actually hung on one spot for several minutes without moving. If ever we were to lose and be broadside to the current, we would be dashed against the rocks and capsize. It seemed an eternity. Then, almost imperceptibly at first, it began to creep forward, climbing between the great rocks. Leaving the rushing channel behind us, we steered into a cove and stopped to let the engines cool and to permit the captain, the crew, and the passengers to recover from the terrific strain.

The Chungking Gorge is so deep and narrow that one must almost lie down to see the slim line of sky between the walls overhead. As we reached the confluence of the Jialing River and the Yangtze, the canyon widened, and we could see the buildings of Chungking climbing the mountain between the two waters. The only way to reach the city was by an ancient, steep mossy stone flight of perhaps a thousand stairs, which zigzagged up the face of the cliff.

We were met at the water's edge by a delegation of Methodist workers who brought with them a fleet of light-weight, open bamboo sedan chairs hung between long bamboo poles and carried by coolies. To walk up a wet, muddy staircase would be frightening enough; to be carried up was worse. Bishop Lewis took it all with good humor, as four strong coolies made his big bulk sail upward; but my heart was in my throat as my chair was lifted by two coolies and tilted back at a terrifying angle. The ascent was so steep that the rear carrier of my sedan chair was about ten feet lower than the man in front. Every moment I feared that my men would slip, sending me and my chair down into the muddy, rushing Yangtze. We constantly had to dodge the stairway traffic--dozens of water carriers who, with buckets dangling from poles, provided the entire water supply for the city of Chungking. When we reached the top of the stairs, we entered a city filled with noisy crowds, bustling markets, colorful banners and jostling sedan chairs.

We spent Christmas, 1916, in the warm and jolly atmosphere of the big Chungking Methodist compound with its church, schools and hospital. There was no snow, but the region was under a cloud bank the whole winter season, so neither sun nor moon could be seen.

After three days in Chungking we set out overland in a caravan of comfortable enclosed sedan chairs on the ten-day, 250-mile journey to Chengtu. The only roads were four or five feet wide, made of large stone slabs laid on the partitions between the rice fields. Coolies transported our food, baggage, and trunks slung from bamboo poles. The periodic "rest stops" were often in places where there was no privacy, and so a potty was carried in each sedan chair. Human functions were accepted as a normal part of life.

The countryside was breathtakingly beautiful. Mirror-like, flooded rice terraces reached from the valley floors to the hilltops. Picturesque farmhouses were surrounded by well-tended vegetable gardens and tall, waving bamboo plumes. "Bamboo must be heaven's gift to China," I thought, for as we passed the farms we could see that it supplied countless needs: material for building houses, roofs, and boats; windbreaks for the fields; household utensils, pipes and tools, all at no cost.

We stopped to eat and sleep at Chinese inns along the way. They were grimy, with rooms opening on a central courtyard. Beds were made of rope crisscrossed on a wooden frame covered by thin padding. But we welcomed them. The food was hot and either pickled or freshly cooked.

I soon became attuned to the rhythm of the sedan chair and was thrilled to be traveling on the same time-worn stones that Marco Polo used centuries earlier on his famous expedition from Persia to Peking. But there were some tense moments when my chair bearers hugged the edge of the path to allow a water buffalo or another sedan chair to pass going in the opposite direction.

After five days' travel we reached the city of Tzechow and the large Methodist teachers' training school. The director had told her cook to make his best cake in honor of the Bishop and his party. At dessert time, a beautiful white cake was brought in, with a pink scroll around the edge in frosting. In the center, carefully copied from a foreign advertising poster, was written, "Pink Pills for Pale People."

Next morning we were underway again. Mr. McCurdy, a local American Methodist, conducted our party over the next portion of the trip. We learned that, since the 1911 revolution which toppled the Manchu Dynasty, China was far from peaceful. Dr. Sun Yat-sen, father of the revolution, wanted to establish a democracy, but he had no national army to keep order. The provincial governors, the "war lords", were fighting among themselves for power. Szechuan Province was known for its agricultural richness and therefore was coveted. A governor who ruled it for even a short time could acquire great wealth in loot and taxes, which he sometimes forced the inhabitants to pay several years in advance.

During this period the penniless soldiers of defeated generals often went off with their guns and ammunition and became bandits. Once, along our way, Mr. McCurdy called our attention to a spot where he and a colleague, Mr. Rapé, had heard bullets fly as they were returning from a conference.

"We dived behind a rice field embankment to avoid stopping one of those bullets," he told us. "The bandits rushed at us, shooting as they came. They were surprised to learn that their intended victims were American educators from the Chungking schools and they promptly apologized and offered us a bargain: If we would pay for the bullets 'wasted' on us, they would let us go on our way in safety. So Mr. Rapé and I gladly paid the $4.85 set as the value and they let us go."

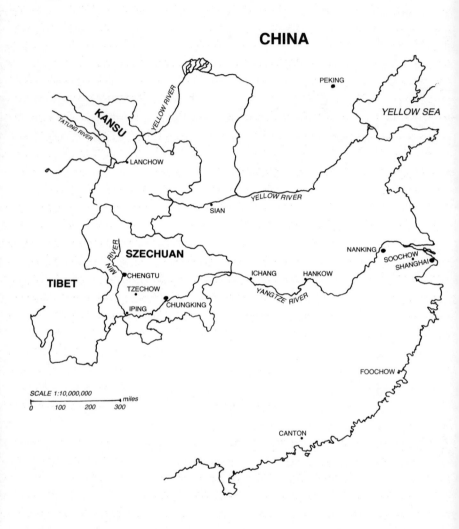

CHAPTER 3
MY NEW HOME IN SZECHUAN (1916-21)

Another five days and we reached our destination, Chengtu. It was a city on a rich agricultural plain surrounded in the distance by high mountains. The low-slung roofs of the farm houses gave off a golden hue of the rice thatch from which they were made, and a mist hung in the air. As we approached the city across the rice paddies we could see the handsome American-supported Union University for men outside the walls, built with the cooperation of the various Protestant denominations working there. Inside the walls were the hospital, administrative headquarters and primary schools for boys and for girls run by the Methodists. There was also a women's compound whose substantial residence and school buildings exceeded all my expectations.

While the girls' newer high school was built of brick, the staff residence had been built of temple wood years before under the personal supervision of the beloved old-timer still in charge, Miss Collier. It provided a private study and bedroom with balcony for each staff member. Miss Collier herself showed me to my room and watched my face glow with pleasure as I walked through the balcony doors and discovered that they opened upon a panorama of six glaciers in the distance in the Tibetan Mountains!

My language studies started almost at once, but I still had time left over. Full of energy and anxious to make myself useful, I urged the others to give me some special task. After meaningful glances among themselves, they assigned me the job of finding out how water was getting into our milk so that we had almost no cream. For one with two brand-new college degrees this seemed a humiliating assignment, but I swallowed my pride. "You can be sure you will have your cream for breakfast tomorrow morning," I told them confidently.

At that time people of interior China knew nothing of germs. The Chinese believed that diseases were caused by devils. Miss Collier required the farmer who tended a Jersey cow for us to drive it into our city compound each afternoon. There, we could provide sanitary utensils, supervise the milking process and pasteurize the milk in our own kitchen. I watched every move the farmer made when he milked, but, to my great chagrin, there was still no cream on the milk next morning. This went on for several days and I was rapidly losing face. My college education had not prepared me for this contest with a Chinese milkman.

Finally one evening, as I watched him milking the cow with the sun behind him, I saw the glistening of water coming from his hand with the stream of milk. I dashed into Miss Collier's study and told her. She came into the courtyard and made the farmer take off his padded coat. There, fastened under his upper arm, hung a bag of water with a small bamboo tube attached. Each time he stripped down the milk, his arm pressed the water bag, and some ran down the tube onto his arm and into the milk! Once the fraud was discovered, we again had cream for coffee and rich milk for our cereal.

About this time, amazingly, a letter arrived from my mother addressed simply to "Miss Inez Marks, West China." Mother had forgotten to put on the full address, but it had actually reached me in that vast country! From the postmarks I could figure out what had happened. The Pasadena post office had sent it to Chinatown, San Francisco. There it had been put in a pouch for Shanghai, where it was delivered to the U.S. Consulate. They must have kept a list of Americans in the country, for the letter was sent up the Yangtze by steamer the thousand miles to Ichang, then by junk for several weeks through the Gorges, then carried overland the ten-day 250-mile journey up to Chengtu, and delivered to our gate!

The days rushed by. I studied Chinese from 9 a.m. to noon and from 2 until 4 in the afternoon with a dear old Chinese teacher. Over the usual Chinese dark trousers he wore a black vest topped by a long brown outer robe. He had the status of a classical scholar in Chinese society and his dignified manner demanded respect. Upon his arrival, we would bow to each other before we entered the study to begin my lessons.

At first we had not one word in common, but soon he had me listening carefully to his pronunciation, then repeating the words and phrases after him until I had them correct. If I made a mistake he would shake his head and say them again for me. He demonstrated how to mix the ink, then had me work with the brush over and over until my Chinese characters were readable. Calligraphy to the Chinese is more than skill. It is an art.

Promptly at four my teacher left and I began the practical aspect of learning the language. Waiting at the compound gate I usually would find my <u>dong sih ren</u> (things man) with his bundle of things to sell, and it was necessary to converse with him entirely in Chinese. The things man was a plain, jolly, plump middle-aged man wearing the commoner's blue cotton pants with a coarsely woven outer robe of dark grey, and a dark blue skull cap. He shared himself as well as his wares, giving me all the time I needed to practice my Chinese on him.

"<u>Nee hau bu hau</u>?" was the common greeting (Are you good, not good?).

"<u>Hau</u> (good)," was the usual answer.

I always invited him into my study where he would spread out on the floor items being sold by some of the defeated Manchu officials who now had no jobs or money since the overthrow of their dynasty.

"<u>Jai go do shao chan</u>?" I would ask. "How much is this?"

"<u>E kawi chan</u>," (a dollar) he might answer.

His offerings included beautiful strings of amber beads, carved ivory beads and beads or pendants of jade. There were choice old dishes and carved ivory figurines. He also laid before me the richly embroidered sleevebands from Manchu gowns and the colorful "Manchu squares" which adorned the front and back of the gowns, indicating civil or military rank. Women wore the insignia, usually an animal, depicting the ranks of their husbands. Sometimes there were handsome brocade and embroidered garments still intact, like new. The needlework was exquisitely done.

All these were being sold at a fraction of their original cost, so that even on my small salary I could collect them. I decorated my study with such treasures, but most of the purchases were sent home to my sister, Winifred, who sold them for me to eager buyers in Pasadena.

"Inez," Winifred wrote me, "by the time you return I will have been able to pay off your entire college debt of $800 with eight percent interest, and have some money left over for you."

Outside study hours I had lots of fun with the Chinese school girls. They knew a few English words and I was fast learning Chinese.

Every Chinese word is monosyllabic and each word, like ma, chee, fen, and ee, may have several different meanings according to the tone in which it is uttered. In West China we generally used four tones: a high tone, a rising tone, an explosive tone dropping at the end, and a steady, low tone. Our Western ears are not adapted to these slight variations, and as a result we make many ridiculous mistakes.

I passed my examination of a thousand characters for reading and three hundred for writing, and became quite proficient in everyday conversation. I memorized some of the sayings of Confucius and Mencius, Chinese proverbs and Bible verses in Chinese. The school girls enjoyed teaching me Chinese slang which I often used without realizing what I was saying.

In China the family name comes first, so I was "Marks Miss." But the closest they could come to Marks was "Ma" and I learned to my amusement that this meant "Miss Horse" in Chinese.

Eager to increase my vocabulary, I carried with me a notebook and pencil and continually asked, "What is this?" In the kitchen I picked up an empty oatmeal can and asked the cook what it was.

"It's all gone," he replied in Chinese, and for weeks I told him to give us "it's all gone" for breakfast. I pointed to the tea kettle and asked "What is this?"

"It's leaky," the cook replied. Henceforth I called the tea kettle "leaky." Later, when I chided the cook for not correcting my mistakes, he answered, "Oh, that was all right with me. I knew what you meant to say."

Chee dza may mean wife or flag or chicken, depending upon tone. One of our American friends traveling by houseboat through a bandit-infested region saw a group of armed men ahead on the riverbank and called to the captain.

"Quick! Get my American flag and hang it on the mast," but what he really said was, "Quick! Get my American wife and hang her on the mast!" The Chinese understood his intent.

After I had been studying the language for six months, one of the high school girls asked if I would like to go shopping with her. "Wait while I put powder on my nose," I meant to reply. The youngster's eyes danced and she looked as though she would explode with laughter.

I had used the wrong tone and had actually said, "Wait while I put fertilizer on my nose." Fertilizer was human waste that had "ripened" in pits before being used on the fields. No wonder she laughed.

Learning their language brought me closer to the Chinese people and they responded to my efforts with the kindness and good humor that was already beginning to endear them to me.

The language study was sometimes interrupted by war. Three months after my arrival a battle took place inside the city walls between the forces of two rival generals. The Chengtu city gates were closed and for five days we lived in the basement of our brick high school while the tops of our buildings were shot full of holes.

Sitting in a basement, with so much excitement going on outside, was the last thing I wanted to do. I would sneak up the three flights to the top floor and look out the dormer windows. Once when I was leaning out counting the fires in the city, machine gun bullets ripped across the tile roof just over my head with a frightening clatter and I dashed back down to the basement three stairs at a time. But faith and curiosity did not let me tremble in the basement. Before long I was back up again watching the battle.

One general had his men burn an exit through the city from his headquarters in the former Manchu palace to each of the four city gates so as to make a quick escape if necessary. Our compound was in a direct line with the south gate and a strong wind was blowing in our direction. Smoke soon enveloped us and it looked as though our wooden buildings would be burned. We were all praying that Shang Ti (The Heaven Father) would spare them when, just as the flames reached our compound wall a change of wind sent the fire off in another direction. The Chinese said that we foreigners were "a people with a great god." They did not say we were "a great people with a god," as we often assume.

Since the city gates were closed, the Americans outside were afraid we had run out of food. Early one morning a fearless young professor had himself hauled up the fifty-foot city wall in a bamboo basket and managed to contact both warring generals. He persuaded them to stop fighting at noon for one hour and to open the south gate so that the five of us American women with our seventy-five school girls could leave. We walked unmolested down the battle-scarred street and outside the city walls to the university. The huge gate clanged shut behind us and the fighting resumed.

The Union University gave us shelter in a partly constructed brick building on the campus, but that night we lay sleepless on the floor while bullets popped like fire-crackers against our outside wall because the fighting had spread. The numerous antiquated cannons on the city wall roared continually, sending out great sheets of flame. Our hearts ached for the crowded city folk inside the walls, for their unprotected homes were burning and they had no place to which they could flee.

Other wars followed, but between them life went on as usual and my daily lessons in Chinese resumed. When I was able to speak the simple language of children, I organized street children into a Sunday school which met in the court-yard of our compound. The little waifs were delighted to be taught songs and to sit on the red benches borrowed from our classrooms. In the streets I soon became known as the "Red Bench Lady."

Then from my teacher I learned that some four hundred years earlier in West China there lived a famous woman named Ch'in Liang-yü who had had a career similar to that of Joan of Arc. It thrilled me to encounter such a woman in history, and I began to ask Chinese scholars about her. Everyone I asked had heard of her military exploits, around which a legend had grown, but no one knew her life story. I now had a new project for myself.

Our home was not far from the Provincial Library where the old official records were kept. When I was too busy to study with my teacher, I sent him there to write down everything he could find about the life of Ch'in Liang-yü. Next time we studied together, he would read me a paragraph about her and have me repeat it back to him until I had it correct in Chinese. Then I wrote it down in English. Her story inspired me. She rose from humble origins to become a valiant commander of an army which under her extraordinary leadership and military genius saved Szechuan from invasion many times. Unlike Joan of Arc, she lived to old age.

Later I heard that the Provincial Library was burned in a battle and I feel quite sure that my version of Ch'in Liang-Yü's story is the only one in existence taken completely from the original sources.

CHAPTER 4
SUMMER IN SZECHUAN PROVINCE

In winter a great cloud bank piled up against the Tibetan mountains. When it lifted, spring came on with a rush. Migrating birds began to appear and the young green leaves and bamboo plumes gave everything a fresh new look. Soon the children and the workers took on a slimmer look, for they were the first to discard the padded winter garments for lighter warm-weather wear. I noticed that many of the boarding school girls carried little trays on their books, on each of which was a green mulberry leaf. When I asked why, the girls pointed to tiny black spots wriggling on the leaves.

"These worms will eat the mulberry leaves," they explained, "and one day grow big enough to make silk."

Anxious to try raising some myself, I asked our cook to buy me three cents' worth. He soon returned with a mulberry leaf on which crawled my wriggly new family. I put it in a dish on my desk and commissioned Amah, the housemaid, to keep the worms fed with fresh leaves from the mulberry tree in our compound garden.

The worms ate day and night, and grew so fast that they soon required a larger nursery. I took pans from the kitchen, but shortly needed more pans, then trays, then all the flat receptacles I could beg or borrow. My study desk and floor were covered with silkworms.

Only by giving half my worm family out for adoption was I able to reach my desk again. The remaining worms continued to grow until they were two or three inches long. They were also changing color, the meaning of which I did not understand. That weekend I went to stay with friends at the university, not dreaming of the wrath which would descend on me from the other ladies in the home when I returned.

Saturday night the biological cycle suddenly compelled my hundreds of worms to stop eating and to crawl off in all directions to every conceivable place where they could take hold--into corners, curtain folds, shoes and dresses, closet interiors, bookcases, and undersides of chairs and window sills in all the bedrooms--and spin themselves into silk cocoons. My colleagues gave me an ultimatum: my cocoons had to go. It took me days and days to collect them and give them away. After that my desire to raise silkworms was gone.

Because the Chengtu summer was hot and sultry, we foreigners sought the cool of the mountains. My first summer several of us planned to stay in a new hostel on Bei Lu Din, a 6,000-foot mountain rising abruptly from the plain. It could only be reached on foot. Mrs. Pilcher, another first-year language student, and I were to hike up a day early with my book boy to see that all was in readiness. The next day her husband and Miss Murdock, the nurse, would arrive with the coolies carrying our loads of clothing, bedding, food and cooking utensils.

Mrs. Pilcher and I started the steep ascent near a temple. The long trail zigzagged upward, offering magnificent views of the valley below with its well-kept rice fields. On reaching the top after four hours, we were shocked to find that the new hostel was far from completed. Since every other place was filled to capacity, we were forced to sleep there on the bare floorboards. A storm came up, and we lay listening to the rain on the roof all night. The next morning it was still pouring, and the mountain trail was treacherous; but we hurried back down to save our companions from making the futile climb, practically sliding in the mud all the way. We reached the temple dripping wet. The priests were friendly;

they served tea and offered us their own wash pans and towels, which we accepted, grimy as they were.

We waited. Darkness came but no one arrived. The temple gong sounded and the thirty priests who lived there gathered for supper, which we were invited to share. Ravenous after our long hike, we ate the steaming hot rice and vegetables with relish, even though we had watched flies walk up and down the chopsticks and in and out of the bowls all afternoon.

"It is long past dark now," Mrs. Pilcher said. "Obviously our party won't arrive tonight."

There was no use trying to make conversation with our hosts; we had exhausted ourselves and our Chinese words long ago. The priests invited us to spend the night in the temple guest room and brought in an old grandmother to act as chaperone. She slept in the adjoining room, and there was a small opening in the wall between us. Our windowless room was off a side court which contained an open cesspool, and the odors coming through the cracks in our wall were unbearable. We drew the heavy bedcurtains aside, filling the room with dust. Without disrobing, we shrinkingly lay down upon the dirty grey linen, with mosquitoes flying about us, singing their hunger song as they prepared to strike. Creeping and jumping creatures in the bed were equally overjoyed by our arrival. The chaperone in the adjoining room chewed the local tobacco and periodically cleared her throat and expectorated with a splash against the other side of our wall.

In desperation I stepped out into the court and picked an armful of fragrant gardenias. We arranged them in wreaths around our faces, then we removed our underskirts and used them to cover our arms against the mosquitoes. Thus we lay the entire night, composing ditties about mosquitoes, bugs, odors, and temples, and doing a great deal of giggling. A sense of humor was an absolute essential for the foreign traveler in those days.

After two days at the temple, we were relieved to welcome Mr. Pilcher and Miss Murdock with their coolies. They had been detained by local fighting and washed-out bridges. It was the custom to give a present of "tea money" in return for a favor, so we gave a generous sum to our hosts and bade them goodbye. The priests had told us that rooms could be rented at Cave Mountain in the "Temple of Hell" a day's journey away. We hiked there and had our first experience of living with idols, each different, and filling the room by the dozens. The painted wooden idols glowered down at us from their pedestals with uplifted swords in hand. Every morning before daybreak the priests would ring bells and pound on gongs to awaken the idols so they would drive away the evil spirits of darkness and be ready for their day's work.

Our quarters, including kitchen and dining rooms, backed into a huge cave presided over by three enormous idols with long flowing beards and whiskers. Every strong breeze brought a shower of ancient dust down into our food. One day I climbed up onto the lap of one idol with water and a brush to give it a lesson in cleanliness. Soon a group of frantic Chinese crowded around, beseeching me to stop immediately, for the god would punish me severely for such sacrilege to his person. I assured them I was not afraid, but when a mob began to gather, discretion made me get down.

Whenever we went to the main gate, we passed a certain section called "Hell." All the wooden figures were life-size and dramatically illustrated punishments dealt out to sinners. One statue showed a man tearing out a woman's tongue, the punishment for a nagging wife. One showed a man with his hand being cut off. He was a thief. Another portrayed a piteous-looking woman being beaten for adultery. Still another figure showed a young man being roasted over a fire because he had disobeyed his father. And so they went, through the long list of human transgressions.

Spirits, I learned, had many peculiarities and could be easily deceived. For example, they could travel only in straight lines, not around curves. That is why most streets in old China were crooked, for a spirit would dash himself to death against a curved wall. For many centuries Chinese architects dealt with the spirits by making roofs curve abruptly upward in the belief that when a spirit landed on a roof it would be shot off into space again by the upward curve.

But some spirits were not so easily tricked and fear of them often prevented Chinese from helping people in distress. Once, returning to Chengtu from the summer recess, a friend and I followed a small river.

"Look, Inez" she cried.

There was a man drowning within ten feet of the bank, while some twenty or more Chinese looked on stolidly.

"Please help him," we pleaded; but nobody moved. Neither of us could swim, so I picked up a stick and tried to reach the victim, but it was not long enough. Just then a farmer came along, leading several cows.

"Quick," I called. "Give us your rope for a minute."

His only response was to beat his animals so they would move away faster, and the man drowned. I was appalled that these people whom I had already learned to love could be so inhumane--that they thought life so cheap. Could they learn to value the individual?

At the dinner table back in our ladies' residence in Chengtu, Miss Collier listened to our account of the incident. Then she explained that the Chinese dreaded the caprice and anger of the river god. They would even let a helpless man drown for fear the god would later claim them in retribution.

"But do not regard the Chinese as primitive or backward," she admonished us. "Their contribution to civilization has been too great for that. Like so many other great peoples, they became trapped by superstition and fear when their culture went into a decline. This experience will help you appreciate the importance of our work. By bringing them a merciful, loving God who values each and every life and believes in the development of the human personality, we are helping to free them from the bondage of ignorance and fear."

China had tried to isolate herself from the world, she went on to remind us. But while the Manchu rulers had discouraged Chinese personal expression and advancement among the general population, foreign political and commercial exploitation deprived the people of their dignity and freedom to develop their own resources. They had been exposed to many of the worst features of Western culture. Having cast off the Manchu yoke, however, the Chinese were now eager for Western advantages.

"We are here at a crucial time in Chinese history," she said. "We have the privilege and the responsibility to offer them the best of our faith, our ideas, our knowledge and technology."

The wheelbarrow was the only wheeled vehicle in the entire Szechuan province of 50 million people. Transportation in Szechuan Province was by sedan chair, wheelbarrow, or--on difficult mountain defiles--by a saddle on a man's back. Nothing moved faster than a man or a water buffalo.

In 1917, the Reverend Mr. Yard of our Men's Board went on furlough to America and brought back with him to China a lightweight motorcycle and a few gallons of gasoline to show the Chinese. Far inland, Chinese leaders had no idea of Western progress in transportation. There was no place to ride the motorcycle except on the military parade grounds. Important dignitaries were invited to go there one afternoon to see this "speed wonder" of the Western world, and to have a ride. What a sight it was to watch those high-ranking Chinese men in their long satin gowns as they took turns being whirled away on the back of the motorcycle for a few moments of adventure.

"Why can't we have these 'itself-go carriages'?" I heard them exclaim.

"You can," Mr. Yard answered, "but you will have to build some roads on which they can run."

Then and there began the "Good Roads Movement" which was to help move West China into the twentieth century. The leaders decided to build the first road from the capital to Kuan Hsien, the site of a famous irrigation works developed 2,100 years before by a great Chinese engineer, Li Bing. Because of his genius, this densely populated plain never suffered from flood or famine. The thirty-mile journey had always been a long day's ride by sedan chair; but the "itself-go carriage" could do it in less than two hours. Everyone was excited about the project. Each official made a pledge to pay for a certain portion of the road. Eventually all areas of Szechuan Province were connected.

Another transportation "first" in Szechuan Province was a rickshaw brought upriver by junk from Shanghai by an American, and then sent overland 250 miles by load carriers. It had soft rubber tires, excellent for traveling on the cobblestone streets of Chengtu and on the level paths around the university campus. One man pulling a rickshaw could take the place of four sedan-chair carriers.

Miss Golish, our principal, was delighted with this opportunity to cut down expenses, and she wanted to be the first to ride in the rickshaw to the university. A strong young carrier brought it over and proudly set down the shafts at our front gate so she could step in. She managed to wedge her 240 pounds into the narrow seat and the carrier picked up the shafts to start running. But just at that moment Miss Golish leaned back, the shafts reared skyward, and she tipped backward onto the cobblestones with her feet waving in the air. The poor carrier clung to the shafts and dangled in mid-air yelling for help. We bystanders were so convulsed with laughter that we were unable to do a thing.

The Chinese have a characteristic expression: <u>Shang-ee-fa-dza</u> (think of a way). After discussing the problem, some members of the crowd rolled the rickshaw onto its side, pulled its massive occupant out sideways and helped her to a standing position. Miss Golish did not find the incident amusing, but you can be sure that the story was told and retold with great zest in the tea shops where Chinese men loved to congregate.

Among the young of China there was a fast-growing fad of doing things the foreign way. Not that they were turning their backs on their own culture, but like young people everywhere they wanted what was new and would give them a sense of independence. They were proud of using English names along with their Chinese names. They openly admired Americans and enjoyed adapting some of our traditions to their own social lives. If sometimes amusing, their efforts were always charming and indicative of their initiative and openness to new ideas.

A university student and one of our high school graduates had a "modern" Chinese wedding. It took place in our school chapel, which was filled with high school girls and university men. While the girls modestly pretended to ignore the presence of the men, the boys eagerly took advantage of their new privilege to eye the girls.

The bride was dressed in pale pink satin instead of the traditional red. (It would not be our traditional white because in much of the Orient white is a sign of mourning.) She entered an hour late because, according to Chinese custom, she must not appear eager to be married. The groom came down the aisle in a high silk hat and a wrinkled American full-dress evening suit, rented from a theatrical company, filling the air with the odor of mothballs as he passed.

The Reverend Mr. Yard performed a beautiful Christian ceremony. The bride and groom then bowed three times to the minister and three times to the guests, an adaptation of the old Chinese custom of Kow-tow. Next, with gusto, the University Glee Club sang in English "Polly Wolly Doodle All the Day"!

To them it was a modern wedding, and the guests went away happy and anxious to describe it in detail to those not fortunate enough to be invited. It was among the first in which young people could do their own planning, and they certainly did.

But our job was not to influence the style of weddings, nor to sightsee. My knowledge of the language had progressed far enough; it was time to get to my principal job of education.

When we returned from the summer break at Cave Mountain I was put in charge of the two Chengtu Methodist primary day schools, one inside our compound and the other outside the city walls. I plunged into the job with enthusiasm and the schools went well. Much of the success was to be due to Pen Sih Ru, an unconquerable soul whom I have always called my "Chinese Little Sister."

The first time I saw her she was yanking on the long braids of a classmate. Temper blazed on her tense face. She was sixteen years old, ten years my junior.

"Who is that?" I asked Miss Golish.

"That is Pen Sih Ru, whom we call Rachel. She is our 'bad girl' of the school. I'm sorry, but we have been unable to reach her, and now she will have to go."

Miss Golish went on to tell me that Rachel Pen was a troublemaker, often deliberately starting fights. After witnessing several of Rachel's misdeeds, I could understand the principal's desire to expel her. On the other hand, I felt a bond with this "bad girl." After all, I myself had once been known as "that minister's bad child."

"Tell me about Rachel's background, Miss Golish," I said.

"Rachel belongs to no one, except this school," she replied. "Her father and mother died when she was a baby. Her grandmother took care of her and when she died, Rachel was brought here by neighbors. This is the only home she knows. We are sending her to some distant relatives."

She told me that Rachel's grandfather was a famous Christian martyr at the time of the Boxer Rebellion. The Boxers ordered the Christians to renounce their religion or be killed. Many did, but he refused. The Boxers drew a cross on the ground and said, "Unless you spit on the cross and stamp it out with your foot, we will cut you up alive." Rachel's grandfather lifted his eyes and replied, "Cut my body to pieces and kill it if you must, but you cannot kill my soul."

The Boxers carried out their threat. After they had gone, those Christians who had denied their belief gathered up his remains and eventually built a monument to him.

"Surely, Miss Golish," I pleaded, "the granddaughter of such a courageous martyr must have something special about her. Do let her stay awhile longer."

But the principal refused. Rachel remained defiant up to the last minute before her departure. The small box containing her belongings was packed and placed in the front hall. The sedan chair had been called to carry her away. Suddenly she broke down and sobbed.

"I know what I need," she said through her tears. "It's not to be sent away from this school. What I need is to let <u>Shang Ti</u> change my heart."

Miss Golish sent Rachel to her room and told her to stay there until a change of heart took place. Two hours later Rachel returned, radiant. She looked as though she felt just as I had a few years earlier when I prayed for guidance under the pepper tree.

"The Heaven Father has changed my heart," she said. We could hardly believe it, but it was true. From that time on she was different. She conscientiously worked at controlling her temper and devoted herself to helping others. I gave her a notebook and every time she felt angry she recorded it with a check mark. At night she looked over each check and prayed to do better the next day. Each week I inspected the book and saw that there were fewer and fewer checks, and then, finally, none at all. Rachel had won her battle with her temper, and the book was laid aside.

Rachel Pen became the most devoted friend I ever had. We often sang duets and I can still hear her beautiful alto voice. She played all the songs in the Chinese hymnal by ear. Often she would say, "I love God first and you next." We were truly sisters under the skin.

That winter I received a severe shock. The doctor told me that Rachel had tuberculosis and might not live through the cold, damp season in the unheated rooms. It was unthinkable to me that her life could be blotted out so soon. Every day I fed her fresh raw eggs and held her nose while I poured large quantities of cod liver oil down her throat. Gradually her health returned. She grew stronger and graduated from high school with top honors.

Until my language ability was adequate for me to go out into the province and open new girls' schools, I remained in charge of the two local primary day schools and Rachel became my assistant. Under her watchful eyes they ran like well-oiled machinery. There were never any serious problems, for she always told me very tactfully what to do and what not to do. She was a genius with children, always maintaining discipline with a low voice and firm, but loving manner. They adored her.

One day I was to lead assembly, but I entered an absolutely empty building. I looked out the back window and gasped in astonishment. There on the earthen floor of the outdoor exercise yard were the 150 youngsters on their knees, neither moving nor talking. The only sound came from the crows in the gingko tree. Not a teacher was in sight.

"Children," I called down to them. "Why are you down there on your knees, and where is Miss Pen?"

One child spoke out: "More things were stolen yesterday," she piped. "Miss Pen told us to stay on our knees and pray until someone confessed or until she returned. The thief must be absent today, for no one has confessed."

The children's total obedience to Rachel was amazing, but the stealing continued and worsened as warm days came and windows were opened wide. A precious American doll given to one of the girls as a prize disappeared. All the tears and pleas of the owner failed to melt the heart of the thief. One day Rachel's glasses were taken from her bedside table. By now we were all desperate to find the thief.

"The situation is undermining the school's morale," I told Rachel. "The teachers blame the students, the students blame the servants, and the servants blame the gateman for not keeping better watch. Everyone is under suspicion."

To Rachel, Shang Ti was not austere and distant but a very personal God concerned with all the individual affairs of daily living. At chapel next day she spoke to the children.

"Only Shang Ti knows this thief, and only He can help us find who it is. We must all pray for His help." And so we did.

The day after the girls prayed, a violent spring storm swept the city. Rain-soaked, a huge crows' nest at least four feet in diameter fell out of a large gingko tree. The storm ceased as suddenly as it had begun, and the girls ran outdoors to investigate the nest. Then there was a screaming commotion as they tore it apart and gleefully held up various articles that had been stolen. There were Rachel's glasses, and the precious American doll! In the nest they also found thirty-two pairs of scissors that had disappeared over the years from the girls' sewing baskets, which they had left out in the courtyard during lunch. This gave me an idea.

"Rachel," I said. "There has never been a kindergarten in this great capital, or in the entire Szechuan Province of fifty million people, for that matter. You have a wonderful way with small children, and you are just the right person to help me start one. The scissors will be our first item of equipment, and we'll have them sharpened at once."

The new kindergarten was a great novelty and its fame spread rapidly. Rich Chinese sent their pampered children to us and were astonished at the transformation the school made in them. Even the governor of the province heard of the kindergarten and of Miss Pen. One morning two officials and three servants appeared at the door with his two youngsters.

"We will accept the governor's children," Rachel told the officials, "but you and the servants must immediately return to the palace and leave them alone with us."

The two children had never been without their attendants and never had been thwarted. When they learned they were to be left alone with us they threw themselves on the floor, kicking and screaming. Rachel ignored their tantrums, simply waiting until they tired themselves out. Then she gently took them to see the dolls and equipment, and had the other children sing songs with them and play games. Gradually the governor's "little problems" became fascinated and began to mix with the others. They never missed a day of school after that.

At morning refreshment time, Rachel taught the children to bow their heads, clasp their hands, and thank <u>Shang Ti</u> for food. Soon word reached us that the governor's children were making their father pronounce the same blessing with them before meals at home in the palace. At the close of that school term, he came with the other parents to see the children perform, and spoke.

"None of us can ever repay Miss Pen for what she has done for our children," he stated. "Today I am donating $1,000 to enlarge this kindergarten so that it can accommodate more children."

During our years of close association I watched Rachel grow in vision and leadership. I also saw China's nationalist movement increase from a mere ripple into a powerful wave roaring across the whole of China. More and more Chinese were being educated, and the advance made by women and girls in the cities was phenomenal. One day several of our high school girls burst into my study.

"Miss Marks," they exclaimed excitedly. "We need you for our chaperone. There's going to be a mass meeting of all students--girls as well as men--and we want to be there! It is a protest against the Japanese 'Twenty-One Demands' for special military and commercial privileges in China. We want to pledge our patriotism and boycott all Japanese goods."

Every detail of that meeting had been carefully planned. Two policemen escorted our schools' seventy-five girls to the Governor's Park, where they joined students from the schools the government had started for the city's elite. All the city's 6,000 male students stood on the left of the platform facing the girls. A moat surrounded the Governor's grounds and kept out curious crowds from the city.

The speeches were impassioned patriotic addresses, with Ngai Kwai ("Love Country") as their motto. To my surprise, a government high school girl stepped calmly to the platform and in a clear, steady voice pledged the patriotism of Chinese women. The vast audience stood very still, eager for each word. Enthusiastic applause followed. When the ceremonies were over the girls were allowed to depart first, then the male students.

That event marked a new day in ancient Chengtu. Men and women met for the first time on an equal basis, asserted their love of country, and formed a unified program of action. This was the first of many experiences which would bring me into close contact with the dramatic emergence of Chinese women as they stepped over the threshold from seclusion into an undreamed of more abundant life.

CHAPTER 5
PIONEERING THE DISTRICT

In 1918, after two happy years studying the language and managing the two city schools in Chengtu, it was time for me to begin my work of opening schools for girls out in the Methodist District. When a village asked for or agreed to have a school, it would be up to me to show them what would be necessary in the way of furniture and equipment, to design the curriculum of study and to provide a teacher from among the girls trained at our Methodist training school.

My first trip was to visit some villages where Methodist men had already established boys' schools, and I was accompanied by Mrs. Lewis, a Chengtu old-timer whose husband worked for the Men's Board. The first thing that struck me was that there was not a single woman or girl with natural feet. Not only had they all been crippled physically by having their feet bound, but they had been deprived of their childhood by early marriages arranged by their parents. It made me heartsick to think of the some eight centuries of suffering. It was to help these women and girls that I had come to China.

Then I received the depressing news that all funds for new Methodist work were cut off because they were diverted to the war effort in Europe. For weeks I waited unhappily in the capital, trying to make myself useful in the primary schools, but always feeling guilty for not doing what I had come to do. Then one day during prayers my mother's motto came to mind: "Nothing can defeat you but yourself." I rose from my knees with determination.

"I will do this work You sent me out here to do," I said to the Lord, "and I will depend on You to help me."

That evening at supper I announced to the other ladies in the Home that I was going out into the District the following morning to take up my work.

"But there is no money," they said.

"That's true," I replied. "I'll use my own savings for this trip and trust the Lord to supply money for the future."

I prepared my sedan chair and notified the chair carriers and load bearers to be ready by dawn. Custom demanded a chaperone, so I arranged for Mrs. Wu, a lovely Chinese widow ten years my junior, to go along with me.

That night I went to bed much happier and was just dropping off to sleep when I heard a clatter down at the gate. Miss Golish went out with a lantern to see who was there. Soon I heard her call out.

"Miss Marks! A telegram has come for you!"

We were a thousand miles beyond the end of the inland railway at the time, but the capital city did have a telegraph service.

"Open it and read it!" I called back, hurrying into my robe.

It was from a Pasadena man visiting China who had heard of my financial difficulties from my mother. The telegram said: "Have this day deposited your account American Oriental Bank Shanghai $385 for your Chengtu District work." That was a lot of money in those days.

We set out next morning in great spirits, traveling on the "Big Road", slabs of stone laid on the partitions between rice fields. The watery fields gleamed in the sunshine and the bamboo waved like great green feathers around the farm houses. The road took the form of steps when it crossed over a pass through the hills into the next valley.

Having Mrs. Wu along gave me extra status, because her youth made me seem older than my twenty-eight years, and age was highly respected in China. Mrs. Wu had studied in our training school after her husband's death, and her feet had been unbound as much as possible. (She was too old to have them completely unbound, as the bones and cartilage had been deformed and could never go unsupported again.)

Mrs. Wu would teach me Chinese customs and help our work with the women however she could. One day I over-heard some village leaders asking her to explain the different Christian denominations that were working in China.

"Oh, they are all the same religion," she told them. "The only difference is in the cermony that takes you in. With the Baptists you get a big wash. With the Methodists you get a little wash; and with the Quakers you get no wash at all."

Four days out we were met by a man dressed in the satin gown of an official. He had heard of us and had walked for several hours to entreat us to come to his large village of Wu Feng Chee and open a girls' school there. He was obviously an influential and progressive man.

"We have already set aside a room in the village temple for the church services and another for a boys' school," he told us. "There is also room for a girls' school. The people of Wu Feng Chee will pay the salary of a woman teacher." Then, to my astonishment, he said, "I have three little girls of my own and I will be willing to unbind their feet and set a precedent."

This offer was indeed remarkable. We changed our plans and accompanied him to Wu Feng Chee. These villagers had never seen a white woman. Children repeatedly ran ahead of us so they could stand and watch us pass by again. I am sure that every youngster in that big village was tripping down the street with us. When we alighted from our sedan chairs at the temple the villagers were not only amazed at my white skin, strange clothes and big feet, but it was clear that they had never dreamed of a Chinese lady with unbound feet like Mrs. Wu's.

Our host proudly took us inside the big temple to inspect the rooms set aside for the boys' school and the church, as well as the one they offered us for a girls' school. It did not seem to bother anyone that the huge idols still stood there, with their altars neglected. I certainly made no objections.

"We will open the school in September," I promised him, "and since you agree to pay the teacher's salary, I will pay for the teacher's chaperone from our Women's Training School." The chaperone could help persuade mothers to unbind the feet of their daughters.

Next day we returned to the "Big Road," and by lunch time we had approached another large village. We were expected, so, according to Chinese custom, people were out on the road to meet us. The carriers set down our chairs and Mrs. Wu and I stood up to return their greetings, bowing and shaking our own hands in the Chinese manner. Then we took to our chairs again and rode into the village.

It was market day and the narrow streets were crowded with people and their baskets of produce. Here, too, the children came running after us. Women reached up to my chair to feel the cloth of my skirts. They chattered in astonishment at my big feet. Obviously no white woman had ever traveled to that village, either.

I usually ate one American-style meal a day, at lunchtime, but that day, to appear less conspicuous, I told my cook boy to stop at the inn and to order local food which I would eat with chopsticks, instead of a knife and fork. We sat down at a table on the side open to the street. Word had spread that I was there, and it seemed that the entire population rushed to have a look. Boys climbed to the beams so they could watch and hung their feet over my table. People stood on tables and on the benches and crowded me so that I could scarcely raise my chopsticks to my mouth. I shall never forget a wrinkled old woman who had pushed her way through the crowd until she could see me.

"Oh, look!" she shouted back to those behind her. "She is civilized and uses chopsticks, just like we do."

At first it was hard to get used to these crowds so curious about my looks and my mannerisms, but with time I came to feel very much at home among the village people. Adding to my self-confidence was a letter which came from Pasadena soon afterward saying that the members of my Mother's Sunday School class had organized an "Inez Marks Club" and a similar club was formed in Fresno to support my educational and mission work.

China had always been a man's world, as reflected by the sayings of the sages. Twenty-five hundred years ago Confucius wrote: "Woman is a human being but is of a lower order than man." There were other well-known sayings:

> The aim of women should be perfect submission
> to man, and not the development of the mind.

> It is a law of nature that women should be kept
> under the control of man and not allowed a will
> of their own.

> A woman should not presume to follow her own
> judgment.

> If a woman would escape rough treatment, let
> her cultivate docility.

The chief function of woman was the bearing of sons for ancestor worship. A bride moved to her husband's family home, and only when she presented her husband with a son did she win some esteem for herself and gain any influence in the household.

Then there was the curse of the bound "lily" feet. Chinese men for some 1,000 years (since the Court of Li-Hou-Chu ca. 970 A.D.) cramped the mental and spiritual development of their women by denying them education and insisting that their feet be bound into the form of "lilies". No one seemed to know the origin of the footbinding custom, but one theory was that a woman so crippled would be forced to remain under the man's roof.

Only two types of women had normal feet: the ladies of the former Manchu ruling class who were originally foreigners, and slaves. I never saw either of these in our part of

China. Actually a law had been passed against footbinding after the outbreak of the "golden lilies" parade in Nanking at the beginning of the revolution, but Sun Yat-sen's poor, weak government could not enforce its laws.   Besides, parents resisted this law because they feared a girl with unbound feet could not get a husband.

The years of suffering involved in producing the "lily" feet are beyond our comprehension. At the age of four or five all the girl's toes except the big toe would be turned under and bound tightly against the ball of the foot. This made it too painful to put the foot down flat, so she would try to walk or run and play on her heels. Then the most painful part of the process began. The big toe was pulled back under the foot toward the heel by a strap which was slowly tightened, month after month and year after year.   This forced the instep up into a hump, curving--and sometimes breaking--the bones until the deformed foot would be only four or five inches long, even after the girl became a grown woman.

There was no social life open to her, and being unable to read, she could only sit and suffer, staring into space. By then she was ready to be married to a man chosen by her parents, one she had never seen. The pitiful little bride hoped for immediate pregnancy and a male child.   The agony of carrying the extra weight of a baby on the crippled feet is sad to contemplate.   To unbind the deformed foot would cause unbearable pain, as the bones and ligaments could no longer function normally.

Chinese women's shoes were made of layers of cloth glued together, so my mother sent me the good sections of cloth from old overcoats she collected. In each of my schools I bribed the mothers with this cloth to make shoes for themselves and their daughters. I also assured each mother that her daughter was now being educated and there would be no trouble finding a husband for her. During my three years traveling the District, I was to have the satisfaction of knowing that 250 of my own students had their feet unbound, and of setting a precedent in each community where I had a school for other courageous mothers to do the same. The cruel custom of footbinding would finally be obliterated.

A young woman journalist from New York who wanted to experience travel in rural China asked to join me on one of my regular trips over the District to inspect my new schools. We both found the trip worthwhile, but after spending twenty nights in heatless school rooms, temples and noisy inns on our camp cots, we longed to reach home in Chengtu Saturday night for a warm bath, hot dinner and to sleep in our own good beds. We listened to a heavy rain all Friday night and Saturday morning we slopped along in the rain and mud. The possibility of not getting home Saturday afternoon was depressing, so I sent my cook boy hurrying on ahead to Chengtu, without a load, to request the city gate police to hold it open for us past the five o'clock closing time. Darkness fell and we continued slipping and sliding along by lantern light. Finally, three hours late, we reached the city wall. The gate was closed. I pushed against it and it squeaked.

"Who is it?" a voice called out in Chinese.

"We are the two American ladies returning home," I called back through the darkness.

Immediately the great gate groaned open. Overcome with gratitude, I asked the men how much they wanted for waiting for us all that time. They refused pay, but we gave them generous tea money, anyway and proceeded to our compound.

We found such consideration often. One spring day I was giving semi-annual examinations to my school girls at the village of Lung Chuan-E when my cook boy burst into the room crying out:

"Soldiers have commandeered all your bearers and are forcing them to carry their loads to Chungking! They are already out on the main road." One could not travel far in Szechuan Province without bearers.

Without hesitation, I raced out the back door and headed across the rice fields on the narrow dirt partitions hoping to catch the convoy before it turned south. What a picture we must have made--a tall, slender white woman running full speed and followed by thirty or forty little students who, with one accord, dashed after me to see what would happen. Those with unbound feet were closest to me, while those whose feet were still bound had to stump along behind on their heels. The line extended almost all the way back to our gate.

A 400-yard dash brought me to the main road just as the soldiers arrived with my bearers. I stopped the soldiers and explained breathlessly who I was.

"I will be helpless without my bearers and unable to get back to my home in the capital," I told them. "Won't you please be so kind as to help me, a guest in your country, and release my men."

By then the whole caravan of soldiers and carriers had come to a stop, surrounded by pleading children.

The soldiers fell into a noisy discussion, after which they ordered all my carriers to unload and return with me. Then some of the soldiers went back to search the streets and teahouses for other carriers. Wherever a door moved they rushed to grab the man behind it. Two farmers had hidden in a large outdoor oven, but they couldn't resist peeking out when they heard the excitement and were promptly caught. The poor draftees were not even given a moment to return home to explain their disappearance and they would receive no remuneration except food for the long, hard journey. The children, my bearers and I watched the convoy pass.

Chair carriers typified Chinese politeness by their behavior in crowded streets. Instead of yelling at people to get out of the way, they called out De dsway, de dsway ("We beg your pardon, we beg your pardon."). They had their own code of honor and would risk their lives to deliver passengers and their possessions safely. I could spend the night in a city temple with no doors to lock, feeling safe in the knowledge that just on the other side of the idols my men were sleeping on mats on the floor.

There were no banks in West China in those years except at the provincial capitals, and no paper money. For small amounts we had strings of "cash"--little coins, each with a hole in the center--but in all other transactions silver dollars were used. To pay the teachers and other school expenses it was necessary at times for me to carry from three to five hundred silver dollars in my sedan chair. My carriers could estimate the amount of money in my chair by the extra weight.

On one occasion when my chair was particularly heavy with silver we entered a large town on market day. I closed my chair curtains and told the carriers to take me and my loads directly into the temple, behind the idols, since that room was seldom used. Once inside, I opened my curtains and stepped out of my chair to find myself in the midst of a group of bandits cleaning their guns! I was stunned, realizing what my load of money would mean to them, and what its loss would mean to me.

"Hau bu hau?" (How are you?)" I greeted the bandits cheerfully, hiding my fear.

I pretended to believe they were the village police and asked whether they objected to my eating there, all the while unpacking my lunch as they stared at me. It so happened that I had with me a can of American peaches and I pointed to the picture on the outside. It was obvious they had never seen a tin can before, and they were intensely curious.

"Watch me open it," I told them.

Then I shared a peach slice with each bandit and let each have a sip of the syrup. Before leaving I gave them the empty tin can, which they examined and fondled with delight. Then I thanked them profusely for their "protection." Had they only known, the bandits could have made the haul of their lives.

On another occasion, I had to carry 500 silver dollars on a six-day trip through the mountains to pay the teachers' salaries and the cost of converting an old building into a girls' school. The weather was exceedingly hot, and I dreaded the journey. When one of the Methodist men told me about a shortcut over the mountains, it appealed to me. There was one drawback: the area was known to be bandit-infested.

Nevertheless, after thinking it over, I decided on the shortcut and to trust the Lord to see my 500 silver dollars through safely.

The first night out we slept in an inn at the foot of the mountain and started the ascent the next morning before sun-up. I helped my men by walking on ahead because of the excessive weight of the silver in my chair. Near the top of the mountain, our narrow road passed between a steep embankment on one side and a giant boulder on the other. Suddenly three bandits with guns drawn, stepped through the gap ahead. I was startled and scared, but there was no turning back.

"Hau bu hau," I cheerfully gave them the traditional greeting. They were surprised to see a lone white woman.

"How far is it to the next place where I can get breakfast?" I asked them.

Then I chatted on, complimenting them on being the local protectors of the area. I saw they were intrigued by my white skin, big feet, and strange accent and they were amazed that we could understand each other. Evidently they were distracted from the idea of robbing me, for while we conversed, my loads and sedan chair passed us silently and continued on through the narrow gap to safety.

"Have a peaceful day!" I shouted to the bandits. Then I hurried on to catch up with my men.

"Shang Ti always takes care of our American lady and her bag of money," they said, still in a state of shock. They had been sure that this time we would be robbed.

My most unnerving experience on the District took place when, once again loaded with silver, I had to sleep in a noisy, crowded village inn. With difficulty I finally dozed off, still half conscious of the heavy bag of money I had placed against my pillow as usual.

Suddenly I felt something moving along my body on top of the covers. I was so frightened my heart seemed to stop beating. I could visualize a hand coming closer and closer to my face and I knew that in another instant something awful would happen. Summoning all my powers, I rose up in bed and screamed.

"<u>Na e go</u>!" ("Who is it?")

Whereupon, a great rat jumped off my bed onto the floor, probably as scared as I was. I lay down again, panting, trying to calm my quivering nerves.

Suddenly, through the thin board partition between me and the adjoining house, there arose a wail that sent chills up and down my spine. It was soon joined by others which I could make out as repeated cries of "<u>Fu Chin whey lai</u>! <u>Fu Chin whey lai</u>!" ("Father, come back!").

Then I realized that the head of the household next door had chosen that night to depart this world for the next. Then the mourners set off firecrackers to clear the air of evil spirits so that the deceased's soul could start on his journey. They sounded like a machine gun going off beside my bed.

A flickering light shone through a knothole in the wooden partition, and I peeked through to see what was going on. The view sent my already shattered nerves into a still worse state, for the family was laying out the departed one on two boards right up against the wall, so there were only a few inches between us.

The corpse and I lay side by side until daylight. It was a miserable nightmare of a night. At dawn I called my men and we cleared out. We hurried on to my girls' school, delivered the silver dollars and headed for home. I had had enough of the District for that trip.

The District work enabled me to experience the beauties of the land in all its season and to know the lovable character of the Chinese, their rich and ready humor and their unfailing kindness to guests. I had the fearlessness of youth, a sense of pride in having an important job to do and the satisfaction of getting it done. Being able to laugh with the people and at myself helped me through some of the touchy times.

Four years after I had traveled to Chengtu with Bishop Lewis and party, the Bishop's daughter, Ida Belle, was appointed president of the new Women's College at Foochow, near the South China coast. He urged her to see interior China before taking up her post. In fact, he wanted her to repeat the tour we had made with him in 1916 by sedan chair from Chungking to Chengtu. Miss Beatty and another worker accompanied Ida Belle through their Chungking district to the border of mine, where I joined them in order to conduct her to Chengtu and show her some of my schools along the way.

Again it was December and Ida Belle was warmly wrapped in a long muskrat fur coat and turban. The rice fields were full of water resembling miniature lakes reflecting the sky, clouds and trees. It was a glorious morning, but rain the night before had made the stone slabs of the Big Road very slippery. As usual, my sedan chair led the rest. Sometime mid-morning I glanced back just in time to see poor Ida Belle's carriers slipping and dragging her and her chair with them into an exceptionally deep rice pond. Emerging from the freezing plunge, she looked like a drowned muskrat in her dripping fur coat. Her fur turban never surfaced.

We could not continue with her wet and shivering, so we took refuge in a nearby farm house. The farmer's wife welcomed us kindly. Since our load bearers had been anxious to reach a certain eating house famous for its soup, I had allowed them to hurry on ahead and they had our baggage. Inside the hut, each of us removed one or more garments so that Ida Belle could wear dry clothing. Then, somewhat warmed but very hungry, we hurried on to the restaurant, where we caught up with our bearers and loads.

We sat down on the backless benches at one of the rough-hewn tables and were immediately served big bowls of delicious steaming noodle soup. While we ate, chickens and a family of pigs searched around under the tables for discarded food morsels. From experience, Miss Beatty and I kept the pigs away by swinging our crossed legs back and forth. Presently I looked at Ida Belle and saw that her chin was quivering and big tears were rolling down her cheeks. Solicitously, I asked what was the matter.

"Oh," she cried, "I am so ashamed of myself, but I just can't stand it any longer. The pigs keep going between my legs to scratch their sides." Holding in our laughter, we showed her what to do.

Despite all the new germs I encountered, my health was remarkably good. The "white medicine" I carried made me famous. When my carriers or students were sick it was surprising how they benefited from a good drink of boiled water with epsom salts, or from soda taken for indigestion or a gargle with warm soda water for sore throat. My quinine capsules, too, were important. Of course I expected them to be swallowed whole and generally explained this, but a few times I forgot. The villagers had never seen such things, so they emptied the capsules, swallowed the bitter pure quinine, and returned the next morning asking for "the little bottles" to be refilled.

The only time I was seriously ill was once when I came down with malaria while traveling out in the countryside near Luan Chuan Sih with Mrs. Wu. When we arrived at the school, I had my cot taken up to the loft for privacy, then climbed up the ladder and lay down. I was soon overcome by high fever and chills. Mrs. Wu brought my quinine and piled all the bedding available on top of me, but my shivering was uncontrollable. Unable to sleep, I lay all night figuring that it would take four days to send for a doctor, or three days for me to be carried to a doctor. I felt too ill to live much longer and began to visualize the Chinese trying to get my stiff, lifeless body through the small opening of the loft and down the ladder.

The climax came about daybreak when the butcher in the shop next door began killing pigs. Their unearthly squeals and dying groans were more than I could stand. With a dramatic surge of energy I got dressed and asked Mrs. Wu to have my sedan chair brought to the foot of the ladder. Somehow I conquered my dizziness, climbed down feebly and got in. With curtains drawn so that people would not stare, we made the three-day journey home to our American doctor at Chengtu.

CHAPTER 6
THE ROAD TO AMERICA

Shortly before my five years were up and my furlough to America was due I was faced with a heavy decision. The wife of a fine man at the Methodist Hospital Compound had died in childbirth, and when his initial grief had passed, we were brought together by mutual friends and common interests. Our relationship was very casual, but I soon learned that he wanted to remarry and to continue working in West China.

To marry this man would give me the two things I most longed for: to remain in China and to have a home of my own. He was a good man, and the life he offered to share was appealing. But I was learning the importance of making the right decisions according to God's plan for my life.

One afternoon I went out on my bedroom balcony to be alone where no one would see me. I gazed out at the glaciers gleaming in the sunlight on the distant mountains and, kneeling, began to pray just as I had prayed as a young girl in California, on that important day under the pepper tree.

"Lord, I want your decision, I will do what You want me to do, regardless of my own desires."

Some believe that prayer is a clearing of the mind or listening to the best in oneself, and perhaps it is. But for me it was a real communication with God, who would guide me if I would just listen. I determined to stay on my knees until He gave me His answer.

Before long came the realization that this marriage was not meant for me. God's plans for my future did not include this man, and his absence would not hinder them. Feeling at peace, I went downstairs. The young man happened to be in the hallway and we exchanged greetings, but I didn't stop to talk with him as usual. Somehow, any romance had fled.

Before departing for America, I took my last tour of the Chengtu Methodist District, especially happy to have Miss Cowan, my replacement, and the Rev. Mr. Yard of the Men's Board, go with me. I had intended that no one should know this was to be my last trip, but the news traveled faster than I could. And so everywhere we went I was honored in the true Chinese style, much to the delight of the Chinese and to my embarrassment.

As I entered or left each city or town, the children of the schools I'd started set off firecrackers to announce our approach, drawing crowds which watched us pass by. When my visit coincided with a market day, hundreds of farmers lined the narrow streets to see the rare sight of an American woman and the forty or fifty little Chinese girls traipsing along beside her, some running free on unbound feet.

I loved all my schools, but two were special: Guan Fu Yan and Wu Fung Chee. We spent four days at Guan Fu Yan, a 2,000-year-old village to which, three years before, two officials had invited Mr. Yard and me after attending one of our prayer meetings in a neighboring city.

"We have always lived the best life we know how according to our consciences," the spokesman had said, "but we never before heard of Shang ti." They had felt that somewhere there must be a Heaven Father, but they did not know how to contact him, so had urged Mr. Yard and me to begin work there. And we did. Typically, they had greeted us at the outskirts of town upon our arrival there, and showed us the old, run-down building they had bought for the boys' school and the chapel. Then, of all things in an out-of-the-way place like this, where there was not a single woman or girl with unbound feet and women had never before met together, they showed us their plans for a girls' school. We had only to provide the teachers.

Now, just three years later, what a transformation! The school building was spacious, cleaned and whitewashed. About fifty little boys studied in the boys' section, and about forty bright-eyed, eager little girls in the girls' section. Many of the girls' feet had been unbound, and they were the first girls of the region to have their own school. They crowded around me and took turns holding my hand. Then we all assembled in the chapel where, at the front, was a huge gold Chinese character for <u>NOAI</u>--Love. Certainly a new kind of love had come to this big village.

The next morning we were guests at an unusual breakfast, in that it was hosted by the robber chiefs of that section of the province. Robbers and villagers had a working understanding between them. The village headman had informed the robbers that we were special friends who were never to be harmed.

The next couple of days we spoke at the women's meetings. The mothers came a hundred at a time, and we talked with them about unbinding girls' feet, about modern hygiene, education and other ways of bettering their lives. They were thrilled to come together and socialize as they never had before we started the schools, but they did not understand a speaker's need for silence. Consequently, when we spoke one sturdy deacon climbed onto a bench and presided over the meeting with a long, slender bamboo rod with which he kept the women from talking by tapping them on the shoulders.

Next we went to the large village of Wu Fung Chee, whose leaders three years before had walked half a day to meet us on the Big Road and ask that we open schools there. Now they were going to show me what they had accomplished. We arrived on market day. Despite my protest, a group of girl students, teachers, and churchmen met me outside the entrance. There the girls draped me with yards of silk and silk rosettes. Then, with bursts of firecrackers, our procession wound through the crowded streets to the big temple.

What a change. The idols had been taken down from their age-old pedestals and crowded into a rear room. On the front wall of this chapel also hung the Chinese character for LOVE. A table served as a pulpit, on which rested a Bible. There were backless benches for perhaps 200 people. I was delighted most by the attractive schoolroom they had built for little girls and the sight of so many with their feet unbound. This tour was followed by a feast and many speeches. I complimented the leading men on the splendid work they had done and their success in raising so much money for buildings and labor, and asked them how they had done it.

One official replied, "Well, we read the Bible and it said to give one-tenth of what we have to Shang Ti, so most of the members now tithe."

What an example for us all!

Finally, after twenty-two days, the sound of firecrackers died away and the feasts of chickens, ducks, fatted lambs and pigs were over. The many gifts, mostly yards of silk, were packed for America. And my "little sister Rachel" was going with me as far as Chungking.

During our years of friendship she, too, had decided against marrying. In the Chinese custom of the time, several fine young men had approached me, as her superior, to ask for Rachel in marriage. I urged her to marry, but she refused them all, saying, "Marriage is all right for others, but for me, no. I have too much work to do for Shang Ti and for my people."

Now that her kindergarten was flourishing, Rachel wanted to take a two-year course which would enable her to train others to organize kindergartens in the many large cities of Szechuan Province.

"Of course you should take it, Rachel," I told her. "You are a born leader who will do much for your people."

The nearest kindergarten training school was at Soochow, near Shanghai, 2,000 miles away. About that same time Miss Golish had prepared a brilliant student for college--Eva Ruan- -who, if we could send her, would be the first girl from the entire province to have a higher education. Unhappily, there was no money to send either one, but I was determined they should realize their dreams, and I had an inspiration. It was like a "postcard from heaven."

"I've figured out how to get the girls downriver to school," I announced happily. "They'll go with me on my houseboat as far as Chungking and my savings will cover their steamer passage from there to the coast. The first-class ocean liner ticket provided for me by the Methodist Mission Board can be exchanged for a second-class ticket, and the refund will cover the girls' first semester's room and board. Once at home in California, I'll raise the tuition money by selling some of the embroideries, amber and jade I've been able to buy so cheaply in Szechuan."

The staff knew me well enough to be sure I'd follow through, and everyone was excited about this wonderful opportunity for Rachel and Eva.

I planned our trip to take us on the more circuitous, but faster way to Chungking--on the spring flood waters, down the Min River, which flows past Chengtu and finally joins the Yangtze above Chungking at Iping. Then our boat would continue on the Yangtze to Chungking, from whence we would take a steamboat to Shanghai.

The best boat I could find was a twenty-five foot junk which looked as old as China itself. I arranged for a new bamboo mat to cover the central section and ordered the entire vessel to be scrubbed with a disinfectant.

As I was checking out our supplies for the trip, the gateman brought me a note from a friend at the university which read: "Charles Wood, editor of the New York Sunday World, and his wife are eager to reach Chungking to catch the next steamer downriver to Shanghai. Not knowing the language, they are as helpless as babes in the wood. Will you take them along on your houseboat?" I agreed, and as soon as we met I knew we would have a happy traveling party, for they had a wonderful sense of humor.

Early the following morning the Woods, Rachel, Eva and I boarded. Then, just before the crew pushed the boat from shore with bamboo poles, the captain killed a rooster and let its blood spill onto the prow to appease the river god. Each time we prepared to embark thereafter, and before we were to pass through any dangerous rapids, the captain observed this custom.   The "sacrificial" rooster was always eaten, however, as the Chinese wasted nothing.

Mr. Wood was a chain smoker, and he always offered a cigarette to each man on board. For almost every cigarette he smoked, ten Chinese oarsmen, two servants, and the captain rejoiced in his generosity.   This meant stopping at every large river village so that our cook boy could go into town and buy up all the available cigarettes.

These were pleasurable days, as we passed through the glorious scenery of the plain, with the white washed farm-houses and the waving bamboo sometimes 100 feet tall. The Chengtu Plain was a fertile and prosperous area from time immemorial. We reached the confluence of the Yangtze and the Min rivers at Iping just when we were eating our lunch on a folding table placed between Mr. and Mrs. Wood's cots. Our boatmen, seeing their first steamboat coming upriver toward us, got so excited that they allowed our junk to get caught in the turbulent wake of the powerful engines. The food was tossed all over us as we rocked and rolled in the troughs of water.   Mr. Wood's noodles and vegetables landed in his lap, while a can of condensed milk gurgled away, happily emptying itself on Mrs. Wood. Afterward, when we realized we were safe, the hilarity caused by our messy appearance somewhat dulled the terrible fright we had experienced when it seemed that our boat would capsize and plunge us into the flooding Yangtze.

Soon after that the captain brought the boat to anchor early at a small village which he declared was the best place to stop for the night. But Mr. Wood was so eager to reach Chungking that, to my later regret, I ordered the captain to continue on for a couple of hours. River boats traveled only in daylight, so late in the afternoon we tied up beside a number of other junks in a cove above the <u>Yeh Tan</u> (Wild Rapids) of the mighty upper Yangtze. Our junk was secured by a bamboo rope weighted down by rocks. The oars were tied, one above the other, to the front and sides of the boat as protection from the night wind.

It was a beautiful night. The tall masts of the numerous big junks moored there made a picturesque sight as they bobbed up and down and side to side. We sang favorite songs until midnight. The exhausted oarsmen seemed to enjoy it, but they soon were snoring loudly. A bit later the Woods were asleep on their cots beneath the roof matting, next to the boatmen. The rear center floor was carpeted with the two Chinese girls and myself, curled up on pallets. The captain, cook and houseboy slept at the rear. As usual, every foot of space was occupied.

At last all aboard our junk was quiet. I fell asleep listening to the distant murmur of the rapids and watching the moving masts silhouetted against the moonlit sky. From time to time our junk gently bumped hulks with others in the choppy waters.

Suddenly I awoke with a terrible premonition of danger. I sat straight up and screamed. The moon was gone. The junks which had been next to us were gone, and the distant sound was no longer a murmur, but a great roar. I realized that our anchor rope must have come loose and we were drifting in total darkness out into the main stream above the wild rapids.

In their deep sleep, the boatmen ignored my frantic calls. In desperation, I stumbled over to where the captain slept and shook him, shouting "Yeh tan! Yeh tan!" (Wild rapids!) He was on his feet in an instant, reaching for his long pole with the big hook on either end.

"Get to your oars," he yelled at the boatmen, who instantly came to life at the sound of his voice. All the time he was dragging his long pole deep in the water in search of the rock ledge he knew to be below the water's surface just outside the cove before the river entered the main current. After what seemed an eternity, the hook of his pole took hold. The boat jerked several times, finally swinging around on the pivot of the captain's pole. We startled passengers all kept to our places as the captain, straining with all his might, held the boat against the terrific pull of the water while the boatmen plunged their oars and frantically rowed us back into the cove. The junk was once again made fast to the shore and we all fell into a sleep of exhaustion and thankfulness.

The next morning, shortly after daylight, we headed for the rapids, with each oarsman standing, facing ahead. Their thousand-year-old rhythmic chant--"ai ya, ai ya, ai ya, ai ya"--rose in crescendo as they stepped up the speed of the oars to exceed that of the current and thus keep control of the boat as we approached closer and closer to the wild rapids.

My breath seemed to stop. I could only pray. In a craft dwarfed by the canyon walls, without life jackets or protection of any kind, we were about to shoot the most dangerous rapids of one of the world's greatest rivers, in flood time. Those strained first moments would determine whether the boat would make the small, narrow, rushing passages among boulders, or crash on them and overturn.

Our boatmen brought us through, and we glided into a momentary smooth stretch of current. I stood at the stern shaken and weak, thanking God for our safety. Looking back, I saw that the next craft to begin the ordeal was a large junk loaded with gold-red mandarin oranges. Aboard were some twenty oarsmen chanting and bending frantically to their oars. Just when their boat should have slid over the standing wave at the bottom of the rapids, the chanting suddenly ceased as boat and boatmen were sucked into the swirling cauldron below. Not a man came to the surface, but soon thousands of oranges were bobbing hysterically on the current of the muddy whirlpool.

Recalling the horror of our own narrow escape from these rapids in the darkness of the previous night, I was suddenly overwhelmed with the awareness of how wonderful it was to be under God's divine protection.

We were yet to reach Chungking, and after that, Ichang, through the gorges. I wondered about that transfer to the steamer at Chungking. When I had gone upriver five years earlier with Bishop Lewis and his party, we had to be carried by sedan chair up a great slippery stone stairway in order to reach the city. However, this time we moored nearer the city buildings, for two-thirds of the stairway was submerged by the spring flood. We parted from the junk, its valiant captain and the crew with feelings of gratitude and admiration and generous tea money. Then we transferred to a steamboat for Ichang.

At Chungking we were joined by some American friends, Mr. and Mrs. Hooker and their two boys, Johnny, age nine and Charles, eleven. Together we stood at the rails watching the spectacular traffic in Chungking waters. The river was alive with vessels. Some were the new steam boats, but most of them were still powered the ancient way, by wind and human power. For centuries men had painfully pulled the heavy junks upstream, fighting the mighty Yangtze for hundreds of miles, straining with ropes step by step on the paths cut in the cliffs of the awesome gorges. For this hazardous job they received only a pittance, for human muscle power was cheap in China. There had always been an oversupply.

From Chungking to Ichang was a four-day journey by steamer through five separate magnificent gorges which cut through mountain ranges. Their precipitous reddish-grey walls, sometimes green with shrubbery, often towered several thousand feet above us. American engineers had estimated that the Yangtze gorges contained more potential hydropower than all the rivers of the United States combined. Amid this fascinating scenery, and enjoying the comparative safety of the steamer over the smaller craft, I thought of the day when the water of the Yangtze would be tamed to turn the wheels of industry.

The Yangtze River begins its 3,000-mile journey in the glacial snow-covered mountains of Tibet. It is comparatively easy-going in winter, but when sunshine melts the accumulated snows and spring rains pour down over the interior of China, then the Yangtze becomes a raging, roaring dragon writhing its way through chasms and gorges, rushing down to the lowlands near the coast, carrying millions of tons of topsoil with it out to sea.

I knew that Chinese boatmen believed that when boats capsized and human life was subjected to the great river, the river god was angry. Not to be denied what he sought, he would claim any rescuers in revenge. I also knew, though, that the foreign steamboat companies had been able to convince Chinese that the river god did not want white people or their luggage, so that there would be rich rewards as incentive for saving us and our goods in case of a disaster. In anticipating the rough waters still ahead, this was at least some selfish consolation.

Mr. Hooker had been in China for some years. He explained the difference we could expect between the time of my ascent with Bishop Lewis' party five years earlier, when the Tibetan mountains slept under blankets of snow, and now, when we were speeding down on spring floods. The river, confined in the gorges, rose 250 feet above the earlier level. Above Ichang this enormous surge of water would shoot us through the final gorge with indescribable force.

He was right. The current the day we came through was terrifying. It seemed miraculous that we were still afloat, and I could scarcely believe that junks could have been pulled up through the gorge by manpower. Just before Ichang the canyon widened giving us for the first time a view of open, hilly country.

Ichang was the point of transfer from small boats and steamers to the great steamboats going down to Shanghai, and vice versa, creating considerable offshore activity. Standing by were the gunboats of foreign powers--some from England and the United States--there to protect their trade. But the port had no docks because the current was so forceful it would crush anything at the river banks. Only the little light sampans could approach the shore with safety. Other vessels had to anchor midstream, each with a landing raft beside it from which passengers and cargo could be transferred to or from sampans. Clever boatmen would guide their sampans downcurrent to the shore, then pole them laboriously upstream one boat-length at a time to a point higher than their destinations, then expertly maneuver them downstream to the ships' landing rafts.

Our party divided up. Eva, Rachel and I climbed in one sampan and sat clutching our hand luggage on our laps. The Hooker family boarded a larger sampan. We reached the river bank and were then poled slowly upstream. One or two men did all the work of pushing each boat, while others did nothing but stand with arms akimbo, pleadingly whistling for the wind to blow and fill the sail to help the boat along. Struggling against the current, our sampans hugged the shore until they were far above the large steamer that would take us to Shanghai. The crew then swung our smaller sampan out and the swift current carried us down to the landing raft, banging us against it with wild force. The boatmen quickly made the sampan fast and unloaded it. Greatly relieved, we climbed the stepladder to the passenger deck and waited there watching the arrival of the Hookers. What happened next was horrifying.

Their sampan crashed against the raft and suddenly capsized, plunging the whole family with their luggage into the rushing river, along with the crew. They all disappeared at once. Some rivermen chased after the trunks and suitcases being carried off by the fast-moving water, while others searched the river for the white people. We were helpless spectators.

The sailors of a United States gunboat, which was lying at anchor some 150 feet downriver, saw the accident. They crowded the deck to take action. When young Charles Hooker suddenly popped to the surface beside the gunboat many arms reached out toward him, but the boy was just beyond their fingertips. Then, as he was being swept beyond the stern, two sailors gripped each other chain-like and flung themselves out across the water. The furthest man caught Charles' arm in the last split second, so the sailors were able to deliver the eleven-year-old, dripping and trembling, to our boat.

No one else came to the surface. Our steamer's captain-- an American--shared our anguish. I stood beside him as with his field glasses he searched the water down to the curve in the river half a mile below for some time. Finally he turned and said sadly, "I guess we've lost them all except Charles.

No one else can come up alive now." He turned away from the stern and walked somberly away. His spirit was crushed at losing three lives, and we were beside ourselves. It had all happened so fast, and there was nothing we could do. We went to our cabins full of sorrow.

Our steamer was to have left that afternoon, but the captain decided to remain until the following day. We retained the faint hope that we could at least recover the bodies.

Several hours later a loud commotion made us dash out to the rail. We would scarcely believe what we saw. It was Mrs. Hooker! She was staggering up the ladder, her wet, long blond hair stringing down to her waist. We rushed to put our arms around her, then led her to a deck chair. Charles, sobbing, ran to his mother and clasped her in a tight hug. We were all weeping for joy. Everyone was asking at once what had happened. The last thing I had seen was Mrs. Hooker's hands stretched upward to ward off the tumbling suitcases from her head as she disappeared under the water. Now she told us that, as the current swept her downward, she had felt her husband's tweed coat, and he had appeared to be swimming strongly upward, but when she tried to grab onto him, the current tore her away. He must have come up under the ship, because otherwise, like Charles, he would have been seen, for hundreds of eyes were searching the water. Only his hat and cane came up. Mrs. Hooker had surfaced in the swift current far downriver and boatmen had pulled her aboard their sampan and laboriously poled her back upriver.

Night fell, and with it all hopes of rescuing Mr. Hooker and Johnny. None of us could sleep. One moment we were overcome with joy at the safe delivery of the two survivors, and the next with grief for those lost.

I was in my cabin the next morning when Eva and Rachel pounded on my door screaming, "Johnny is here! Johnny is here!

Could it be? I rushed out to the rail. It was true. There was nine-year-old Johnny climbing up the ladder from the ship's loading raft. How had he managed to escape the river god?

He told us of holding fast to his seat when the sampan turned over and that he came up with his head in the pocket of air trapped beneath the boat. For hours he hung there, fingers cramping and muscles aching, in the darkness as the boat was carried along by the swift current. He hadn't given up, because he remembered from previous trips that eventually, somewhere below Ichang, the Yangtze enters a large lake. Sure enough, the current slowed and his boat drifted into quiet water. By this time most of the air had been used up and he was becoming drowsy.

It was almost dark when two fishermen, returning home across the upper end of the lake, saw the capsized boat and went after it. They arrived at the moment that Johnny, afraid of falling asleep and drowning, decided to get out from under, and his blond head popped to the surface beside the boat. The startled fishermen hauled him in and spent the whole night poling upstream to return him to the ship.

When we asked Johnny what he had done during those long, dark hours in the rushing waters, he answered simply, "I was praying."

That afternoon we left Ichang, with all its tragedy and miracles, for the last thousand miles of our voyage to Shanghai.

CHAPTER 7
WEST MEETS EAST

We sailed past the picturesque walled city of Nanking set in gentle hills on which we could see temples and gardens, then down into the estuary at a good speed with the help of a fresh breeze and the outgoing sea tide. Soon we could see Shanghai, with its six- and seven-story buildings built down to the water's edge, such a contrast to the cities of the interior. It was 1921. The World War was over and Shanghai had become bigger, busier, and more crowded than ever.

As soon as we disembarked, I went directly to the shipping company office and easily received a refund for changing my first-class ticket on the S.S. Empress of Asia to second class. I breathed a sigh of relief. Rachel and Eva's first semester expenses were taken care of. From there we went to a mission hostel.

The weather was unbearably hot, so I suggested that we go to the park for the afternoon. We had rickshaws drop us near the entrance, and the coolies hurried away. At the gate, a British Empire policeman, an Indian Sikh, directed his club toward Rachel and Eva and said, "No Chinese can enter."

"But why not?" I cried. "These girls are like my own sisters!"

His answer was to thrust out his club, take a few steps toward us and repeat, "Chinese cannot enter." Then he pointed to an English sign over the park entrance:

NO WHEELED VEHICLES ALLOWED
NO CHINESE ALLOWED
NO DOGS ALLOWED

My pleading was in vain. My disgust with the British, members of a Christian nation, of all people, to exclude citizens from their own park was unforgiveable. There was nothing we could do but walk back, in the boiling sun, to the city to get rickshaws to return us to our suffocatingly hot rooms.

Eva, with tears in her eyes, explained, "China has never been a military nation. The soldier has always been considered the lowest of the five classes of society. But now, since the foreigners have come here, we realize that we must make ourselves into a strong military force. Only then will the foreign nations show us respect or allow us to rule our own country."

What could I say?

It never entered my mind that the International Settlement of Shanghai was a place of foreign privilege and exploitation. I learned that Westerners dealt with or operated ghastly sweat shops and enjoyed a status which made them immune from Chinese law, regardless of what they did to the Chinese. In spite of the fact that foreigners made up over half of the population, the Chinese paid eighty-five percent of the taxes. The British controlled the customs and post office and claimed all the revenues. No wonder Chinese called white people yang juei tzu (foreign devils) behind their backs.

I could not understand how foreigners had come to regard the Chinese as inferior. How does one judge a nation's greatness? By the length of its history? China was a great nation long before Babylon. Her culture has continued without interruption from antiquity to modern times, never sliding into oblivion like other civilizations.

Is population an indication of greatness? China has always had more people than any other country. Is it territory? For centuries, China governed all the lands from Burma to Korea. Even after other nations have taken so much from her, China still has the second largest land area in the world.

No country has equalled China in culture and education. Since her Golden Age 2,000 years ago, her poetry, art, ceramics, sculpture, and painting have been unsurpassed. Until the overthrow of the Manchus, not even a minor offical could hold office without passing an examination in the classics. To get this, he had to memorize vast amounts of literature. Long before our ancestors had emerged from the forests of northern Europe wearing animal skins, the Chinese had produced silk and linen and a cuisine which were the envy of the ancient world.

By trial and error, and without the benefit of modern science, Chinese farmers learned to produce food for enormous populations and to keep their fields at excellent production levels continuously for more than 4,000 years. China would have committed suicide centuries ago had her farmers not developed techniques of cultivation that included using animal and human waste which put back into the earth the nutrients necessary to keep it fertile.

The Chinese called their country Chung Kuo (Center of the Universe). Over the centuries they had secluded themselves from the rest of the world. They invented the compass, gunpowder, printing and porcelain.

The Western world, meantime, slept in the Dark Ages. Then it stirred, awakened, and had a Renaissance. It developed technology and built steamships and massive armaments. The Industrial Revolution followed, with mass production which needed markets. The West pounded loudly on China's doors with cannon, demanding open doors and commerce-- including the right to market opium in the country--a curse on an already desperate people which the Chinese resented in particular. The Chinese resisted, but the Western powers prevailed. They humiliated the Chinese even more by taking over their ports and crippling them with unjust taxes.

No wonder Chinese nationalism was on the rise!

On May 1, 1921, Rachel and Eva with some other friends saw me off to America. They stood on the dock and waved, and I waved back as long as I could see them, tears running down my face. What if I never saw them again, or never returned to China at all?

My departure was made easier by getting acquainted with a young student from the Methodist High School in Nanking. His name was Hahn Chee Chin, but his English class had given him the name of Clarence. We talked in English, which he spoke fairly well, and sometimes in Chinese, but I was puzzled by a feeling that my Chinese was better than his.

When our ship docked at Nagasaki and Yokohama in Japan, I thought Clarence would go ashore with me to see the sights, since I did not want to go alone. But he took to his cabin and stayed there the entire time we were in each port. I was disgruntled, but he must have had his reasons.

As soon as we put out to sea again, Clarence appeared on deck as though nothing had happened. His behavior was mysterious to me, but in the days that followed, we had wonderful conversations. We not only became good friends, but I realized that he was brilliant, and I invited him to visit my family in Pasadena. I was sure I could get him a scholarship at my alma mater, the University of Southern California.

It was not until the evening before our eighteenth day at sea that he again acted strangely. As we prepared for landing at Victoria, British Columbia, the transfer point for Seattle, he whispered to me, "I must talk to you. Please follow me."

He led the way to the very back of the second-class deck, among the pipes and smokestacks. When we could go no further, he spoke.

"Now our voices will go out to sea and no one can hear our words. There is something I must tell you. I am not Chinese. I am Korean."

I immediately understood the situation. Korea was under Japanese rule at the time. That was why he had hidden in his cabin when we entered Japanese waters. If he had gone ashore and been recognized as a Korean, he would have been arrested and maybe tortured and killed. It also explained why his Chinese was inferior to mine.

"Japan will not permit any Korean to go above the eighth grade in school," he said. "They are afraid if we are educated we will revolt. But I am determined to attend college. I left Korea on foot and walked all the way to Nanking when I was sixteen years old. I went to the Nanking high school in order to pass as a Chinese and buy a Chinese passport so that I could go to America. The Japanese have spies everywhere and if they had picked me up, I'd probably be dead now. It has happened to others. Tomorrow we'll land in Canada. There may be difficulties with my passport. I will need a friend."

"Clarence," I assured him, "I will stand by you regardless of what happens."

The next morning we docked in Vancouver where the passengers for the United States and their baggage were transferred to the boat for Seattle. However, all except Clarence had received their passports from the purser to go on. I stayed with him, wondering what in the world to do.

The boat whistled its departure, and soon our baggage was headed for Seattle. Then the Vancouver immigration officials jailed Clarence for landing without proper papers. I ran frantically from one office to another, demanding to see the highest immigration official in the port. When I found him I was tired, frustrated, indignant and determined.

"Clarence is innocent of any wrongdoing. The ship's purser failed to give him his passport and he must get to Seattle." I added, "I am coming home after five years in China and bringing this student from China with me to go to my university--where I am getting him a scholarship!"

The official contacted our ship and was given the news that the purser had sent the passport to the captain of the boat that went without us. Then, to my astonishment, he released Clarence Hahn into my custody on my verbal promise to take him on the next boat to Seattle, where his passport would be waiting. To get us away from any further questions, I phoned a friend in Vancouver who came down to the port in her car and took us sightseeing. After a wonderful day we boarded the night boat and arrived in Seattle the next morning.

Clarence went to retrieve his passport and I started through customs with the boxes on which Rachel and Eva's schooling depended. Since the mob of passengers from the Empress of Asia had gone through customs the day before, I was terrified they would go through everything and charge me an enormous amount of duty. I had, besides my train ticket to Pasadena, only five American dollars left in my purse. As the first box was opened, the official unwrapped an interesting old wooden idol. I immediately began a lecture on its history.

"The Manchus were parasites living off the Chinese people," I said. "Now that they have been overthrown, and because they never learned how to earn a living, they are selling one thing after another. That's why I could buy these things so cheaply."

Other inspectors gathered around and listened while I entertained them for two hours describing various articles and telling stories about China. I dropped frequent hints about my Chinese girls being dependent upon the sale of these artifacts to pay for their schooling, praying all the time that the charges would not exceed my five dollars. While they figured the duty I held my breath, and when they handed me the slip I was afraid to look at it. It was only $4.50. I was so thankful I wanted to shout for joy.

As I waited for my change, Clarence joined me and then, as we were leaving the customs shed, an overjoyed shipping company official greeted us profusely. Apparently a shipping company was fined $2,000 if it failed to deliver anyone on one of its ship's passenger list, and Clarence had been missing from the Empress of Asia. The official thanked me heartily for delivering Clarence!

At home in Pasadena I met my two beautiful little nieces for the first time--Elizabeth and Miriam--who had been born to my sister, Beatrice and her husband, Charles Moody. I learned that my older sister, Winifred, had sold enough of the Chinese embroideries and amber I had sent home to pay off my college debt and start a bank account for me. She had accumulated one thousand dollars. This I gave to her.

Because of her poor health it was the first cash she had ever earned and she was thrilled. My parents were obviously proud of me and it was good to be able to thank the members of the Inez Marks Club for all they had done to make the schools in China possible. It was a joyous homecoming.

My young Korean friend was welcomed warmly and henceforth treated like a member of our family. It was not difficult to get a scholarship for him and I found him a place to work for his board and room and loaned him money for books and essentials. I knew Clarence Hahn was bright, but I didn't dream he was to work his way through the University of Southern California and earn his Ph.D. in just seven years, return to Korea and marry and have four children, and then go on to become one of his country's leaders.

CHAPTER 8
ROMANCE AND HONEYMOON TO CHINA (1921-22)

Before I went to China and through the years I was there, Walter Lowdermilk and I had corresponded on and off--mostly off. At the time we had met in Wilcox, Arizona, I was a girl of eighteen, a high school dropout, uncertain of my potential, never dreaming he would consider me seriously. He had been interested that I went on to receive my B.A. and M.A. degrees with some honors and enjoyed receiving my letters describing some of my experiences in far West China. His infrequent letters mentioned especially my descriptions of the countryside, the wars, shooting of the rapids, and my encounters with bandits. But I told myself that his interest was just gentlemanly.

Meanwhile, Walter had graduated from Oxford with honors in forestry and had worked with Herbert Hoover to help alleviate wartime famine conditions in Belgium. When America entered the war, he had returned home to volunteer for the army and served in France with the Tenth Engineers. He was now a regional Forest research officer headquartered in Missoula, Montana.

I had written to tell him the date of my return, not really expecting an answer, but disappointed that none came. After I had been home for several months, I went to Minneapolis to speak at a church convention. On the way back to California my train passed through Missoula, stopping for more than two hours to take on coal and water. It was a beautiful Sunday morning, and the railway platform was filled with the men of the town who customarily came down to get the Sunday paper from the bundle brought by the train. Could Walter be among them? If so, it would be the first time in eleven years that he and I had been in the same place at the same time. I looked at the faces in the crowd hoping to see his, but he was not there. What had happened to him over the years? Perhaps he was married. I decided I would not try to find him.

However, when the train resumed winding its way through the Rocky Mountains, the thought of returning to China for another five years without seeing Walter saddened me. I had bought a penny postcard at Missoula, so I used it to remind him of our long ago meeting in Wilcox, mentioning that I was staying in Pasadena, but saying nothing of myself or my plans. I mailed the card at a small stop in Idaho called Horse Heaven.

Soon after my return to Pasadena a letter came from Walter saying, "I have not been home for Christmas in Arizona for several years and I would like also to see the Rose Parade and the Rose Bowl football game in Pasadena. May I visit you at that time?"

I was excited. Would he find me interesting after all these years? Both of us must have changed greatly.

We met New Year's morning at the Pasadena depot. The Prince Charming I remembered surpassed my expectations. He seemed taller, even more handsome. He was also very much the polished Oxford gentleman. We watched the parade and later the football game, standing and yelling at each successful play made by our team. It rained, but nothing could dampen our spirits. Afterward we walked to my family home, where he was staying, snuggled side by side under a small umbrella.

Early the third morning we rode the tramway up Mt. Lowe to see the magnificent views of Los Angeles and Catalina Island from Inspiration Point. There, just forty-eight hours after our reunion, and without any preliminaries, Walter asked me to marry him. It seemed trite to say, "This is so sudden," because I realized that ever since I had known Walter he was the man of whom I wanted to be worthy. I had prayed for him often, hoping that his unusual talents would be put to the best possible use. I now told him so.

"If you have felt the same toward me, Walter," I said, "then it must be that heaven meant us for each other."

Inwardly I marvelled that this disciplined scientist who prided himself on never making decisions "without all the facts," should take this plunge knowing so little about the woman he was asking to share his life. (Later he said that my courage in talking the bandits out of robbing me, plus my shapely ankles, helped him make up his mind.)

After accepting Walter's proposal, my first question was "Will you go back to China with me?" He couldn't answer as quickly as I had answered him.

Knowing how China needed men of Walter's training to deal with erosion, floods, and famines, I told him about the new Famine Prevention project the United States was developing in connection with the American Union University at Nanking. During the last terrible famine in China a relief fund had been raised in America, but that year the rains came early, bringing extra large crops. There was $2.5 million left over to be used strictly for the benefit of Chinese farmers in the enormous battle against hunger. The group of experts now being appointed was to decide the program. The salary would not be high, but there would be other compensations for Walter and me if he joined the project. I could manage the family finances on the $1,300 per year salary, I assured him.

Walter looked a bit doubtful, for he was already climbing rapidly in the U.S. Forest Service; but I knew in my "bones" that we would go to China together. "This is an enormous challenge," I said enthusiastically. "Think of the contribution you could make there." I suggested that he write the Fund's administrators at once and he agreed.

We jubilantly came down from our mountain top, hardly needing the tram for we were floating on air. We hurried home to tell my parents of our engagement.

Mother was clearly shocked that I would consider marriage at this point, for she had invested a great deal of effort in supporting my "faith" schools in China and she expected me to fulfill her own dream of service. Besides, she considered Walter practically a stranger, so she did not conceal her disapproval. When my father started to object, I interrupted him:

"But, Daddy, I am sure our marriage was made in heaven."

"Yes," was his reply. "It must have been made in heaven, because there wasn't time to make it on earth."

Two days later Walter gave me a beautiful diamond ring. Then, after a total of just five days, he returned to Montana. We wrote each other every day. He considered the work in China and decided it was what he wanted to do. He applied to the Famine Prevention Commission and was accepted. We decided to be married August fifteenth, 1922, the same day of my parents' fortieth wedding anniversary and Beatrice and Charlie Moody's tenth, and then to leave for China immediately after our honeymoon.

Walter arrived five days ahead of time for the festivities. My excited friends organized parties and brought useful gifts for our home in China: a patchwork comforter embroidered with the name of each friend; linens, and nice cooking dishes. Herbert Hoover sent us a large silver bowl.

Eight months after Walter's proposal the wedding took place in our Washington Street church. Friends built a large, flower-covered arch under which Walter and I stood, and another arch on either side for my parents and my sister and her husband to stand, for they took part in the service. My father performed the ceremony, tying a "good, strong knot" before the church full of well-wishers. Then he gave us the same advice he had offered all the couples he had married before:

"Always keep two little bears in your home and let them loose in all the rooms. Then you will have a happy marriage. Their names are 'Bear' and 'Forebear'."

With rice in our hair we took off for the Los Angeles railway depot to go to Santa Barbara for a short honeymoon. We were late, so Walter suggested that I go ahead with the baggage and tell the gateman that he would follow with the tickets. I boarded the first car, selected shaded seats and sat down to wait for Walter. I waited, and waited. There was no bridegroom. When the brakeman called, "All aboard!" I was in a panic. Should I jump off? If I did, all the baggage would go on without us. Should I remain on the train and start my honeymoon alone? Impossible. By this time the train had gotten under way. It was too late to do anything.

Suddenly, Walter, out of breath, dropped onto the seat beside me. He had managed to jump aboard the last car and come through the entire length of the train to find me. I couldn't imagine what had happened and he seemed reluctant to explain. Finally, at my insistence, he said, "Well, Sweetheart, it was this way: When I got to the gate I realized I had been so absorbed by thoughts of you that I had only one ticket, the one I bought for you. I had entirely forgotten to buy one for myself, so I had to go back to the ticket window and get another."

With these sweet words he got out of the predicament much better than he did on future occasions when he was so absorbed in his work he totally forgot he had a wife.

From Santa Barbara we went to San Francisco where we spent three delightful days before boarding the President liner for the Orient. As the ship sailed through the Golden Gate into an exhilarating breeze from the Pacific, I stood on deck beside my husband, thrilled at the prospect of our new life together. Then my mood changed abruptly. The moment we began to plow through the first big ocean swell, I was forced to make a sudden dash for the stateroom. During the furious storms of my first Pacific crossing I had written home of "throwing up everything but my appointment to China," but I never dreamed of being seasick on my honeymoon. I remained in the stateroom throughout the trip, utterly helpless. Walter, on the other hand, loved the sea and ships. He was invigorated by the ocean air and ate three enormous meals a day with snacks in between. Whenever he came down to inquire about me, I could only encourage him to meet people and to enjoy our honeymoon as best he could.

He was usually seated at the captain's table near Mrs. Fay Cooper Cole, the charming wife of a distinguished anthropologist, who was going to Japan to meet her husband. She, too, was a good sailor. So, in the following days, she and Walter walked miles around the deck, either waiting for meals or walking them off.

Years later I was introduced to Mrs. Cole in Washington and she said to me, "Oh, Mrs. Lowdermilk. I am so glad to meet you. I spent your honeymoon with your husband."

Before our ship had ever left San Francisco harbor, I had an inkling that even an Oxford gentleman could be difficult and it would be up to me to smooth things. Passengers and guests were still gaily milling around on deck when I had proudly introduced my new husband to Miss Ogborn, a greatly respected old-timer who had been in China long before the Empress Dowager died in 1906.

"This is my husband, Walter Lowdermilk, Miss Ogborn."

"Do you say your name the same as buttermilk or clabbermilk?" Miss Ogborn lightly asked Walter.

But Walter openly resented her seeming to make fun of his name, and he turned his back on us both. I wanted so much for us to have happy associations with the Americans in Nanking and was so afraid of what Miss Ogborn might say about Walter after his rudeness that later, in our cabin, I began to cry.

"What do you want me to do?" he asked.

"Please go up on deck and locate Miss Ogborn," I begged him, "and see if you can find something nice about her."

"Well, all right," he said grudgingly, and left. He did not return and did not return. Finally, all glowing and happy, he burst into our cabin, very proud of himself.

"Oh, I've had the most wonderful time," he told me. "We've walked miles around the deck and I've never heard more fascinating experiences. Actually, Miss Ogborn is one of the most remarkable women I have ever met."

That had begun a wonderful, deep friendship that lasted many years.

What a relief it was to get off the ship at Yokohama. We toured Japan by train, then joined our ship at Nagasaki. Seventy-five miles from the China coast we reached the famous "Golden Pathway" that I remembered so well. The yellow, silt-laden water still marked the way to the mouth of the Yangtze River. Walter watched it intently, pulling out the notebook he always carried to record the important things he observed and his reactions to them. It was as though the problems of China were coming out to meet him.

The sights, sounds, and smells of China were welcome and familiar to me, not to Walter. As he looked over the ship's railing at Shanghai he remarked, "It seems strange to be in a place so different from anywhere else I've been, and where I know no one and no one knows me!"

We disembarked and went by rickshaws to our hotel in the International Settlement, where they gave us a large room with overstuffed British furniture and big, overhead fans. Then we went out to open an account at the American Oriental Bank.

We had gone scarcely a block when a voice called, "Lowdy! Lowdy!"

There was one of Walter's American army buddies rushing toward him. Then who should be the teller at the bank but Walter's college roommate from Arizona! These encounters resulted in immediate invitations to dinner. Within a few days, Walter was convinced that it was not true that "East is East and West is West and never the twain shall meet." Everywhere we went there were friends from different parts of the world and a host of new friends in the making. China was considered the place of opportunity by many young Westerners, especially in business.

Walter was eager to reach Nanking and get started on his work. For myself, my ambition was to stand with him to the best of my abilities so that he could use his remarkable training and talents.

A few days later we took the overnight train from Shanghai to Nanking. There we were lodged temporarily in the large home of John Reisner, head of the Famine Prevention Project and Dean of the University's Department of Agriculture.

It was to be expected that Walter and I, especially as newlyweds in a foreign land, would have some adjustments to make. After all, we had written only a few letters during the eleven years after we first met, and had just five days together to get reacquainted before the wedding took place. Both of us were set in our ways. I was thirty-two and Walter was thirty-four. But we had married "for better or for worse." Divorce was rare then, and unthinkable for us, so it was up to us to make the marriage work.

There were a few similarities in our backgrounds. Both families had been held together to a large degree by admiration for and love of the mother. Walter's mother was a minister's daughter and had instilled in him the desire for scholarship. Neither family had much money. Other than that, everything was different. My family had been accustomed to doing everything together, while Walter's family members were not close and when there was friction they might not speak to one another for weeks or even months. Naturally this was reflected in Walter's behavior after we were first married. He did not expect the openly-expressed love and support I was accustomed both to getting and giving, and doubtless his Oxford education also trained him to be reserved.

I idolized him, but he was irritated and embarrassed when I bragged about his accomplishments. My uninhibited enthusiasm about almost everything made him nervous at first because, as a scientist, he believed in soberly examining all the facts before making up his mind about anything.

One particular problem we had during our first months in Nanking seemed unsolvable. Around the house Walter continually smoked a pipe. This was distasteful to me not only because of my Methodist upbringing, but because it made it very hard to understand what he was saying. He was used to being independent and I could see it would do no good to nag him about it, so finally, one day, I chose one of his smaller pipes and went into his study with it hanging from my mouth.

"If this pipe smoking is so nice and means so much to you, Walter," I said, clenching it between my teeth, "then I want to enjoy it with you. As long as you smoke a pipe, I will. When you stop smoking, I will also stop."

He withstood that pipe hanging from my lips for about three days. Then he put his pipe down and never smoked again.

CHAPTER 9
LIFE IN NANKING (1922-7)

Our first winter in Nanking was miserable. Walter declared he was colder there than he had been in Missoula, Montana. The big Reisner house had no central heating--just fireplaces in the dining and living rooms. Sometimes we carried around little ceramic or clay ho-pans containing small pieces of glowing live charcoal to keep ourselves warm.

Cold or not, Walter insisted he must have his daily bath. The bathtub pipes were frozen, so every morning the houseboy filled a bucket from the kitchen pump for Walter to splash over himself, as he had done since Oxford days. That water would freeze in the tub, but Walter would dump another bucketful over himself each day, standing on the ice, until it was about twelve inches thick. It did not melt until the sun began to shine some weeks later.

Nanking, with its 400 Americans and 200 British in residence, had developed a fine language school for the foreigners. It was not easy for grown men like Walter to go back to school and, like children, repeat after the teacher the Chinese words for book, bag, school, house, baby. Yet in twelve months he had a good working knowledge of the language. He felt he could not wait until the year's end to start working with the Chinese students, though, because he saw the need to teach them calisthenics right away. He had learned that for centuries Chinese scholars had considered physical effort beneath the dignity of the educated. The students even hired coolies to carry their hymn books to church on Sundays. They could not understand why American professors would exert so much effort to chase little tennis balls when they could hire coolies to do it. Walter was determined to teach the value of exercise and so began to give physical fitness lessons at the University.

Walter was part of the Famine Prevention team which included professors who were trying to eradicate wheat rust, produce disease-free seed, improve the fiber crops and control silkworm disease. They believed that by producing cotton and silk, the farmers would be able to buy food if their own crops should fail.

The Chinese produced some of the finest silk in the world. But for generations farmers had lost up to ninety percent of their crop because the silkworms would die just as they were ready to spin. The farmers thought that a devil got into the worms and produced the disease now known as pebrine. When the farmers were provided with disease-free eggs they harvested a very profitable crop. To further encourage the market, the Silk Commission of America put up $50,000 to construct a fireproof building to be used as a "silkworm hotel." I visited the place often. It housed more than three million silkworms which consumed ten tons of mulberry leaves daily. Several times a day the worms were moved, by hand, onto fresh new leaves by 112 students who were hired as waiters to cater to the silkworms' needs.

Other urgent projects China needed--concerning floods, erosion and forestry--had been delayed because as yet no qualified experts had been found. When Dean Reisner discovered that Walter was qualified in all three fields, ample research funds were made available to him. Walter explored Northwest China. His assignment: to find the causes of the Yellow River floods which destroyed the crops.

Walter studied the old official records and made preparations for his first expedition in August of 1923. He left with O.J. Todd of Palo Alto, California (the American engineer who would rechannel the runaway Yellow River after the great flood of 1932), two foreign experts and several young Chinese scientists. They wanted to examine the site where, in 1852, the river had broken through its enormous system of dikes, changed course and gone 400 miles to the north, emptying into the Gulf of Chihli instead of into the Yellow Sea.

They headed to Honan and the Yellow River but, when they reached the great plain through which the river flowed, there was no water to be seen. Instead, they saw the outer dike--a gargantuan, flat-topped shelf forty to fifty feet high, stretching as far as the eye could see. When they mounted this dike they faced an inner dike, set atop the first, seven miles from the edge. Only after climbing this were they able to look down into the silt-laden river! There the reason for this hidden river became clear. Having no means of dredging to keep the channel clear, the Chinese had built the dikes higher as the bed of the river rose with yearly silt deposits filling the channel. Over the generations, the gigantic flow had literally been lifted above the plain along 400 miles of its course. Without machines or engines, steel, timber, or stone, millions of farmers, over centuries of time, had accomplished this stupendous monument to the human will by carrying earth in little baskets from their own farms to raise the dikes of the river.

Despite their heroic efforts, the river would sometimes still flood, killing by drowning and subsequent famine untold millions on the densely populated plain below. No wonder the Yellow River was called "China's Sorrow."

Returning to Nanking, Walter pored over the data evening after evening. He described the problem to me, tracing the history of it on the maps spread out over his desk.

"The villain is erosion," he declared. "I must find its source!"

And so the following spring he led his team on a 2,000-mile survey into the vast northwest provinces where China had had a capital--Sian--and a Golden Age of agriculture over 2,000 years before. As always, he wrote a daily diary in the form of letters to me in which he detailed his experiences, investigations, findings and conclusions. These he mailed in packets whenever his group reached a town large enough to have a post office. He was shocked, he wrote, to see poverty everywhere. Some of the walled cities were almost depopulated. Many other scientists were then attributing northwest China's decay to an adverse change of climate, but when Walter found forest trees flourishing naturally inside the protection of temple walls, he knew that the destructive force was not climate.

Pushing on, he found millions of acres of formerly rich food-growing lands literally eaten away, traversed by gullies sometimes 200-400 feet deep. The erosion of soil had started during the time of prosperity when the rich, lightweight, wind-deposited loess topsoil was exposed to the weather by ploughing, even the sides of foothills, to meet the food demands of a large, growing population. The farmers had no technical knowledge, nor even the stones to build strong terraces for holding back the earth. Erosion accelerated out of control and for centuries the Yellow River tributaries had been washing the good soil off the farmlands and into the main river where it was carried in the form of silt and deposited down on the plain.

Walter called the devastated area a "man-made desert"-- a term that became widely used as his theories proved true and applicable to other parts of the world as well.

Walter wrote well, and when he was deeply stirred his reports became dramatic, even poetic. From Northwest China he described the conditions of starvation. To him there was no more horrible way to die.

"Food riots are terrifying," he wrote. "Starving people will not keep the peace; neither will they stay within their own borders nor honor their treaties. A starving farmer will even eat his seed grain, knowing that it is disastrous for his future to do so. Parents will sell their children for a little food for themselves in the hope that the children will be kept alive by others. In time of famine the entire fabric of society falls apart. The law of the jungle rules when people must fight for food.

"Finally, in the last stages of starvation, people become tragically silent. They remain almost motionless as they wait out the long days and nights for slow death."

When Walter returned from his expedition, he said to me, "Now I know what my life work is to be. I must study the relation of peoples to their lands and how, by destruction of food-growing lands and raw resources, they undermine their cultures and their civilizations and bring disaster to all the generations that follow. In the last analysis, all things are purchased with food."

While Walter was on expeditions things were very busy for me. Not long after our arrival in Nanking the University constructed a large house for us on the campus. Since I had been brought up in the spirit of hospitality and Walter and I both enjoyed visitors, we found ourselves frequently acting as hosts. Hotel rooms in Nanking were scarce and when people came with nowhere to stay I could not turn them away. Accommodating others, at a modest cost, supplemented some of Walter's salary and it certainly increased our knowledge of human nature. All kinds of people wanted to see China in those days, including journalists, artists and many others.

Because the U.S. Navy personnel from the river gunboats were moved around like chessmen they never could establish homes, so they were grateful when their wives could stay with us for a few weeks while their vessels plied the lower Yangtze. We knew that if ever trouble came, they would be there to protect us.

The mother of one of the navy men we knew came to Nanking on a writing assignment for a popular American weekly to do an article on "What It Costs the Chinese to Worship Their Ancestors." Every day she would come to my house and pick my brains for material. I saw that she and her editor were really interested in understanding the financial and spiritual burden the people were under because of ancestor worship.

One day she didn't come and I learned later that she suddenly had a stroke and died. I was sad and shocked. She had become a good friend who cared about the Chinese and wanted to bring into the open a very complex problem. I was disappointed that her work would never be completed.

"Why shouldn't I finish that assignment?" I asked Walter. "Americans have no idea what is involved in the religion of the Chinese."

Walter was not optimistic, but I decided to introduce myself to the editor and ask for the job. I sat down at my typewriter and wrote six pages on "The Experiences of an American Woman in the Interior of China 1916-1921" and sent it to him as background material and as a sample of my writing. Since there was no airmail, it took weeks for mail to reach America and just as long to receive a reply. I had almost forgotten about the article when a letter arrived from the editor. I opened it and, to my surprise, out dropped a check for seventy-five dollars for the short article I had sent. He also asked me to write the report on Chinese ancestors.

I combined official information with my personal experiences with Chinese funerals and customs. The subject had interested me for a long time because of my concern for the economic as well as the educational needs of the Chinese people. We were shocked to discover how extensively ancestor worship, with its obsession for sons and more sons, was responsible for a long train of ills in China. It had placed upon the Chinese people one of the heaviest economic burdens a people had ever been compelled to bear, and the custom of looking backward for centuries produced the dead weight of conservatism from which modern China had to extricate itself.

The death of every adult Chinese male produced a new ancestor for whom custom demanded a heavy wooden casket, and an elaborate, expensive funeral with feasts, bands and ceremonies lasting for days before the final procession took place. I saw hundreds of Chinese funerals. The thick, heavy caskets consumed a large portion of China's much needed timber. The grave sites were many times the size of the average American plot, so that a man's final resting place, unless he was very poor, took up more land than was required to support him during his lifetime.

All this was a tremendous drain on the national resources. In many places that silent population outnumbered the living and there were large areas where the good lands seemed to grow little more than tombs. Some valleys were a maze of mounds. China's food-growing lands increasingly were limited by the demands of space for the dead. In addition, there was the huge cost of the yearly ceremonies, gifts and sacrifices which had to be borne by the survivors.

China has long held the tradition of razing all graves at the change of each dynasty. The Manchus, whose reign began in 1644, had ended this custom. It was not resumed when China became a republic in 1911, because the Chinese feared that it would be treating their ancestors "undemocratically." By the 1920s, graves had been increasing for 700 years. Dead men were made into gods, and women were placed into a kind of slavery, whose only self-esteem came in the production of sons.

Once I had assembled the material I worked hard and fast and sent the story off. To my delight a huge check for $250 came back in payment. The editor asked me to send more articles on China, and I continued to write for him until we left there several years later.

I also wrote an article on "The Outrage of May 30, 1925," about a momentous strike and subsequent events which, I predicted, heralded the downfall of the foreigner in China. I wanted the world to know why there were problems and who was to blame. I gave the background as I had learned it there personally.

The greed of the British and Japanese factory owners was greater in China than anywhere else; working conditions were intolerable and wages shameful. Finally the Chinese had led a strike at a Japanese cotton mill. Student leaders who demonstrated on the workers' behalf were arrested. When a large group of their fellow students, unarmed, marched in protest to the jail in the International Settlement at Shanghai, the British opened fire, killing and wounding many. At that moment the flame of anti-white resentment flared up all over China. Students occupied all the telegraph offices and sent out the message to the world: "Foreigners shoot and kill unarmed students in Shanghai." They organized demonstrations in every town and village, held huge parades and carried placards denouncing the cruelties inflicted on their people by the foreigners. That marked the end of the era when outsiders could beat and humiliate the Chinese at will.

On a summer break from the heat of the plain Walter and I went to the mountain resort of Gu-ling in Lu Shan mountains on the southern bank of the Yangtze where we were joined by Rachel Pen, my "Chinese little sister." We had kept in touch during her two-year kindergarten training course at Soochow and also when she returned to Chengtu to train a corps of kindergarten teachers to open new kindergartens.

One day she and I were hiking, enjoying the superb scenery, when we came upon a clear mountain stream. We were both very thirsty. I was afraid to drink unboiled water, but Rachel took a chance. Very shortly thereafter her temperature rose alarmingly and her eyes glazed. She had typhoid fever.

We rushed her down to our hospital in Nanking. She was given the best treatment and care that our Chinese-American staff could offer and I visited her daily, but she lay for weeks, making no progress. Then she developed pneumonia. The doctor told me to have her casket prepared and I was thoroughly shaken. I wondered, was God taking my "Little Sister"?

But Rachel hung on. The nurses and doctors were amazed. "Shang Ti must have some special work for Rachel," they said. "Otherwise, how could she be so near to heaven yet remain with us?"

Finally she began to recover, and I was allowed to take her to our house. As she regained her health we had many talks about education for women, about her hopes for her people and the wonderful opportunities which democracy would offer them if only China could get established among the free nations. More and more I could see that she was developing great vision and was the kind of leader who is rare in any land--a national treasure. When she regained full strength she returned to her teachers at Chengtu.

I was sad to see her go, but she had rekindled memories of my years in Chengtu. I missed my work there--opening schools and helping girls to prepare for life in the twentieth century. I had loved the challenge of every town, the excitement of the progress I had helped to build, and the close association with people I had learned to love so much. I once more yearned to help modernize the status of Chinese women, to improve the lot of the people as a whole, and to bring about better understanding between Americans and Chinese.

All one winter I spent an afternoon each week at the Governor's Palace across the city teaching English to the governor's wife, Mrs. Chee. The poor woman had not yet given her husband the son demanded for ancestor worship, but she was protected from divorce for three years, because she was in mourning for her husband's mother.

Mrs. Chee and I had great fun discussing the many ways we did things in almost totally opposite ways. For example, American books begin at the top of the page and read left to right, while Chinese books begin at the right and read from the top down. We put footnotes at the bottom of the page, while they put theirs at the top. The Chinese made the first compass with the hand pointing south to the magnetic pole; when we invented the instrument much later, we made it point to the north.

She thought it was odd to call a person "Mr. Smith," when the Chinese would put the family name first and say "Smith Mr." How could our postal system be efficient, she wondered, when we write the address backward? The Chinese put the country first, then the city, town, street number, and name.

Teaching individuals was satisfying, but the best way that I, and other American women, found to express our interest in the Chinese people was by organizing the Nanking University Faculty Wives Club, which dedicated itself to social work. To start with, we each contributed five dollars, making a fund of $500. With this we purchased pieces of the famous Nanking tapestries and made them into cushions and bags to sell to to tourists. Within two and a half years we had raised over $9,000. We had already built our faculty house especially for Chinese teachers and were starting on another.

When I became president of the Faculty Wives Club in 1925, we organized a social service club among some of the leading Chinese women and affiliated them with our American Women's Club. It was probably the first club of its kind in China. It was not easy for the traditionally shy, secluded Chinese woman to take part in public life, so we worked gently with them at first, then encouraged them to become independent. After all, it was their country.

One of our first projects was to arrange for the wealthier Chinese women to open their gate houses at least one day a week during the cold weather and to provide tubs, hot water and soap so that the poor women could bathe their children in comfort.

Through this club the Chinese and Americans of the University community became like a big family. Every semester each faculty wife entertained thirty-five junior class boys for tea, ten senior class college boys to a light meal, and had a number of Chinese faculty members to dinner. In addition, there was an "open tea" at some home every day so that no one, either Chinese or American, was ever without a place to go and be among friends.

Walter and I were planning a family of our own, but we had been in China almost two years when the doctor said it was not likely we could have children. Both Walter and I were praying for guidance and help when I heard that occasionally the Shanghai YWCA received babies for adoption. I contacted a secretary I knew there and before long she wrote me saying that a young nurse from Scotland, newly widowed, might be giving up her baby.

I took the train for Shanghai at once and went to see the mother at the hospital. She was a lovely woman whose story was even more sad than I expected. We sat down together and I held her hand as she told me that it began when she lost her first child, a three year-old boy, in Scotland. This had so saddened her that her husband, a musician, thought they should leave the country and go to the international city of Shanghai to escape the memories. All the travel arrangements were made when her husband, too, died.

Nearly crushed by the dual loss, she nevertheless decided to go and make a new life for herself in China. On the sea voyage she discovered that she was pregnant. Being a devout Christian, she contacted the YWCA immediately upon landing, for advice and help. They found a position for her after the birth and advised her to adopt out the baby. There was no way she could make a living without leaving him with a Chinese amah all day long, and the simple Chinese women at that time knew nothing of the sanitation and nutrition necessary to keep an infant alive and healthy.

Before leaving, I let her know that my husband and I were longing for a son. "If you would consider us," I told her, "I will take you to Nanking to live with us for three weeks so that you can see the kind of loving family and home your baby will have."

"Several people want my son," she answered, "but you are the first to have any sympathy or feeling for me."

She agreed, and we returned together. It was assumed by everybody that she was a nurse who came to help me learn how to care for this new arrival, and no one suspected otherwise. She was satisfied that ours was the right home and after three weeks the legal adoption took place.

We were excited and happy beyond words. To the Chinese, the arrival of a son was a blessing from the gods. To us he was the answer to our prayers. By the time Billy was a year old he could walk and already had a small vocabulary in two languages. He spoke to us in English and to the servants in Chinese, using the correct tones. Billy never ceased to surprise us.

We never had any pets in China for fear of disease, but one day when a friend came riding by on a beautiful horse, I held Billy up so he could pet the horse's nose. He was thrilled and excited. His regular nightly prayer was, "God bless Daddy, Mommy, Billy and the world, Amen," but that night as

I put him to bed he would only say "God bless the horse's nose." "All right, Billy," I sighed, "God bless the horse's nose." Then he happily repeated it and continued with his regular prayer.

Every afternoon about four o'clock, if Walter was not away on an expedition, he would put Billy on his shoulders and take him up to the University weather station to read the anemometer registering windspeed. One day when some guests for tea overstayed their welcome, Billy, two years old by then, came into the living room.

"Come on, Daddy," he said clearly. "Let's go up to the University and read the anemometer."

The guests were amused to hear him use those big words. They also got the message and left.

Meantime, one of my neighbors, Pearl Buck, who was married to an agricultural expert, experienced the heartbreak of having their baby born severely retarded. On the low salary Pearl's husband made, they could not afford to send the child to a suitable school in America. To earn money, Pearl began writing about the Chinese people she had come to love, and eventually was so successful that they could take their daughter to America to support her in an appropriate institution.

Pearl Buck found she could never have more children, and when she saw the joy that Billy was to us and how promising he was in every way, she decided to adopt a baby, too. Since her baby would have to grow up with her older, defective child, Pearl sent to a New York orphanage and asked for a baby that no one else would take. They gave her a neglected, unwanted little girl who thrived on the love and care Pearl lavished on her. She was such a joy that as Pearl began to make real money with her books she adopted several other children. Later, after the United States was involved in several wars in Asia, Pearl's heart was especially touched by the plight of the thousands of babies our American soldiers were leaving fatherless in Korea, Japan and Vietnam. Most of them were never acknowledged by their fathers or by the U.S. Government. She used her increasing fame to promote a foundation for the adoption and education of these youngsters.

As our lives became busier and busier I found myself looking for time to be alone with Walter. One little incident turned out to give us some of that precious time on a regular basis for years to come. We had a barber come to our home regularly to cut Walter's hair. However, Walter was so busy that he sometimes forgot the appointment. One day, when we were to go to an important Chinese Social function, I saw that his hair looked terrible, but it was too late to get a barber.

"Walter," I said, "You sit down this minute and let me see what I can do to improve your looks."

Like a sheep to the shearer, he sat down and I began with my scissors as I had seen my mother cut my father's hair all during my girlhood. When I had finished Walter was delighted.

"You do a better job than the barber!" he exclaimed.

Henceforth, each week for the next fifty years, unless Walter was traveling without me, one of us would say, "It is time for another 'snip-up'," and while I cut his hair, we would have ten or fifteen minutes of uninterrupted time together communicating on personal, national, or international subjects. I appreciated the payment for my service, too. It was always a loving thank-you kiss.

*****

In the fall of 1925, an opportunity came our way that widened our experience in the Orient. The Japanese government was holding a Pan-Pacific Science Congress in Tokyo and invited the leading scientific organizations from the nations on the Pacific Rim to participate. It was Japan's "coming out party" for foreign visitors to see that, in science, the Japanese had caught up with the Western world. Delegates and their wives were invited to be guests of the Imperial Government of Japan for an entire month. The United States asked Walter to go as its forestry and land conservation representative. We left Billy in the care of neighbors and set sail.

The Japanese were extraordinary hosts. On shipboard we were welcomed to their shores by radio. Upon disembarking, every one of the 175 foreign delegates was greeted by a Japanese official and presented with a 30-day railway pass to see Japan and a 14-day pass for Korea. We were all housed in the large, earthquake-proof Imperial Hotel designed by the young American architect, Frank Lloyd Wright--the only public structure that had survived the great earthquake of 1923. Our hosts included the Emperor, several of Japan's most powerful princes, the President of the Imperial University, the President of the House of Peers, several barons, and the Mayor of Tokyo. We were invited to innumerable garden parties, luncheons, theater parties and tours.

Everywhere the architecture and landscaping reflected Japanese religious fervor and love of beauty, but it was their remarkable work in erosion control and reforestation that excited Walter. He frequently gave up a party or tour in order to see more of it. The Japanese had so little level food-producing land that they could not afford to lose a single acre and they were determined to hold the mountain soils in place. In fact, Japan's progress in every field of science astonished the foreign visitors.

Special entertainment was offered wives while our husbands attended conference sessions with the 400 Japanese delegates. I was becoming so familiar with Walter's work that I would have enjoyed the scientific lectures, but the events for women were superb and we could share the experiences later and thereby experience twice as much. Together we saw the riotous autumn colors at Hakone and at Matsushima Bay with its 249 little isles, and sailed through the Inland Sea to Kyoto, with her ancient palaces and matchless gardens. We saw Lake Chuzenji, toured the lakes at the foot of Mount Fujiyama by auto and yacht, then had the thrilling drive to near its summit.

We went up to Nikko by train, crossing and recrossing the famous twenty-one mile avenue of giant cryptomeria trees. I learned the history of these famous trees: long ago, to honor the first Togkugawa <u>Shogun,</u> each <u>daimyo</u> (provincial lord) was to bring a gift for his shrine. Those with large, rich provinces brought elaborate gifts, but one daimyo was from a poor province. His modest offering consisted of cryptomeria saplings. He had 20,000 of them planted for the <u>Shogun</u> along the road to Nikko. Nobody remembers the other gifts, they say, but any Japanese school child will tell you that Masatsuna Natsuidaira, Lord of Kawagoe, was responsible for this glorious avenue of trees.

The social affairs were a demonstration both of Japanese respect for tradition and their determination to meet the West with dignity. A welcoming reception was given the delegates and their wives at the palace of Emperor Taisho by his brother. Walter wore the prescribed high silk hat and cutaway coat and I wore my best silk hat and afternoon dress of blue chiffon tiers over a narrow silk skirt. Inside, we were received by waiting Japanese nobles, men in western-style formal afternoon clothes and their ladies in traditional kimonos. Ahead of us in the audience room, the Japanese guests bowed very low before the prince. I became very nervous at the prospect of performing this feat in my tight skirt and was debating whether to risk it when, to my great relief, he extended his arm to shake my hand.

Next we were invited to one of Japan's greatest social functions of the year, the Emperor's Chrysanthemum Party, held on November tenth at his palace. Once inside the walls, we walked about half a mile through the majestic old garden, then ascended stone stairs to the great flower exhibition pavilion, where, for variety and artistry in the display of flowers, the Japanese have no peers.

The several thousand guests were politely kept to the prescribed route by courtiers in velvet dress, and we walked in procession to a great, open reception area. There we were told that the ailing old emperor had sent his regrets. Yet, on the minute of three o'clock, the Prince Regent whom we knew soon would be emperor, appeared with his wife at some distance from the guests to head the procession through the rest of the garden. They did not look at us, for the immediate royal family considered themselves divine and were worshiped as such. (Many years later, after the defeat of Japan in World War II, this prince, then emperor, came down from his divine pedestal to "become a human being." He and Walter met at a tree-planting ceremony when Walter was advisor to General MacArthur's Flood Control Commission for Japan. That time they not only shook hands, but talked man-to-man about Japan's food-production problems.)

At the end of our month in Japan, Walter went on to Korea for two weeks to inspect the reforestation and erosion control measures Japan had taken there, and I returned home to Nanking and to Billy to revel in having been treated so royally. My childhood of austerity had not prepared me to ever expect such privilege and opulence. I had been dazzled, but remained always willing to share good fortune.

It was morning, just seven days before Christmas, 1926. Nanking was bitterly cold. Our large living room was cozy and warm, with gay decorations and a lovely tree in the bay window, with beribboned packages tied among its branches just above the reach of our eager, starry-eyed Billy. Outside, the sharp wind blew from over the ice and snow in Siberia, but some important errands were waiting. Wearing two sweaters and a heavy overcoat, I stepped into my rickshaw, doubled my heavy steamer rug and tucked it around my lap. Despite my protests, the rickshaw man would wear only one padded garment because he claimed that his running kept him warm. He picked up the shafts and began to run through the narrow streets.

As we wound our way between the high walls of one street, we passed an open gate through which I caught a fleeting glimpse of some children huddled together, dressed only in rags. In an instant we were past the gate and all I could see was the usual dingy wall, its whitewash gone except in patches.

"What place is that behind the wall?" I called out to my rickshaw man.

"It is the city orphanage," he called back, without losing a step, "the place where 'Nobody's Children' live."

I thought of all the happy children around the world celebrating the birthday of the Christ Child who came to bring joy to all children, but there was no joy for these youngsters.

"Turn around," I told him. "Return to the gate and take me inside to the superintendent."

Inside the compound we passed huddled groups of children standing motionless. Through their rags their skin showed purple with cold. They watched us with listless eyes and solemn faces. They were terribly thin. The superintendent was startled by this unexpected morning call from a foreigner and politely waited for me to speak.

I explained that I was interested in children and wanted to know about those in his charge. He told me that 250 orphans lived there. They received no regular schooling, and no, they had never had a Christmas party.

"Would there be any objection to our giving 'Nobody's Children' a Christmas party?" I asked.

His eyes lit up. "How much money will the American woman give for the party?" he unctuously inquired. He must have been thinking that I was a rich American and a generous sum for the food would provide him with a large "squeeze," as the Chinese called taking a share for oneself. His face fell when he learned that we would cook the food ourselves and bring some high school girls with us to serve it.

That evening when I told Walter about the idea, he was just as excited as I was. As soon as we told our friends and neighbors about it, they put aside their own Christmas preparations to help. We collected some money. Then we made 250 bags of thin, red net cloth and stuffed each one with a bright red apple, a mandarin orange, a handful of peanuts, some hard candy and a ball of candied popcorn that we made in my kitchen. We also provided a pair of warm stockings for each child.

Meantime, Walter was busy arranging with Chinese caterers for huge barrels of fluffy steamed rice. This would be a treat, for when I had visited the home a second time I learned that the children usually were fed only a soupy rice mixture.

At eleven o'clock on Christmas morning a cavalcade of rickshaws left our compound with eight high school girls and myself loaded with presents. We met Walter with his carloads of food at the orphanage gate. When we arrived, the yard was empty. Inside, the children were sitting on rough benches around tables, waiting. The superintendent said they had been there for two hours, wondering if we were really coming to give them a party.

We sent the orphans into the yard with the high school girls who told them the Christmas story and taught them songs while we put a colorful bag of goodies at each place. In the center of the tables we set huge steaming bowls of fish, vegetables with beef, and vegetables with pork. Then we asked the children to file past Walter on the way in. Their faces lit up as he dipped empty bowls into the fragrant rice barrels, down and up again as fast as he could, trying to keep up with the eager little hands stretched out toward him. His cheeks were flushed and perspiring in spite of the cold, and his eyes glowed with satisfaction. When the children reached their tables their eyes opened with disbelief. Obviously they had never dreamed of such a feast and so many treats. We told them they could refill their bowls as many times as they wished. Finally, every child was chi bao lo (filled up to the neck) and still there was some food left.

Then they all went out into the yard with their gifts and goodies except for one small fellow who remained alone at his table. Great tears rolled down his pinched little face. I sent one of our high school girls to find out what was wrong. She returned, smiling.

"When I asked him why he was crying he sobbed, 'Just look at all that good food left, and I am too full to eat any more!'"

Suddenly I, too, felt like crying. We had enjoyed giving them what was probably the happiest memory in their dull little lives, but what was their future, after all?

CHAPTER 10
COMMUNISM COMES TO CHINA:
THE NANKING INCIDENT (1927)

Though we had never suffered from it personally, during our years in China we were aware of a growing antiforeign bitterness which we could fully understand. It stemmed chiefly from the nineteenth century Opium Wars, started by China's resistance to foreign opium trade on her territory; and the Boxer Rebellion, which tried to end foreign influence in China altogether. Both these efforts failed, but the bitterness was fanned by the subsequent occupation of Chinese territory by foreign troops and the commercial exploitation, crushing taxes, indemnities and other humiliations laid upon the Chinese by outsiders.

We had always thought of ourselves as being in a different category of foreigners. We were making friendships and helping the Chinese people achieve a better life in which they could stand independently and meet the outside world on equal terms in medicine, agriculture, education, commerce, and technology. But the event of 1925, when British troops gunned down unarmed Chinese students, had shown that the days of the white man's presence in China, good or bad, were numbered.

Why were democratic friends of the Chinese such as America also included? Because our leaders failed to understand our kinship to the Chinese in their aspirations. In 1911, the Western world should have been thrilled when Sun Yat-sen successfully organized the overthrow of the corrupt Manchu Ch'ing dynasty and set up a republic. Instead, the foreign powers did their best to keep the new government weak so it could not interfere with their commercial activities. Sun's continuing struggle for Chinese independence was beset with overwhelming problems. China's revenues from customs and salt tax were already pledged to repay foreign loans and indemnities, and foreign gunboats were there to protect their interests. Revenues from railways and land were being syphoned off by local warlords who constantly involved the population in battles among themselves, and corruption was rampant.

The army was still in the hands of Yuan Shi-kai, who had been commander under the Empress Dowager. Hoping to get strength behind the new republic, Dr. Sun resigned as president (unwisely) in Yuan's favor. But Yuan used the opportunity to attempt to set himself up as emperor of his own dynasty and betray the republic. Fortunately this plan failed and he soon died ("by request," Walter was later told by a high-ranking Chinese official--which meant by poison). However, Yuan's maneuvers had helped to split the country into two rival factions. One was in the north, a reactionary clique centered around Peking and supported by a group of warlords, some of whom even cooperated with the Japanese to the detriment of their own countrymen. The other faction was in the south, centering around Dr. Sun and his then democratically-minded Kuomintang Party, to which students and young workers were rallying.

In a desperate effort to save his country from chaos, Dr. Sun appealed to Great Britain for a $10 million loan to finance an army to restore order, but this was refused. Next he approached the United States, and in addition to the loan, he requested that we undertake to turn China into a democratic republic as we were doing for the Philippines. Britain persuaded the United States to turn him down. Thus we lost our greatest opportunity of the twentieth century. Our refusal meant that Dr. Sun had no choice; in 1924 he turned to the Soviet Union for help.

The Russians not only agreed to provide the $10 million but made it an outright gift. They also agreed to train China's new army. They voluntarily returned Chinese territory taken by the Tsar and gave up their commercial concessions in China, all this in exchange for China's acceptance of Soviet advisors and unlimited Soviet propaganda privileges in the country. At that time Soviet tactics were poorly understood. Sun Yat-sen was desperate, and the deal was made. Chinese officers went to Moscow for training (among them was Chiang Kai-shek) and Russian officers began training Chinese soldiers near Canton. Soviet Commissar Michael Borodin was put in charge of Soviet propaganda.

Our life was scarcely affected by all this because Nanking was a well-defended, walled city with a strong government which had not been involved in internecine wars, and the province had a good governor. Probably the presence of American business, backed by gunboats in the river, had an effect on keeping order. We Americans at the University naturally pinned our hopes on the democratic cause of Dr. Sun Yat-sen.

Then Dr. Sun died in 1925 and the Kuomintang Party leadership fell to Chiang Kai-shek who, with the help of a Russian general, set out on a campaign to defeat the warlords and unify China. The Chinese people were so weary of the infighting and corruption that they flocked to Chiang's side. Cities often fell without a shot fired. In the following months the Peking government was discredited and its armies were pushed north by Chiang's Revolutionary Army. The country had an air of jubilation.

On March 20, 1927, a beautiful early spring day, the whole city of Nanking seemed delighted to learn that Generalissimo Chiang Kai-shek's Revolutionary Army was sweeping north from Canton. Then we also learned that fleeing before him were over 200,000 Peking northern troops who would have to come through Nanking in order to get enough boats to cross the Yangtze. We feared they would loot and burn their way through, but we hoped that Chiang's troops would arrive in time, for we associated Chiang's troops with Dr. Sun's Western ideals and did not doubt that they would protect us. In fact, University officials made plans to go out to the entrance of the University and welcome them with the customary tea as soon as they were spotted.

However, the captains of the U.S. destroyers Preston and Noa, standing in Nanking waters, had their instructions not to take any chances with the American civilians. The captains appointed Walter as liaison between themselves and our Americans in the University area in case of trouble. Next they told the U.S. Consul, Mr. Davis, to put all American women and children aboard the gunboats for a few days until the northern soldiers had completed their retreat across the river and it would be safe to return. Walter had the unpleasant task of getting the women to leave their homes. I was not afraid, having been through so many battles in Szechuan. Besides, at age 37 I was finally pregnant, and I rebelled at this inconvenience. But Walter said that he would never get the others to go if I refused, so reluctantly I packed the one small suitcase each woman was allowed, confident this was only going to a temporary measure.

On the morning of March 24, 1927, I took Billy in a carriage and left with some others for the port, four miles away. We could see that some looting had taken place as the fleeing northerners ran through the city to make their escape across the river by boat. But the local guard had moved in to keep order and anyone caught looting near the port was immediately beheaded. As we approached the river, I began doing tricks with my hands in a frantic effort to distract Billy from the sight of the heads hanging from telephone poles, sometimes enclosed in bird cages. We were soon joined by more foreign women and children and American sailors awaiting us at the dock took us to the ships. On the heels of the fleeing northerners came some of Chiang's troops, reaching the University area just as we women and children were safely aboard ship.

What nobody knew was that Chiang's spectacular victories, popular personality and influence with the West would make him impossible for the Soviets to control. They

decided on a plan to discredit him with the Western powers so
he would get no backing from them. To do this, Borodin had
organized a secret cadre in Chiang's army who would do
Borodin's bidding only. They were the first Kuomintang troops
to reach Nanking. Instead of following Chiang's orders to
protect all foreign life and property in Nanking, they were
ordered by Borodin to destroy all foreign life and property
and to set up guns on the city walls from where they could
fire down upon the American ships and business houses.

Knowing none of this, the thirteen of us women and
children who were taken to the Noa now found ourselves
wedged into a space in the prow intended for six sailors. We
waited there impatiently for two days. Then we heard the
sound of guns firing from within the city and soon a pall of
smoke hung over Nanking. We did not know who was fighting
whom. We had to keep our portholes closed because bullets
from the Nanking shore were popping against that side of the
ship. Just before 3:30 on the afternoon of March the 24th, a
sailor ran down the ladder and threw some cotton on the
table.

"Stuff the children's ears," he shouted breathlessly.
"We're going to open fire and it will burst their eardrums if
you don't."

We grabbed our children to do as we·were told. The gun
deck was just eighteen inches above my head and I explained
to Billy that the big gun right up there was going to talk.
Then I stuffed his ears and put my hands over them. In a few
moments a terrific explosion shattered all electric light
bulbs, leaving us in total darkness with our screaming youngsters. Then the empty shell case hit the steel plate above and
we heard the shell exploding far away, inside the city. This
angered me. I loved the Chinese and was appalled to think of
white men, especially Americans, bombing their lovely city.
Of course we did not realize that the Americans were
returning the fire of Borodin's guns. I counted as our destroyer fired sixty rounds in all, each one followed by the crash of
the empty shell to the deck and the explosion in the distance.

When the shooting ended and night fell, we were still behind closed portholes and beginning to gasp for air. I went up to the main deck to find an officer. I kept to the side away from Nanking and could see the town of Pu Kow in flames on the opposite, distant shore. The retreating northern soldiers who had crossed the river were, as anticipated, looting and burning. The poor inhabitants were silhouetted against the light of their burning homes as they fled along the riverbank carrying their children and their possessions on their backs.

I found an officer and pleaded, "We are stifling down there. May we open a porthole?"

"No, lady," he replied. "There is too much shooting. About midnight we are going to move you to a refugee ship bound for Shanghai. You will just have to put up with it until then."

I hated the idea of leaving for Shanghai without knowing what was happening to Walter, but at midnight the sailors started loading us into a small open motorboat. While I was standing with Billy waiting to go down the ladder I heard a sailor call to the officer above:

"Don't load the boat too heavy. The engine's on the blink tonight."

My heart stopped. We were in terrible danger. At Nanking the Yangtze meets the incoming ocean tides and the turbulence of the water is violent. The tide was coming in and the river current flowing against it made rough, choppy waves. In the open boat we were entirely exposed to the elements. It was bitterly cold and a strong wind blew stinging sleet in our faces.

We had expected a short ride, perhaps one of thirty minutes, but we had a rude shock. All ships on the Yangtze were blacked out, and as their great hulks loomed up in the darkness there was no way of knowing whether they were U.S. ships or not. Our American sailors had started out without knowing exactly where the refugee ship was anchored. Out in the open water our engine stopped. The sailors worked on it, using a flashlight they tried to hide with their caps, but bullets from shore immediately began splashing around us. The engine finally started and we moved on.

As we approached each darkened vessel our sailors would call out, "Are you expecting any refugee women and children tonight?"

The men on the ships would generally reply with some unprintable expression, indicating an emphatic "No!"

We were lost in the blackness of night out on the turbulent Yangtze, unable either to find the refugee ship or return to the destroyer. Our small boat tossed about helplessly and water was beginning to pour into the bottom. We were thoroughly cold and miserable. I prayed that if it capsized we would die quickly without further suffering.

Once again our engine went dead and this time the sailors could not restart it. We thought we saw an occasional flash of light far downriver, so they took up oars and guided our powerless boat down the current, hoping this was the refugee vessel signaling to us. We followed the flashes until we reached the landing raft on the sheltered side of the ship. It was the right ship this time.

I was too frozen to lift Billy from my lap or even to stand alone, so a member of the ship's crew carried him up the ladder and another helped me. It was now 3:30 in the morning. We had been tossing around out there in the cold and darkness for three hours.

At the top of the steps, Consul Davis was on deck to meet us. I immediately asked him about the Americans still in the city.

"The only news I have is from your husband," he replied. "He phoned me at eight o'clock yesterday morning to tell me that soldiers had arrived whom they expected to be friendly, but who were attacking foreigners and had already killed the University Vice President, Dr. Williams. He is trying to assemble the Americans at Bailie Hall. He said he would try to keep in touch with me, but the phone went dead. I have heard nothing more from there. Our Chinese contacts already told us that some Americans have been killed and that all the homes of foreigners have been looted and many burned."

I was heartsick, but I knew that Walter would be doing the best job of protecting the University people that anybody could do under the circumstances. He had designed Bailie Hall himself and had it built of brick, so he knew it was fireproof and the safest place for them to go.

Already aboard the refugee ship were the seventy-five American residents of the Sacony Hill area of Nanking, location of the U.S. Consulate and most of the businessmen's homes. Consul Davis had been trying to arrange their evacuation when he learned about the guns being mounted around Sacony Hill to wipe out the foreign community. He sent a Navy guard up onto the consulate roof to signal the Noa to open fire to destroy enemy gun emplacements, but to leave a section of the city wall free of fire so that the Americans could escape. They did so by sliding down fifty feet of rope made from bedclothes, then making it to where the Navy's small boats were waiting to pick them up. Among them was Alice Tisdale Hobart, wife of an American businessman who later wrote some best-selling books about China.

The ship was built to hold eighty-five officers and men. Now it carried 275 of us and we were all hungry. The sailors made huge piles of sandwiches and we ate standing or sitting on the floor. We all exchanged experiences and were horrified by the stories of brutality. One man had been wearing a ring that would not come off, so a soldier chopped off his finger. Another man was killed while resisting robbery. One woman announced that some foreigners had been killed in the port area and we feared they might be our loved ones trying to escape.

Our ship left Nanking for Shanghai before daybreak, and we had no idea whether our husbands were alive or dead. After three anxious days in Shanghai we received news that the survivors were arriving from Nanking on American and British destroyers. Billy and I waited with the others at the docks to greet them, confident Walter was a survivor.

The first man to disembark was our former neighbor, Professor Holroyd, extremely pale and trembling. He was a big, strapping man and I could not imagine what had done this to him. After him came Dean Reisner, wearing a lady's coat and my winter hat. He, too, was pale and shaking. I asked him what had happened.

"Walter is coming ashore on the next boat," he answered wearily. "He will tell you."

I was confidant that courageous, disciplined Walter would not go to pieces in war, but when he arrived he looked as bad as the others. I gently led him to a bench and asked, "What in the world has happened to all you men?"

Then he told me. He had eaten practically nothing for three days while he was rounding up the Americans and getting them onto the ships. They were all starving when the first meal was served on board. Incredibly, the tinned meat they were given was bad, and they were all stricken with ptomaine poisoning. The most seriously ill were taken directly to the hospital. Walter should have gone with them, but I had secured the last two reservations on a ship leaving for America in two days, so he refused treatment. We took him to our hotel room where he could rest. All his possessions including his watch and glasses had been stolen. Weak, and practically in shock, he staggered around making preparations to leave and bit by bit he told me what took place in the University of Nanking after Billy and I left.

"There was considerable confusion when soldiers approached the University in Kuomintang uniforms. President Bowen, Vice-President Dr. Williams and I went out to welcome them with the customary invitation for tea...but instead of a greeting, they stuck out their bayonets and demanded our valuables. Dr. Williams begged them not to take the watch his mother had given him...he was shot dead at my feet. Dr. Bowen was robbed, and the two of us were stood to be shot...I could hear the clicks of the triggers cocking. I was thinking only that there would be one more widow when the officer suddenly said, 'Don't shoot now,' and they trooped away."

"I knew something was very wrong if <u>Chiang</u>'s troops were anti-foreign, and I realized that we were utterly without

protection. There was by then looting and burning all over
the university campus and residential area." Our 10-room
home had been looted of all furniture and of all our belongings.

Walter said that he gathered together some of his trusted
Chinese students and told them to find all the other
Americans and tell them to disguise themselves as Chinese
and hurry to the top floor of Bailie Hall.

They came, straggling up the stairs wearing all sorts of
disguises: dressed as Chinese laborers, farmers, even men
dressed as Chinese women. Each told a chilling story of
brutality and narrow escape. Pearl Buck and her daughter
had been hidden by some poor Chinese neighbors about
twenty-four hours before they were finally rescued. As they
arrived Walter had each one sign his or her name of the back
of a large map, which I still have in my possession--quite an
historic document.

When the phone went dead at 8:00 A.M. during his
conversation with the consul, Walter realized that he and
those for whom he was responsible were trapped in the city,
surrounded by hostile mobs of soldiers determined to rob and
kill them. To make matters worse, there were still some
people missing, including women and children. But the
Americans were not safe even in Bailie Hall. Ferocious
looking soldiers armed with rifles and beheading knives went
up and down the stairs terrorizing them. Frightened children
stood trembling with their tiny hands in the air as they were
robbed even of their little shoes. The soldiers constantly
threatened to kill the hostages if they did not produce more
valuables. Just before 3:30 P.M. President Bowan, listening
through the lattice under the eves of the building, overheard
the soldiers decide to go up and demand 1,000 yuan for each
of the hostages or they would kill them. Immediately soldiers
came dashing up the stairs yelling and firing their guns.

This was the moment when Consul Davis had sent a sailor
up onto the roof of the consulate to signal the Noa to open
fire. The thundering explosions from American guns four
miles away shook the whole building. The startled soldiers

stopped. They must have realized that these were not Chinese guns. The officers blew their whistles to recall all the soldiers in the neighborhood and marched them away in formation, which proved to Walter that the looting and killing had been done under orders. After sixty rounds the American bombardment ceased and all was quiet.

Fortunately General Chiang learned of Borodin's duplicity and issued new orders for his soldiers to protect foreign life and property in Nanking. Contingents of these loyal soldiers began to arrive and they offered Walter their help.

There were still thirty of our American university people unaccounted for. Walter asked his colleague, Dr. Li, to secure a car. Accompanied by two of Chiang's soldiers, they set out to find the missing Americans. Many of the looted buildings were still burning and smoldering. Walter would stop and call out as loudly as he could the names of the people who might be hiding there, hoping they would recognize an American voice and come out. He found some of them in cisterns and some hiding in the back of a police station covered with dirty padded winter garments discarded by police. Late that night they found Anne Moffat, a courageous young teacher, under a pile of straw in a bamboo grove where she had been hidden by Chinese friends. She was barely alive. She had been shot twice in the abdomen and had lain there unattended for fifteen hours. They rushed her back to Bailie Hall where Dr. Daniels was able to remove the bullets and save her life.

By noon the next day Walter was able to report to Dr. Bowan that all the missing Americans had been found. Then he and Dr. Roberts made the perilous four-mile trip to the port to contact our naval forces and arrange for their rescue. The anti-foreign feeling stimulated by Borodin's communist soldiers had infected the general population. The two men had to go on foot through crowds of sullen, scowling faces. At the port they passed the street poles, hung with heads of looters caught by the local guard trying to keep order before Borodin's soldiers arrived. They hurriedly picked their way among the corpses of soldiers and animals to reach the waterfront.

The destroyers were anchored far off in the middle of the river so they hired a boat; but each time they tried to leave the shore it was peppered with bullets by Borodin's snipers. Then they asked a Japanese landing party to signal the U.S. destroyer, and soon a launch carrying Consul Davis and a contingent of heavily armed marines came ashore and took the two men to Admiral Hough on the U.S. flagship. They had arrived just in time, for earlier the admiral had given an ultimatum to the Chinese on shore to deliver all Americans by eleven that morning, or he would shell the entire city. Fortunately, Consul Davis had persuaded him to wait for another three hours. The admiral ordered Walter to go back and evacuate all Americans immediately.

Walter and Dr. Roberts returned to Bailie Hall and, with the help of Chinese students and faculty, assembled a long line of horse carriages and rickshaws. Other Chinese friends brought hot food and gathered up looted garments to help the victims ward off the cold. Walter led the cavalcade and Dr. Roberts brought up the rear to see that no one was left behind. As they left Bailie Hall, they passed between double lines of Chinese colleagues, students, and other friends. Many were weeping and all showed unspeakable grief in their faces as they realized that the Americans were all leaving, possibly never to return.

Darkness fell, and still Walter's party had not reached the port. Finally, three hours overdue, they passed through the city gates and came within sight of our destroyer. The admiral sent small boats which transported them to American and British ships. The once happy international family of Nanking was safe at last, except for the eight dead left behind.

The sun was shining when we put our pathetically few belongings on the President liner in Shanghai. As we sailed for America we wondered what would happen to our Chinese friends in the turmoil of civil war.

Soon we were out of the river estuary. When we entered the Yellow Sea the full force of a typhoon suddenly lashed our ship. All the joys of going home left us, as well as everything in our stomachs. All of us, even Walter, lay helpless with seasickness all the way to Honolulu, for the typhoon stayed with us for the whole of that trip and the ship rolled and pitched with relentless monotony. Unable to move, we watched and listened to our closet door swing open and bang shut, hour after hour, day after day. A jar of medicine rolled back and forth across our stateroom floor with exasperating regularity as the vessel convulsed without ceasing. From time to time, the ship's steward brought us food, but Walter and I were too weak to eat. I could not even reach Billy, so I asked him to pretend he was a little doggie and crawl to where the food was set on the floor and eat as best he could.

Walter estimated that the ship was rising and falling sixty feet into the troughs between the huge waves. Our cabin was on the second deck above the machinery deck, yet we were often left in darkness as waves covered the entire vessel and the ship struggled, shuddering back to the surface. Walter and Billy were miserable, and I felt willing to die. Once, when an enormous wave slapped at our ship with a bang down into total darkness we thought the end had come. Walter reared up from his bunk and said, "If the boat sinks, I can't try to save you." Bad as I felt, I couldn't help but laugh at Walter's resignation. But heaven was with us and it quivered back up to daylight. What a relief to finally reach Honolulu!

From San Francisco we took the train to my family home in Pasadena. We arrived utterly stunned and bewildered. We found that our little son had contracted measles in Shanghai and now had pneumonia as well. We were penniless, and without possessions except for the few essentials given us in Shanghai, and we were expecting a baby. My parents and two sisters welcomed us with open arms and loving hearts. Without them life would have seemed unbearable.

Knowing that I had been instrumental in getting Walter to give up his career in government service to go to China, I asked him, "Are you sorry that you went to China?"

"Not for one minute," was his immediate reply. "I shall always feel that China did more for me that I could ever have done for China."

.

CHAPTER 11
GETTING A NEW START (1927-37)

Breathes there the man with soul so dead
Who never to himself hath said
"This is mine own, my native land"
Whose heart hath ne'er within him burned
As homeward his footsteps he hath turned
From wandering in a foreign land?
                                    --Sir Walter Scott

What blessings are family loyalty and love! My mother and father, and my sisters, Winifred and Beatrice with her family, were all living together in our old home. They welcomed us and helped us in every way possible.

We were the first refugees from the Nanking Affair to reach California and much was written in the papers about our escape. One day a lovely elderly woman came to our door asking for me. She had read of our losses and brought me a beautiful coat. She also left a check for $100. Such touching acts reminded me that the Lord was still with us and my spirits were lifted.

Walter had been depressed on the voyage home, because he was convinced that after five years away he would be obliged to resume his work in the U.S. Forest Service at a lower grade, but he was soon offered several well-paying positions, including two as head of forest experiment stations. He was about to make his choice and start work when he was contacted by officials of the University of California. They had read his report, the first to present a scientific measurement of erosion, and had been impressed by the dramatic statement he made about conditions in Northwest China: "Civilization is running a race with famine and the outcome is very much in doubt."

Newly aware that America's food-growing lands, too, were diminishing, they offered him ample funds to continue his research and suggested he could obtain his Ph.D. at the same time. The urge to continue his research was great and he wanted to accept, but he was concerned about supporting his growing family.

"Walter," I said, "this is the time for you to go on with your research and complete your doctorate. If you should begin a new job now at age 39, you may never go back for that degree. Billy and I can remain in Pasadena with my family until after our new baby comes, and you can go to Berkeley and give your full attention to your studies."

It was decided. Meantime, the Forest Service proposed that Walter undertake a surveying fellowship in the San Bernardino Mountains which would count toward his degree and continue until his classes at Berkeley began. For that summer, Walter, Billy, and I lived in a tent in Devil's Canyon among the flies, mosquitoes and dust. Then Billy and I moved to the family home in Pasadena to await the birth of our child and our reunion with Walter.

His letters showed he loved Berkeley from the start. "This seems more like my home town than any other place I've ever lived," he wrote. "I want to live and die in Berkeley."

Walter worked desperately hard to get his degree in double-quick time while I remained in Pasadena until six months after our daughter was born. We named her Winifred Esther, after two of her aunts who had no children. Billy adored his sister. He would run his little legs tired doing errands for her care. At first he could only say "Wee Esther," which became Westher--her name ever since. By the time the family was united in a rented house on Glen Avenue in Berkeley in the summer of 1928, Walter had nearly completed his degree and had already taken a full time job with the Forest Service. His station would be in Berkeley.

After ten years in China with servants and being involved in social service, it was quite an adjustment to a daily life for me of preparing meals, washing diapers and cleaning. But being elected president of the Trinity Methodist Church Women's Overseas Work broadened my scope of activities. For every meeting I carried little Westher on my hip down the hill to the bus, and while I presided at the meetings she played quietly at my feet.

Before long I, too, loved Berkeley, and we decided to put down roots and buy a home. The Wickham Havens Company was developing the entire hill tract north of the university and selling lots. They must have considered us a good prospect because they offered to build us a house, according to our own plans, on easy payment terms if we could pay cash for the lot. We were paying installments on a car and second-hand furniture. Nevertheless, we decided to take the plunge. We borrowed money from relatives, paid for the lot and began building.

However, the lots did not sell as well as expected. So in September, 1929, we found ourselves moving into a lonesome house among the tall eucalyptus trees on the mountainside, with our nearest neighbor more than a quarter of a mile away. The wind howled, dense and blinding fog rolled in. At this time Walter had to be at Bass Lake in the Sierra and in the San Bernardino Mountains seeing after his research plots, and I did not know how to drive, so we three at home were often completely isolated.

In October, 1929, the stock market crashed. The Great Depression began. All government salaries were immediately cut fifteen percent. In general, Walter left our business affairs to me but, despite my economies, we could not meet the payments on the house. Overdrafts became a nightmare. Like most everybody else we listened to the radio in the evening and we heard Amos tell Andy, who was experiencing the same difficulties as ours, that he ought to talk with his banker even though all he had to talk about was overdrafts.

The next day Walter went to our banker. He told Walter that if he could spare ten dollars he would send the bank assessor to look over our place and advise us. We managed to put together the ten dollars and awaited his report.

"The place will not be worth what you paid for it for at least ten years," he told us. "Sell it. Get rid of it!"

We left no stone unturned in the effort to sell, but too many others were in the same situation. The Wickham Havens Company notified us to either pay up by the end of the month or they would garnishee Walter's salary, leaving us with practically nothing to live on. We lay awake talking the whole of that night before Wickham Havens were due to begin court proceedings.

"You must do something!" Walter told me.

"I have done everything possible, Walter. Now we must turn it over to the Lord."

The next morning when Walter was at his office a professor walked in and said to him, "I hear you have a place up on the hill you want to sell. I have two boys who need a big outdoors in which to play."

It was already dark when the professor came with his family that evening. They looked over the house and without further discussion he said, "We will trade you this house with its mortgage for our Spring Way house with its much smaller mortgage. It is rented right now; but if you live elsewhere the rent will pay the interest on your mortgage. You will lose the equity in the house you sell us, but at least you will have cash equity of about $1600 in mine."

The next morning Wickham Havens received a joyful call from me with the news.

From the time it became clear we could never be happy in our house on the hill, I had been looking at vacant lots.

There were many because in 1922 a fire had swept down over the hills north of the campus and burned everything within fifty-four blocks. I knew exactly the spot for our permanent home--at Cedar and Le Roy, on a large corner double lot that was the lookout point of the area. It was almost level, below the fog belt, and had magnificent views of more than half a circle of San Francisco Bay. It was only five blocks from the university and one block from the Hillside School and Kindergarten--perfect. But it was not for sale.

I found out that its owner, Miss Alexander, lived nearby and had a house to rent next to her own, which we rented. Even though we had not saved a cent, I would often say to her when we were both out gardening, "If you ever decide to sell your corner lot, give us an option on the south half." I would even take guests onto the patio of the house we rented from Miss Alexander and tell them, "Some day we are going to have a home on that south section."

"Now, Ina May," Walter would chide me. "You know that is impossible," and he played upon the Bible story of Jacob and Esau: "We sold our birthright for a mess of pottage on the hill."

But nothing shook my confidence that our dream home would one day be built on that sunny lot.

One afternoon, during the depths of the Depression, Miss Alexander came to me in the garden and said, "It makes me heartsick, but I have to raise some money in the next ten days. If you can pay me $5,350 cash, I will sell you the lot you want."

Here was part of the answer to my prayers, but where could we get the money? With no security to offer except our word, I appealed to relatives. My sister Winifred was holding two small mortgages at that time and she called them in so as to be able to lend us the money. Another friend risked her precious savings to help us. A day ahead of time I was able to march over to Miss Alexander's with a check for $5,350--the largest check I had ever seen.

To begin building, we got a loan of $8,500, the last given by the Acacia Life Insurance Company, for the depression had deepened, and insurance companies had stopped lending money on real estate. We economized further by moving into a cheaper apartment nearby.

At the same time, the Chiang Kai-shek government in China had deposited money in Chinese banks for partial compensation to the foreigners who had lost their homes in the Nanking Incident. Half the value of the Chinese money would be lost in the process of exchanging it for U.S. dollars, so I decided to get the full value by having Chinese friends purchase and ship to me exquisitely carved chests, tables, carpets and other Oriental items. These could be sold in California cheaply enough that people would buy, even in the Depression. Then I anxiously looked forward to the shipment's arrival so we would begin making money, because now was the time to build. We could get the best of carpenters, plumbers, electricians and painters for just $4 a day, and the contractor would charge us just six percent above cost.

Walter did well in whatever he undertook and he drew up the plans for a Mediterranean-style house which we knew would be "a thing of beauty and a joy forever." He made huge picture windows with single panes of glass, unusual in those days, to capture the view. Large, hand-hewn redwood beams were used to support the thirty-foot long living room ceiling. The contractor said that redwood was so cheap and so much was stacked up at the mills that it could scarcely be given away.

Walter was to landscape and care for the garden so that it would surround the house with flowers all year. On the street he made a desert garden, which was separated from the tropical patio at the front entrance by a low brick wall and a wrought iron gate. The back garden had lawn and old-fashioned flower beds and overlooked the campus and the Bay. He appointed me weed puller, but one of the first things I did was to plant a coast redwood sapling on the sloping corner of our lot behind the house.

Then the contractor announced that he had to have more money. There was still no sign of my shipment from China.

We were tired out from hard work and worry. Our apartment was cold and drafty. Walter contracted the flu and I came down with both flu and mumps.

Then came staggering news. The old sewer pipes for our rented Spring Way place which ran down through the next door lot facing Arch Street had begun to leak and the neighbor insisted they be moved off his property. That would cost us hundreds of dollars. We lay in our beds discussing the apparently hopeless situation when I suddenly got an idea. It was just like getting a postcard from heaven. The neighbor was a carpenter and because of that, there was a solution. I dressed and went to see him with a suggestion:

"If you buy our place and add it to yours, you can put up at least two small houses to rent to married students."

He saw the advantages of the idea and accepted the proposition. He not only took the leaky pipe problem off our hands, but provided the money to finish our house. Soon thereafter shipments of fine cloth, ceramics and furniture began to arrive from China. They supplied more money as I could sell them from our home.

Shortly after moving in we held a little ceremony dedicating the house to our family, our friends and our community. Our house had become a home. It was secure, despite the stresses and strains we had undergone. Perhaps in the back of my mind was the realization that if Walter was to be the great man I believed he could be, his work would take him far afield and, more than most families, we would need a strong home base.

We wanted the house to be more than a beautiful possession--a symbol of the strength of the family. As the children grew up we tried to share with them our pride in home and country, to make them feel secure in the permanence of the family and to be successful, happy human beings.

Furnishing the house went slowly, because we wanted nothing but beautiful things and these we would have to buy second-hand. Always on the lookout for bargains, every once in a while I would find a handsome piece and by needle-pointing a cushion or cover could bring it back to life. I made the draperies and curtains and as the China shipments came, we kept some of the choice items.

Walter appreciated a lovely home and a hospitable wife and I wanted to make a proper setting for him and his work, for he accomplished a great deal in relaxed conversations at home. Besides, I loved meeting people, too.

Gradually we began to entertain. Scientific organizations often held meetings in Berkeley and it seemed that Walter always had special friends to bring home. One of our first big parties was for the Oxford Rhodes Scholars of the Bay Region, honoring Sir Francis and Lady Wiley, who in England had been in charge of American Rhodes Scholars when Walter was there. I made only one rule for Walter regarding these occasions: "You must always greet the guests, Walter, so that I can do all the last-minute things. I don't want the women crowding into my messy kitchen trying to help, for that makes things all the harder."

Each night we had special guests: raccoons that came down from the hills for handouts after we finished dinner. We never failed to put out food for them. When we were out of town we even had a "raccoon sitter!"

However, Walter did much more than entertain guests and feed raccoons; he was becoming immersed in his research. He was ingenious at creating simple mechanisms to help get at the heart of a research problem. He devised a system for creating "artificial rainfall" that could be geared for any desired intensity so that he could scientifically measure the effects of erosion. In the 1930s, Los Angeles was already expanding its population far beyond what an arid region would normally support and wanted to obtain the maximum amount of water from the nearby mountains. Walter was appointed to set up the largest hydrologic watershed experiment ever undertaken. He was probably the first to use aerial photography in selecting a land-use area. He chose a triple watershed near the San Dimas Forest Experiment Station and was given the services of 200 boys from the Civilian Conservation Corps (CCC) camps.

The Forest Service said it would take six months just to get the buildings for the project planned and approved, but Walter knew that because of the Depression, the government needed to put men to work. He secured a fine architect at carpenter's wages--fifty cents an hour--to draw plans for buildings which would fit into the landscape as well as meet the needs of the research instead of the drab standardized buildings. He presented the blueprints, and headquarters agreed to them. The next day men were put to work on construction.

Walter worked out extensive scientific methods and equipment for measuring the rainfall and runoff in the experimental area in order to determine which method would conserve the greatest amount of water. Each of the three watersheds were to be treated differently. The first was used as the control and left as it was, the second was burned off, and the third was planted with intensifed vegetation and trees. The CCC boys put in trails and installed rainfall and runoff gauges which showed exactly what happened. On each stream Walter used the system he had developed in China: tipping buckets connected with a device which recorded the number of times the buckets refilled.

Many scientists and government people came to see what he was doing. Among them was Rexford Tugwell, the "brain truster" President Roosevelt was sending around the country to be his eyes and ears. Knowles Ryerson, an interested official in the Department of Agriculture, accompanied Tugwell. The second day they were at the project, the President phoned Tugwell, asking if he recommended that the job of Chief of the new Soil Conservation Service be given to Hugh Bennett.

"Do so only if you appoint Walter Lowdermilk as Associate Chief. He is the man out here with the grey matter," was Tugwell's reply. President Roosevelt personally asked for Walter's immediate release from the Forest Service, and early in 1933 Walter was off to Washington.

As Associate Chief of the newly established U.S. Soil Conservation Service, Walter was especially concerned about another catastrophe with far-reaching consequences for America--a stupendous drought that was followed by wind and water erosion on the grand scale that created the great Dust Bowl. To its credit, the federal government recognized that immediate corrective measures were imperative. The terrible unemployment problem of the cities and towns in the Depression was made worse by farmers having to abandon their ruined lands. Reclamation of both people and their resources had to be tackled together.

The first soil surveys showed that in our rapid drive westward across the continent we Americans had destroyed, beyond further cultivation, more than fifty million acres of our good food-growing lands, and that 200 million more acres were being degraded by water and wind erosion with no preventive measures under way. With his experience in China in mind, Walter plunged into the work at hand.

The sad fact was that we in America had degraded our natural resources at a faster pace than any other nation. During those early years of the Soil Conservation Service, many organizations, editors and schools did their best to inform the public about what was happening to our forests and lands. They followed Walter in his travels and helped him by pointing out in their articles that we had permitted erosion to gulley the watersheds and farm fields or blow away top soils until some depleted lands could no longer support our farmers and their families.

America was learning rapidly. In a farm magazine contest for the best 100-word description of a picture of a deserted house in a gullied field, an American Indian won the first prize with the following terse commentary:

> Picture show white man crazy. Cut down trees, make big tepee. Plough hill. Water wash. Wind blow soil. Grass gone. Door gone. Whole place gone. Money gone. Papoose gone. Squaw, too. No chuckaway. No pigs. No corn. No plough. No hay. No pony.

Indian no plough land. Keep grass. Buffalo eat
grass. Indian eat buffalo. Hides make tepee.
Make moccasin. Indian no make terrace. No
make dam. All time eat. No hunt job. No
hitch hike. No ask relief. No shoot pig. Great
Spirit make grass. Indian no waste anything.
Indian no work. White man crazy.

Since he was required to travel a great deal that first
year, I stayed in Berkeley with the children and Walter made
his headquarters at the Cosmos Club in Washington, where he
was a member. Being proud that Walter was making an
important contribution to the nation at this desperate time,
we accepted this temporary separation. But as soon as his
schedule settled down and it was logical to interrupt the
children's schooling, we rented a large brick house in
Washington across from Rock Creek Park on Colorado
Avenue. The year was 1936, not long after the second
election of President Franklin Roosevelt.

The government was still relatively small. Walter's
position as Associate Chief of the Soil Conservation Service
brought us numerous invitations to the White House. At our
first dance in the East Room, an orchestra played as we stood
in the President's reception line. Our former presidents and
their first ladies looked down at us from large portraits
around the walls. President Roosevelt, crippled by polio,
leaned against a tall stool. When we were presented, he gave
me his famous smile, took my hand in a delightful gesture,
looked into the my eyes and said, "Oh, Mrs. Lowdermilk, I am
so glad that you could come tonight."

Of course I realized that he did not care a hoot whether I
was there or not. But I knew that part of his great political
skill was relating to people, and he certainly made each
introduction seem personally important. His wife, Eleanor,
was equally gracious. She invited me to a women's luncheon
and to a number of afternoon small gatherings. Once at a
White House garden party I watched her stand and smilingly
shake hands with 1,500 people. She was the only first lady I
met who gave so generously of herself.

Life in our national capital not only gave Walter a chance to serve his country through the work he had prepared himself to do, but it was an inspiration to our young family. As had our country's founding fathers, we enjoyed the springtime around the tidal basin, the blooming dogwood and redbud and the bare trees suddenly bursting forth from their winter sleep with fresh green beauty in the first warm days of spring.

Walter took the children on long walks and explained the meaning of his work so they would not only appreciate their country, but would in the future work against further wastage of our resources and be responsible citizens and enjoy our national treasures, both natural and manmade.

As for my part, rather than raising the children on tales and fairy stories, I told the children Bible stories at bedtime. They loved those from the Old Testament and knew them by heart. Seldom did I finish one without Westher begging, "Tell it again." When the Washington, D.C. churches had a city-wide contest for telling Bible stories, our nine-year old Westher won first place.

Although Walter was a thoughtful father and devoted husband, on rare occasions he would forget that I existed. Each Friday evening during the winter lecture season he would come from his office and join me at the exclusively male Cosmos Club. We would enjoy dinner with friends in the main dining room where ladies were admitted, then we would all go into the lecture hall.

One night after the lecture Walter said to me, "I'll go through the men's section and get my coat and hat, and you wait for me outside on the corner."

It had grown cold and it was sleeting. I waited on that corner getting colder and colder, unable to re-enter because the women's entrance was now locked. Finally I stood on tiptoe and peered through the window of the men's parlor and saw my husband standing before the roaring fire in the great fireplace, laughing and talking with a group of men as they drank beer. I watched this lovely, glowing picture with the sleet stinging my face, boiling inside. Not for half an hour did Walter remember he had a wife. Then he dashed out, warm and full of apologies.

From a woman's point of view, Walter was sometimes too conscientious and a stickler for rules. Once he forgot it was Christmas Eve and called a meeting of his staff, leaving all the wives alone at home with youngsters and holiday preparations.

Another time I was to accompany him on a trip West, but he wouldn't let me ride in the car with him because of a rule against using government vehicles for private transport. So he put me on a bus and I had to sit up for three days and nights all the way to Pasadena, while he continued on his Soil Conservation tour. I was hurt, because I worked so hard to support the programs of Walter's department.

When he arrived in Texas, the women of the area where he was to speak had arranged for me to address women's clubs and had large audiences ready, and a beautiful luncheon besides. Walter was of course very sorry and told me so.

I won't pretend that living with a great man was always easy, but its rewards far outweighed its few disadvantages. Besides, Walter also had to show patience. I was a trial to him in certain ways, being an extrovert, very talkative, and never able to resist telling others about his achievements, even in his presence. He was modest and would reprove me, but never in anger. My enthusiasm would sometimes get the best of me and once, after one of our parties, Walter chided me for overdoing it.

"Inez," he declared, "you get to taking about something and you go on and on as though you had been vaccinated with a phonograph needle!"

And so it was that we handled each other's faults with humor and love.

"You two never seem to run out of kisses," said Pearl Buck once when she was staying with us, seeing how Walter always kissed me when leaving for the office, put his cheek down to be kissed or give me a quick one as we passed each other in the house.

We shared work as well as love and humor. At that time, the Department of Agriculture ran a fifteen-minute national radio broadcast every weekday under the direction of Milton

Eisenhower. Because of my close assocation with Walter's work, he asked me to give a series of broadcasts. After my first broadcast, entitled "Farmers of Forty Centuries Speak to the Farm Families of America," about our nation's great potential in food production, he told me that the department had received more requests for copies of it than for any other broadcast and they would like me to do more. My next talk, entitled "What About Dust Storms?" explained how the Dust Bowl was created, and was equally well received.

"Don't you feel nervous talking to five million people?" someone asked me in the studio one day.

"No," I replied. "I just think of my family gathered around the radio and forget about the rest of the five million."

One letter enquired how a woman could dare speak with such authority on soil conservation. My response was to explain my close association with Walter's work ever since China.

It was true. Since our marriage I had been witness to the birth of some of Walter's ideas which later proved permanent contributions to better agriculture at home and abroad. I heard him say, as he worked over the Soil Conservation Act of 1935 night after night, "I must make this law so broad and comprehensive that 100 years from now, the government will be able to do whatever is necessary to maintain and improve the lands of the nation."

Next came legislation for flood control. The Navajo Indians of Arizona and Utah were nearing starvation because their lands were being ruined. Walter examined the San Simon Wash in Arizona, a great gully some sixty miles long and 1,000-3,000 feet wide. Once its small stream had drained beautiful alluvial mountain valleys, but overgrazing of the sloping grasslands above had caused floods to erode the land like a cancer. Now the wash emptied into the Gila River and terrible floods were damaging valuable earth and filling the reservoir with sediment.

The Army Corps of Engineers were responsible for flood control on big rivers, but there was no provision for it on watersheds and the upper drainages of smaller rivers, where the real causes of damage were to be found. Walter made surveys and took a draft of the law that was needed to Arizona's Senator Hayden.

"If you can get this provision passed through Congress," he told the senator, "it will be the most constructive measure of this decade."

The result was the Omnibus Flood Control Act of 1936 which gave the Department of Agriculture responsibility for treating headwaters of rivers and streams with conservation measures such as check dams, diversion dams and forestation.

CCC boys were used for a great deal of this work out West. While I was waiting in the car for Walter one day in front of a Soil Conservation headquarters station in Arizona I suddenly laughed out loud at the sense of humor our American youngsters had. There, on an electric light pole was written:

> Say we to the gullies, 'We'll dam you.'
> Say the gullies to us, 'We'll be dammed if you do.'

A different problem was the Dust Bowl, nature's punishment for reckless plowing of the Great Plains which left the soils unprotected by the native grass. After several years of drought, winds carried the dry, fine topsoil in blinding blizzards which darkened the skies all the way to Washington.

Congress got the message when its members began to choke and cough. Money was granted for immediate measures to save what soils were left. The program included developing a permanent cover of vegetation on some fields and a great shelter belt of trees. Two hundred million trees were planted on some 30,000 farms. These formed more than 18,000 miles of shelter which gave protection against the wind and helped retain water and prevent further erosion. (In 1981 some of these shelter belts were ripped up as the 1930s were forgotten. Why don't people learn!)

Walter also encouraged farm families nationwide to have farm ponds for water storage and emergency use. He was tireless in traveling for personal contact with the farmers which brought about a mutual understanding with government as to what could be done for the farmers and their families and what they could do for themselves and their country.

He established districts within which farmers could organize to decide just what was needed on their lands and, under the Standard Act, request help from government experts.

"I must get the right man to administer these soil conservation districts," Walter said over and over. "I would be willing to pay such a man a bigger salary than I get."

He found the right person in Dillon Meyers, who built up a fine organization in cooperation with the farmers. The response to the whole program has been excellent nationwide.

It was nearly ten years since our departure from China in 1927. Despite the distressing circumstances under which we left, our love for the Chinese never wavered, and we realized more and more the value of our experience there. We avidly followed events of the Sino-Japanese war in China through news reports, correspondence and people passing through.

Twice Pearl Buck, our former Nanking neighbor, stayed with us. She had become a prolific writer, and because of our friendship and my knowledge of China, I was frequently called upon as a speaker to review her new books on China for Washington ladies' clubs. When she was with us she told us of the agonizing internal strife China was undergoing. In spite of it, Rachel Pen and others were carrying on the educational work we had begun, and Walter's former students and colleagues were doing their best to keep alive the program started by the Famine Prevention team.

The year we left China, Chiang Kai-shek had broken with the Russians. His Kuomintang party had set up a government in Nanking, but the Communist Party under Mao Tse-tung set up a government at Kiangsi, and later, after the famous Long March, at Shensi. As Generalissimo of the Chinese Army, Chiang had relentlessly fought the communist elements in China until 1936, when the civil war was suspended in the face of Japanese invasion.

Walter and I were deeply grieved over the constant Japanese attacks on China and ashamed that America had actually been supplying Japan with iron and oil, in fact, with everything but the aviators to bomb the helpless Chinese who did not even have anti-aircraft guns to protect their crowded cities.

The Japanese military campaigns took a terrible toll in China. On the newsreels in our Washington movie houses we saw city after city fall. We read with horror of the fall of Shanghai and of Nanking and the ghastly atrocities that took place.

Daily life goes on despite world conflicts, and about that time I realized that I was to have what the Apostle Paul would call a "thorn in the flesh".

A few days after one of Pearl's visits the children came running into the kitchen where I was working one day and cried, "There, Mother, that's the song we've been telling you about. Hear it?"

I couldn't hear a thing. I went through the rooms until I was nearer the radio, but it was obvious my hearing was impaired.

After examining me, the doctor gave his prognosis: "Evidently the large amounts of quinine you took in China to control malaria damaged the nerves. I'm sorry to tell you, Mrs. Lowdermilk, nothing can be done. Your hearing will get worse with age."

I was forty-five years old. Was I to have increasing difficulty hearing for the rest of my life? How would it affect my public life? I would have to start learning to minimize my handicap right away. So I concentrated on "hearing" in other ways, like watching lips. I also developed the habit of laughing when others laughed, sometimes without the faintest notion of what was funny. As my hearing worsened, the intense concentration needed to hear for long periods of time became difficult and I miss much of what people say.

Walter's only "thorn" was, ironically enough, the very thing which should have pleased his department chief: his immense popularity with America's stockmen and farmers, their confidence in him and his ability to get important matters done in the Congress. At one point he was offered the job of department chief, but it was not his nature to sit at headquarters. He wanted to be out seeing after such projects as placement of various dams for the Navajo and shelter belts and water storage ponds for the farmers, so he refused the position. But his very enthusiasm and modesty seemed to irritate one of his important associates. Once at a banquet where Walter was being praised, the man noisily stalked out halfway through the speech.

Walter's habit was to do his best and to ignore any slights, expecting the best of people; but underneath, he must have been increasingly hurt. It was good, then, that he was about to have a change.

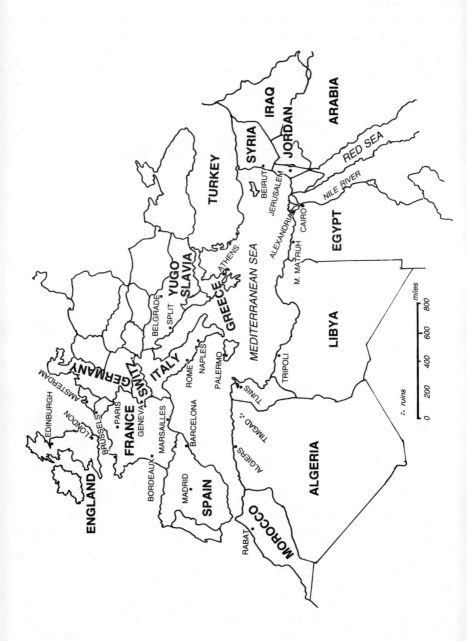

CHAPTER 12
OFF FOR OLD ROMAN LANDS (1938-9)

By the summer of 1938, the U.S. Soil Conservation Service was well established and laws had been enacted to facilitate cooperation between farmers and government. Secretary of Agriculture Henry Wallace began to take an interest in the history of agriculture, recognizing its significance as Walter had in China. It was well known that the Roman colonies had produced vast quantities of agricultural goods which not only fed large populations but made Rome wealthy. Some of those lands produced through the centuries, but others became deserts, reducing their people and their cities to poverty or extinction.

"What can we find in the successes and failures in land use during and since the Roman Empire that might be advantageous to the stockmen and farmers of America?" Wallace asked.

He decided that the U.S. Department of Agriculture would have Walter make an eighteen-month survey of agriculture, past and present, in the lands once part of the Roman Empire.

I was happy to see Walter get a change, but I did not want our family to be separated for a year and a half. Furthermore, such a trip would give our children the chance of a lifetime to learn something about the world in which they were growing up, in a way they never could see it as tourists. Walter was to take along a secretary, Cleveland McKnight whom we called "Mac," and the travel expenses of both would be paid. I urged Walter to have the family go along at our own expense.

"I will help in writing up your notes and reports in each country while you and Mac are in the field with officials," I suggested. "We can ship our Buick and take my niece, Elizabeth Moody, along with us. She is twenty-one years old now and can help organize the thousands of photographs you will be taking and she can also assist Billy and Westher in their school work along the way."

At first Walter objected, but finally he agreed that this scientific safari would be good for the whole family. The itinerary was to take us through Great Britain and Europe, from Holland to Sicily, then across the Mediterranean to North Africa and the Middle East, then through Turkey and the Balkans--eighteen wonderful months.

We boarded the USS Manhattan August 8, 1938 with our car riding along on the deck. At Plymouth, England, we disembarked, the Buick was unloaded and we packed up and were off in a gay mood, headed for a scientific conference at Cambridge. Our Buick accommodated six people, six suitcases, six overnight bags, two typewriters, three cameras, two tripods, an accordion, a box of supplies, a hat box, extra blankets, emergency food and numerous other things.

Walter drove, and I thought he would have heart failure at the autos rushing at him around curves and passing on what was to him the wrong side, since in Britain they drive on the left. British cars were taxed according to horsepower, so big cars were rare. The little Austins scurried about like small spiders. The first time we stopped at an inn for lunch, our large American car was the only one around. We came out to find it surrounded by five or six little Austins.

Westher called out, "Oh, Mother just look. While we were gone our Buick has had a litter of little ones!"

Walter and Mac attended the British Conference for the Advancement of Science at Cambridge University, and then spent a great deal of time in the field with British agricultural officials. The children and I explored the campus and punted on the River Cam, which ran through the campus. We knew there was a "Christ College" and a "Jesus College" at Cambridge. Still, it was startling to hear the enthusiastic students on the bank yelling, "Go to it, Christ!" or "Lick 'em, Jesus!" or "Bump 'em, Christ!"

Next we spent several interesting, merry days exploring the town of Oxford, where Walter had spent three years as a Rhodes Scholar. He showed the children a lovely old spire, and laughingly recounted how, as a freshman, emerging from Wadham, his college, he saw a group of students around the spire looking up and laughing. The pinnacle was crowned with a "potty." Some nimble student had succeeded in elevating this humble but useful vessel to lofty heights. No one had the courage to climb the spire, and the culprit refused to reveal himself, so the school authorities were finally obliged to shoot the unseemly decoration down.

As we drove through England Walter pointed out occasional remnants--roads or walls--of the Roman occupation of Britain which began in 43 A.D. He quoted the English historian, H.G. Welles, as saying that the basic diet in those days was fish or game, and grains were mostly a "patch" crop until an army of occupation had to be fed. Under the Romans, the peasant or small cultivator was either a worried debtor or a spiritless serf, or was unable to compete with production by slaves. But by the time Britain was abandoned by Rome in 407 A.D., its people had been largely Romanized, and so must the Roman soldiers have been Britainized; for many of them remained to settle on the land.

"There developed in Britain a love for the land which led to a highly productive agriculture," Walter said. He had much to tell us from his studies in England and called our attention to the ageless stone farm structures. "The law of primogeniture, whereby land passes from generation to generation to the eldest son, has given British agriculture and its buildings stability and continuity. As trustees of the land, farmers of each generation have wanted to contribute to the prosperity of their descendants. The fine masonry of barns, walls, manor houses, even the humblest of homes, have been built to last for centuries."

We saw no signs of erosion anywhere, probably because most of England's rain comes in the form of mist, not torrents, and the stone fences made by clearing the rocky terrain have enclosed the fields, protecting the soil. Elizabeth asked Walter why England was so green while California was so dry. Walter replied, to see if we were paying attention, "Because not much dust blows off the Atlantic!"

We drove up through Scotland, where the heather in full bloom and the gardens kept fresh by constant showers were a joy to see. Edinburgh surpassed all our expectations in its beauty and the sense of history it conveyed. Billy was intrigued by the castles, especially the castle walls from which he heard hot oil was once poured down upon the enemies' heads.

Back in England, while Walter attended final conferences, we were free to tour the important sights, our noses continuously drippy from the cold and damp. We finally wound up in the church of John Wesley, founder of Methodism. When the people at Asbury learned I was a Methodist from America, they invited us to tea. It gave me a wonderful feeling to be "at home," where the church that had played such a part in my life began.

Two days later we ferried across the Channel to the Netherlands, which the Romans had conquered in the time of Julius Caesar when it was still largely under water. The Romans found primitive mounds and dikes built by the Fresians to increase their food supply. What Walter came to see, however, were the modern polders made by the great dike system which had brought into cultivation large tracts of land reclaimed from the sea by the Dutch.

We saw new fields, for the Dutch had just created an extra half million acres of cultivable land out of the North Sea by closing one of the greatest of their dikes, draining and desalinizing the soil. We slept in the first village inside the big dike of the Zuider Zee, sixteen feet below sea level, with the waves pounding against the other side. Our admiration for the Dutch knew no bounds, especially when we learned that even when the land was still under water, the engineers had determined what the soil under the ocean was best suited for, forestry or agriculture, and had planned accordingly.

"The Lord may have made the earth," Walter remarked, "but the Dutch have made Holland."

We fell in love with Holland. To remember the important facts about each country on the trip we had put together a statement and memorized it with the children. Driving through Holland, we repeated together a description of the land with the official figures of 1938:

"Holland is a fascinating, colorful country composed of 8 1/4 million acres of land, water and dykes, located above and below the level of the North Sea, and inhabited by 8 million people who live in spotlessly clean houses, ride 3 million bicycles, milk 2 1/2 million black and white cows and export millions of cheeses and tulip bulbs through Rotterdam, their largest port."

But a gloom marred the land we were actually seeing. When we arrived in Belgium in the fall of 1938 there was a tension in the air that was familiar to Walter and me, because we had both experienced the feeling of a country at war in China. This was a dress rehearsal for World War II. The Belgians were making frantic defense preparations. We heard that 150,000 troops had already been sent to the German border and reserves were being mobilized. We saw the women walking along beside their husbands as far as they could, and the tragic farewells were heartbreaking to watch.

On our very first night in Brussels we were awakened by pounding on doors and a commotion in the street. The cook in our hotel had been suddenly taken away for army service and the loud weeping of the women of his family who gathered outside expressed to me to sorrow and heartache of countless people in all the mobilizing nations. Wailing was heard all over the city--thousands of women wailing.

We went on to France, and all the way to Paris the roads were clogged with troops, cavalry horses and farm wagons overloaded with people and their possessions. Belgium was on the move. The women could weep, I thought, but what were the men thinking as they trudged along, so sober, silent and submissive?

> In Flanders fields the poppies blow
> Between the crosses, row on row.

I had learned John McCrae's poem in college, but it did not really prepare me for the American cemeteries we saw in Belgium and in France, acres upon acres of green grass with row upon row of thousands of white crosses marking the dead from the First World War. Instead of name and regiment carved into the white marble, some crosses bore only the official inscription, "Here lies in honored glory an American soldier known but to God." America lost 82,000 sons in Europe. The bodies of many were returned to their families, but the remainder lay under the markers, row upon row upon row.

Most of the men in my University of Southern California graduating class of 1916 fought in that war beside the French. While reading through the list of names at the beautiful monument overlooking one of the cemeteries, I was saddened to recognize those of three classmates--vital young men who would have become outstanding citizens.

"What a treasure of life--character, talent, ability and leadership--was lost to the world in that carnage," I thought aloud, "for a cause which we who lived did not fulfill. That war did not make the world safe for democracy. Instead, it produced a Hitler."

The children stood silently beside us, scarcely able to comprehend the enormous tragedy. Even Mac and Elizabeth, in their twenties, couldn't grasp its full meaning. I wept inside, all the rest of the day.

The public squares of Paris were completely darkened and the street lights were hooded to permit only cracks of light to be directed down onto the sidewalks. Autos were allowed to use only parking lights. The treasures of the Louvre and other museums had been placed underground in bomb shelters, for the city was expecting an attack from the air at any hour.

Hotels were almost empty. The government secured for us excellent accommodations directly across from the National Assembly buildings in a small but charming old hotel where we were practically alone. Tourists had fled. The population, including the reduced hotel staff, were terribly frightened. Men of fighting age were nearly all gone, and soon there were almost no women or children in the streets, for they had sought safety in the countryside.

Our hotel was just a few doors from the residence of Premier Daladier and were among the crowd that cheered him as he returned from Munich and declared that he had brought back "peace for this generation." The same day, British Prime Minister Chamberlain arrived in London, announcing that he had "brought back peace with honor." But when we heard how they had carved up the courageous little democrary of Czechoslovakia and handed it over to Hitler, Walter was stunned. Then he blurted, "Peace with honor? I consider that they have brought back honor in pieces!" He knew that September 30, 1938 marked a major setback for freedom and democracy.

How could it have happened? Czechoslovakia had deployed seventy-five divisions on the German border and, at the request of Britain and France, had spent more than $100 million to defend the line. Then, with all the odds seemingly on the side of democracies, Premiers Daladier and Chamberlain had gone to the Munich conference to speak for the free world and for Czechoslovakia--the nation most involved--not otherwise represented. Instead, she was denied even the chance to fight and was handed to Hitler on a silver platter by her friends. Walter talked with some Czech refugees who were being forced by the French government to go back. Their words rang in his ears for a long time:

"You are still free. You can go away. But freedom for us had ended."

"Democracy's sacred principles are being abandoned by its own representatives," I said sadly to Walter.

Nonetheless, with the immediate crisis over, the French capital again became "Gay Paree." The mantle of darkness lifted, the squares were brilliantly lighted, people returned to the streets, and the art treasures reappeared in the Louvre. Walter was given a private office at the Ministry of Agriculture and offered every assistance in his research into France's agriculture and forestry since Roman times. He worked steadily for three weeks while Elizabeth and I toured the city with the children.

We Americans weren't so knowledgeable about foreign countries in those days, so we had many surprises. A certain physical propensity--one might guess weakness--of the male appeared to be a universal feature of France. I wouldn't have imagined signs posted behind statues and in recesses of public buildings on the streets of Washington, D.C. reading "Do not urinate here," but in France they were. There were "les pissoirs" for men in all the public squares and along the sidewalks of city streets. They were covered with tin roofs and screened the occupants only from the knees to the shoulders so that men inside could continue their conversations with friends outside on the sidewalk. Billy invariably counted legs and informed us of the exact number of men inside.

We also spent much time in the French countryside among the friendly farm people while Walter inspected their methods of land use. The houses and barns were frequently combined, the door into the living room often only a few feet from the barn door. The flies obviously enjoyed the "pile of gold" with its oozing liquid accumulated for use on the fields, which occupied a prominent front yard position on the French farm. I knew that it was an important resource but couldn't help wondering how it would be in the States to invite friends to tea and have them "wade in" to my front door, holding their noses.

Throughout France we saw many old women dressed mostly in black working in the fields, pulling carts, carrying loads, collecting firewood, tending sheep in the cold and knitting socks and sweaters. I asked Walter why they were treated like that.

"In World War I, France lost more than a million and a-half of her men," he explained. "These are the widows who have had to live with their relatives and earn their keep. It's easy to understand why they are still in mourning."

But we couldn't let these sights depress us; these memories and misery were in the midst of beauty. Day after day we traveled through living tunnels of trees gorgeously colored by the autumn leaves which rained down upon us and swirled in clouds after we swished by. Napoleon had thousands of miles of roads planted with trees in order to camouflage his troop movements.

In the magnificent French Alps, our hotel windows looked out on Mont Blanc. Walter studied the government's torrent control operations there and became more and more proficient with the cameras. We were met by officials in Bordeaux who wanted to show him the remarkable government project of anchoring the huge coastal area of sand dunes with grass, so that it could be forested with trees producing highly profitable resins and turpentine.

In the evenings Bill was sometimes encouraged to get out his accordion and play for us and our new-found friends. Elizabeth worked out a system to catalogue the photos. I helped Walter make the most of his time by organizing his notes so Mac could type up his reports to Washington.

In the south of France we went with Walter to study the intensive cultivation on hill terraces, probably begun by Phoenicians who had come from the eastern Mediterranean when their population growth outgrew their own lands' capacity to feed them. The Phoenicians made terraces to prevent erosion after forests were cut down. France had produced food on these terraces ever since. A country like Greece, Walter told us, which had suffered erosion with no attempt to terrace the land, had but small areas of productive land left. We also saw in Southern France the wonderful Roman aqueducts bringing water to irrigate the vineyards and supply the cities.

Leaving France we traveled down the west coast of Italy, using the route the Roman Legions followed into Gaul and

Spain over 2,000 years earlier. Without dynamite, Hannibal had cut the road to attack Rome across the great cliffs by driving wooden pegs into holes drilled into solid rock and wetting them so their expansion shattered it.

We arrived in Naples on December 25th and decided to spend Christmas going up Mt. Vesuvius. The famous volcano dominated the blue Bay of Naples. Above her perpetual mantle of ermine-like snow, a blanket of smoke lay on her shoulders. Ten days previously she had suffered her worst spell of indigestion in years and had belched forth enough red-hot rock to cover more than 200 acres below. She was still groaning and spewing forth black breath and occasional tongues of red fire.

We found a good-natured Italian guide and drove up the switchback road past the snowline, but our car wheels soon started spinning and skidding. Other cars were turning back, but the children were not to be stopped. They clamored to reach the top on foot. So we bundled up against the piercing cold and left the car. We staggered and puffed upward through the snow until we reached the edge of the old crater where our guide carefully led us around the deep lava chasms. The crust was still so hot from the last eruption that it not only dried our clothes but burned the soles off our overshoes.

We stopped about 100 feet away from the base of the new volcanic cone and looked at the slow-boiling streams of molten stone. Then, peering down the outer crater edge, we saw our car silhouetted against the white snow 1500 feet below. In another moment we all hilariously slid, rolled and tumbled our way down the snow-covered mountain, short-cutting the road by miles.

While Walter and Mac were with the Minister of Agriculture in Rome the rest of us went sightseeing. I tried to imagine the passing of a tempestuous surge of almost 3,000 years of life as we walked the long, smooth stones of the Appian Way; the power of the emperors, and the devastation and disintegration in the centuries that followed.

"Here the Apostle Paul walked in chains on his way to be beheaded," I read to the children from our guidebook, "and

Peter had his vision of 'Quo Vadis,' then went into the city to be crucified. Here, too, marched all the triumphant legions of Rome, dragging their spoils of war and their captives, including the 30,000 Jews taken at the fall of Jerusalem."

On the Triumphal Arch of Titus, friezes depicted the Jews trudging to their doom as Nero's slaves, to labor for eight years building the enormous Colosseum. I had never been much aware of Jewish people in modern life because as far as I knew we had no Jewish acquaintances. But this made me think of how they had also built the capital city of Ramses II in Egypt and how, through Moses, God had freed them and given them the Holy Land.

In the evenings the family would be all together, and Walter would share some of what he had learned from officials in preparation for what we were to see. Italy's leader, Mussolini, had obviously made impressive progress in public works, but Walter constantly pointed out the evidence that it was being achieved at the expense of freedom. The words Duce, Duce, Duce (leader) were painted on almost every wall, and huge posters with the slogan "Obey, Believe, Fight" were along every street. The dictator was bribing Italian women to bear more children and there were so many children swarming the countryside that we called the villages "Mussolini's Incubators."

Italy had done a great deal in land reclamation. We saw the site of the former Pontine Marshes, which had been malarial swamps before the Italians transformed them in just five years into beautiful farmland.

Mussolini was also building for the ages. He had ordered more than 4,000 reinforced concrete farmhouses and several model towns constructed entirely of concrete and marble. Italy was not only setting her own house in order, but working strenuously toward a Great Italy--she had already embarked on conquest to rebuild Rome's African Empire, beginning with Ethiopia and Libya. What would this eventually mean for the rest of the world?

Our European tour ended in Sicily, where there were over 10 million orange and lemon trees on mountain terraces also dating from the Phoenicians. The day we left, the usually blue Mediterranean was stormy, dashing itself into a white foam against the rocky coastline. From Palermo we took an overnight car ferry to North Africa. We were tired and hungry, but the sea won out and, as usual, I had to flee the ship's dining room before the first course was served.

North Africa was a great challenge for Walter because it had dramatic examples of vanished populations, cities, and agriculture. Was the change of climate since Roman times responsible? Or was it, as Walter had found in Northwest China, that man had put too many demands upon his resources? He was there to find the answers from the past. However, we could not escape the history being made at that moment.

With the colonial powers heading for war in Europe, their territories in Africa would inevitably become embroiled. Italy already controlled Libya and Ethiopia, and we arrived in the French protectorate of Tunisia amid rumors that the Italians were about to invade. As we drove by the Italian consulate at Tunis, the capital, crowds of Arabs were demonstrating outside the gate. Crowds were shouting and shaking their fists. It looked as if it might get out of hand.

Billy pointed out the window, "Look, Daddy! People are smashing ink bottles against the building!" Billy, at 14, saw only the excitement and not the possible results.

We drove on to our hotel with some anxiety, but there were no problems there, except in a personal way. After the cold of Europe in winter, we had looked forward to the sunshine of North Africa, but we were to be even less comfortable there because the hotels had stone or tile floors and absolutely no heat. As soon as we were settled, I went to the dining room and ordered a cup of hot water in order to warm my hands.

Intense war preparations were under way. Soldiers manned their guns behind rolls of barbed wire separating Italian, French and British territories and looked upon all travelers with suspicion. We were often the hapless victims of their mutual discourtesies. At some border points we were held up for hours. This sometimes forced us to travel in darkness for many miles on unknown roads to find a place to sleep. However, we impressed upon the children that they were seeing history.

They found it all boring and exciting at the same time-- boring when the officials made us unload the carefully packed car, including the top roped luggage, just to see if we would. But hardships were also exciting, as when Billy helped to change a tire that had blown out when nails were thrown in front of the car.

While Walter and Mac met with French colonial officials, Elizabeth and I took Westher and Billy to the native bazaars-- the souks. We watched the rug weavers, the silver craftsmen, the artisans pounding copper into decorative utensils, and listened to the strange music wafting through the air. White- robed denizens rested dreamily against the sunlit walls, or drifted in and out of the deep shadows of the ancient arch- ways. Everything seemed mysterious, especially because the women were heavily veiled.

The mosques rose like giant bubbles above all other buildings in the beautiful white-washed cities of North Africa. The French Colonial government officials treated us well, inviting us to many dinners. They even arranged for us to meet Arab royalty.

We visited the Bey of Tunis at his palace who greeted us in Western clothes against a backdrop of exquisite gardens and Arabic architecture, arches and blue-tiled fountains. He and Walter conversed in French, which I could not understand. Then we were given sumptuous refreshments of pastries with honey and nuts and sweet mint tea to drink.

However, Arab men never ate with us. To the outsider, their women were either publicly veiled or nonexistent. The only women we ever met were French. An Arab woman in Morocco and Algieria could not even show both eyes as in Tunisia but was only allowed to pull the veil aside to look through one eye. The more I learned about the status of Arab women, the less status they seemed to have from our point of view--in society, religion, or even in the home.

An Arab scholar living at our same hotel gave me the following translation of a Moslem philosopher's comments: "Woman is the toy with which man plays when and as he wishes. In him is light and understanding, in her is darkness and ignorance. Man is the center of everything and woman is an insignificant part of that everything."

He explained that Islam allows a man four wives at any given time if he is able to support them. He can divorce one by saying before a witness, "I divorce you" four times; but a wife cannot divorce her husband without his consent.

"A man can even kill his wife with impunity," he told me, "should he suspect her to be unfaithful."

My heart went out to North Africa's women.

One day we found the store of a wealthy and intriguing young rug merchant named Ben Saada, a cousin of the Bey. In typical Arab hospitality he made us comfortable on cushions, and had servants bring us sweet mint tea while we enjoyed viewing one after the other of his superb carpet collection. For a land where few ladies' faces were ever seen in public, our beautiful Elizabeth, sweet and demure, had attracted attention everywhere. I was not surprised when, as we paid for our purchases and prepared to leave, Ben Saada gave Elizabeth a small gift and asked to see her again.

New Year's Eve rolled around and we all celebrated at a big crowded nightclub as Ben Saada's guests. The few other women present were obviously foreigners like ourselves. The featured entertainment was belly dancing which highly excited the males in the audience. The more dripping with fat were the dancers, the more they were cheered. The technique of shaking their plumpness up and down, out and around, made the children goggle-eyed.

We drove west across French North Africa--Tunisia, Algeria, and to the borders of Morocco--and shook hands all the way. High rank or low, rich or poor, clean or dirty--it made no difference. Men always shook hands. Whenever we stopped for tea, the host shook our hands. When we went into a shop to buy something we were expected to shake hands, fold our legs on soft rugs or cushions on the floor and drink sweet mint tea until a price was agreed upon. Then the shopkeeper would jump up to shake hands and congratulate us on the bargain he had given us. The germs we exchanged everywhere must have been friendly, for we suffered very little illness.

As we arrived at each capital city Walter reported promptly to the government and officials were both coopera- tive and hospitable. They were glad to show him the evidence of food production in ancient times but, because of his position in the United States Department of Agriculture, they wanted to show him their modern efforts at development and to get his advice. At each place he was busy in the field much of the time while I worked on his notes and Elizabeth helped the children with their school work.

Then we headed eastward across North Africa from Morocco to return to Tunis. In the northwest we saw the cork oak forests. Monkeys, dozens of them, were swinging back and forth across the road just in front of our car to the children's great delight.

We emerged from the forest on a wandering road as the sun was going down, night swooped down on us the moment it set. We had no food and were still hours away from shelter for the night. Hour after hour we traveled in darkness, first through cultivated mountains, then through dense cork forests again. A terrific wind came up and it was bitterly cold. We were thankful that at least we had the protection of the car.

Once in a forest clearing, we passed a sign reading, "Lambert Lodge-Guests." The place was in darkness, but looking back, I was sure I saw a flicker of light through the trees. I talked about this light for about two miles until finally Walter turned the car around on a dangerously narrow mountain road and we drove back to investigate. As he got out of the car the wind literally blew him into the yard. When he opened the lodge door we saw to our great joy a fire inside and a promise of food.

The owner opened the barn door and we drove in among the complaining cows and sheep, who were mooing and baaing bitterly at our late arrival and the gusts of cold wind we brought in with us. It took all the strength of the two men to get the barn door closed again in the face of the gale. The owner could not speak English, but Walter spoke four languages and always found some way to make our needs known.

The next day we drove to where Walter could meet the Kabyle people. Ages ago the Kabyle had been pushed into a mountainous area of Algeria. Farming almost like Stone Age people, they were poverty-stricken on their pitiful, eroded hillside lands. Walter and Mac interviewed some of the villagers and Walter analyzed their situation, hoping to see some way to help them. We all visited several Christian mission stations serving these people, with orphanages, bible schools and cultural help.

No one ever fussed about being crowded in the Buick, but the packing of that car, inside and out, had become an art. There didn't seem to be an inch to spare, and we couldn't have imagined taking on any more. As we went through the streets of Algiers on a cold January day, we saw a ragged teenage boy trying to sell a tiny, shivering Bedouin pup wearing a blue ribbon. Our children were beside themselves with eagerness to buy it. It made absolutely no sense to take on another passenger but Walter could rarely turn the children down and I was no more than a child myself when it came to adorable animals. Billy did the bargaining in French, and got the price down to 90 cents. He quickly became the proud, protecting father of the mutt, although Westher demanded an equal share in feeding and caring for its needs.

We named this smooth-haired brown puppy Mektube, which we were told meant "Allah has willed it; it has been decreed." Mektube literally fell into six laps of love and attention and our Buick was to be the only home he ever knew. For 10,500 miles he was to share our laps and our food. His cute puppy ways, then his adolescent pranks, entertained us throughout the long hours of desert travel.

Back again in Tunis we were greeted by Ben Saada, the rug merchant, as though we were the oldest of friends. We had returned to the shop to buy more rugs. Ben Saada requested we come to the rooftop for photographs, with

Elizabeth in a harem outfit.   Later, seated on the natural colored Kairoun rugs sipping mint tea, Ben Saada asked Elizabeth to step into the next room to view another speciality. She did not return promptly and my fears were aroused. I had a "feeling in my bones" that I had to find Elizabeth. Stepping into an adjoining room, Elizabeth was emerging somewhat agitated and with red eyes. In private she told us that Ben Saada had proposed marriage to her, and had promised to divorce his other wives if she would marry him.

I was terrified. Ben Saada had boasted to us that he had always gotten what he wanted and officials had told us that colonial policy was never to interfere with Arab men in matters of women. If Elizabeth were to be snatched and put behind harem bars, we might never hear of her again. It was too terrible to contemplate.

I hunted up Walter and called him out of the meeting, telling him in urgent whispers what I had learned. He recognized the dangerous implications of the situation at once, excused himself from the meeting, and he and Mac left with me. Within a few hours we had packed our car, checked out of the hotel and were well on our way down the coast.

As we traveled fast toward Tripoli, some Arabs driving towards us frantically waved and shouted something to us which, of course, we could not understand. Then a dip in the road plunged us into a wadi in flood from a sudden rainstorm in the hills. The muddy waters splashed up over the top of our car, totally blinding us, but Walter kept a steady hold on the wheel and delivered us to the opposite bank.

Shortly we came to another flooding wadi, this one two or three hundred feet wide. When a Frenchman came along driving a huge truck Walter asked him to tow us through, but he refused. So, when he started across, Walter nudged our Buick's engine up under the back of his truck bed and drove in the grooves the truck tires were pressing into the mud until we got across. We had to drive until 9 P.M. before we could find a place for the night. We were exhausted and hungry, but thankful to be safe before facing the next flood.

Then we drove on to the excavations of Timgad (Themugadi) and Djemila (Cuicul), great cities built by the Romans. As we approached across the desert, El Djem's colosseum loomed high above the horizon even though about one-third of it was buried in the sand which through the centuries had covered the entire city. The size of this structure indicated the presence at one time of an enormous population.

The excavations at Timgad and Djemila revealed a number of the cities' features. We took pictures of the marble forums, temples, public baths, palaces, paved streets and the carved marble toilets constructed so that their seats were over a stream of running water. In all this ancient grandeur, the only sign of modern life was a clutter of Bedouin huts.

We had dreaded Libyan desert travel, but after our car bumped along through the no-man's land between French Tunisia and Italian Libya, we suddenly found ourselves on an excellent road.

"This can't be!" we all exclaimed. "This can't last!" But it did--for 1,500 miles. We had been unaware of Mussolini's efficiency and speed in his determination to recreate the old Roman Empire. He was driving his people to do in Africa as they were doing in Italy. This great "autostrada" stretched across Libya from Tunisia to Egypt. It had been completed in ten months and ran like a ribbon off into the horizon. Every thirty miles there was a service station where a family lived, and they provided gas, oil, food and shelter for travelers. On the average we passed another car every 200 to 300 miles. Speed was limited only by the power of a car's engine. Obviously Mussolini had built this road to enable the speedy movement of troops and arms from the French border of Tunisia to the British border of Egypt.

At one stop, Bill pulled out his accordion after supper and we all sang. The station family gathered around and soon they told us the wonders of Mussolini. The father explained that there was one 500 mile stretch of autostrada without a single turn! Another member of the family, a colonial official, described the astonishing new Italian Colonization Deluxe, on the eastern portion of the autostrada in Cyrenica.

He said that between 1937 and 1939 the government had built thousands of reinforced concrete houses, provided wells for irrigation water, cleared lands and prepared gardens for the planting of vegetables upon the arrival of Italian colonists. Each farm had its own barn and storerooms. The first 50,000 Italians had arrived by ship in the morning--two of their cousins and a great-uncle were in the group--and by evening every family was established in its new home. Each house had been furnished, beds made, food in the cupboards, tools ready for use, livestock in the barn, and a pail out for the new owner to milk the cow. Mussolini was certainly trying to surpass the accomplishments of his Roman ancestors in his colonization of Africa.

Walter decided to have a look at the life of the desert tribes and we left the centers of modern civilization to travel into the northern Sahara. The roads were often just bumpy tracks made by camels, but we learned to love its vastness and its emerald oases. These wound like green threads along the rare water courses, or centered around wells or springs or where there was underground water close enough to the surface that palms could stretch down their thirsty roots and drink. After approaching an oasis over the hot sand from a long, long way off, it was refreshing to drive out of the sun's glare to the cool shade under the canopy of waving palm fronds. Oases are rated on the map not by population but by their number of date palms. Their fruits are closely guarded until harvest time as an important part of each family's staple diet. Ground date pits were even used to feed the animals!

Camels were by far the most interesting of the animal life we saw. They have personality-plus. They are also indispensable to man, as they take the place of freight cars or automobiles. In dire emergency the camel is a source of food and water. It has a reserve water tank somewhere at the bottom of its long neck. The male "gargles" with this water with a disgusting noise when he wants to impress a female.

We saw long caravans of camels while on the way to see Leptis Magna in Libya, an excavation which showed the most magnificent Roman baths of all the great ruined cities. It had pools and rooms that could almost be used today. As the Roman civilization of North Africa was overrun by conquerors, the vineyards and orchards were no longer cared for. Overgrazing by nomadic herds laid bare the soil to the winds, and the careful agriculture that had supported millions vanished. Like Timgad, Djemila and El Djem, Leptis Magna had been swallowed by sand until twentieth century archaeologists had begun to excavate it.

Walking among these ruins, we pondered the sense of might and power that Romans must have felt, never dreaming that their civilization would fall into decay. Would our civilization have the same end?

We knew that only the future could tell. As we stood thoughtfully on the desert sands covering a once magnificent city, even the children seemed to realize that, as Santayana expressed it, "Those who do not learn from the mistakes of the past are bound to repeat them."

CHAPTER 13
ENTERING THE WORLD OF THE BIBLE (1939)

After ending our 1,500 miles of travel across Libya we spent a weekend at Marsa Matruh, on the Mediterranean coast. It is clear why Cleopatra seduced Anthony into meeting her there. It was the most beautiful spot imaginable, with a harp-shaped cove surrounded by clean, white sands and at the entrance to the sea great rocks dashed incoming waves high into the air.

When we arrived at the Egyptian border, the Egyptian officials held us up for several hours and it was nearly dusk when at last we started across the no-man's land between Libya and Egypt. Barbed wire denoted hostility on both sides.

Walter's co-workers had often joked that he brought rain wherever he went, and this trip was no exception. In the dark we often had to have Mac get out of the car and go ahead on foot with a flashlight to find the dirt road between the puddles of water.

Westher was very ill with a high fever, and every jounce of the bumpy road was painful. I tried to cushion her by holding her during the hours on no man's land. We had stayed an extra day at Marsa Matruh so she could get well, but the children, healthy or sick, could not hold up the trip. They became somewhat stoical. After 17 hours in the car we were grateful to reach a hotel on the Alexandria-Cairo paved highway, and we slept soundly.

The next day we reached Cairo where it was hot and sultry. We stopped at the American Embassy and picked up our mail from home. While Walter consulted officials and exchanged American money for local currency, we sat smothering in the hot car. After some time, a peddler came by with a box on his shoulder calling out for customers.

"Mother!" the children clamored. "He has Washington apples. Please, get us some."

I motioned for the man to come to the car before realizing I had no Egyptian money. I was trying to tell him that I could not buy when a shopkeeper nearby stepped over to the car and asked us in English, "May I help you to bargain?"

I explained my predicament and he answered, "Please let me bargain for you and I will pay."

I agreed if he would let me bring the money to his shop when Walter returned, and we soon had our laps full of apples. As the stranger turned to go, he seemed somehow different from others we had met there so I asked him if he was Egyptian.

He hesitated just one moment, then answered, "I am an Egyptian Jew."

This was the first time I had consciously realized there were non-Islamic minorities in the Arab world. He saw that I was intrigued and added, "The Jewish community of Cairo is over 2,000 years old."

Our next destination was Palestine. But, like the Children of Israel, we first had to get out of Egypt, and the rulers refused to let us go, this time due to terrorism along the border. We did not set plagues on them as did Moses, but Walter did plague the Egyptian officials daily with applications for a permit to cross the Sinai Desert into Palestine.

While these negotiations were going on, we climbed the pyramids inside and out and rode camels around the Sphinx. British archaeologist Reisner took us underground to see an elaborate group of tombs recently discovered. The lid was off one of the deeply carved stone caskets and we looked down upon the bones within.

"You will be interested in this fellow," he told us. "The hieroglyphics have just been read. He was the Chief Lictor of the slave drivers at the time the Children of Israel were enslaved in Egypt, more than 3,000 years ago." Seeing Billy's eyes light up, he said, "Take whatever you want, son."

Billy looked at me as if to say, "Shall I?" and I nodded yes. We both knew it would be good for an "A" report in school. He chose a leg bone first. It was small; the cruel lictor must have been a very short man, but it was too big to take with us, so he chose a smaller bone.

In the great National Museum in Cairo our eyes bulged with wonder at the glittering gold and jewels and art from the tomb of King Tutankhamen and marvelled that 4,000 years ago people had the capacity for such exquisite workmanship. We saw such remarkable paintings and carvings in the tomb of Ti, at Sakhara, built 6,000 years ago, that I wondered, "Have we equalled them yet?"

Toward the end of our Egyptian stay we visited the Great Mosque of Cairo, where female foreign tourists were admitted with guides. Seeing that the Moslem women were relegated to a dismal balcony with bare floor boards, I asked our Moslem guide, "If at last, as you say, you have decided that women have souls and can come into the mosques to pray, why then must they pray in that unattractive place? Why not here on these nice mats and rugs which the men are using?"

"Oh, that would never do," he answered. "If the men saw the women kneeling to say their prayers they would have evil thoughts and be unable to say their own prayers."

Finally government officials promised to furnish us exit permits if we agreed to go at our own risk, for no car had crossed the Sinai Desert for six months. British-controlled Palestine was experiencing increasing terrorism from Arabs resisting the League of Nations mandate facilitating the creation of a homeland for Jews in Palestine. All border stations had been blown up. Telephone lines had been destroyed and roads might be mined. We left the Land of Egypt two days later, before daylight, and like the Israelites, we were well loaded with provisions. We drove down the Nile past Memphis and crossed the lower portion of the Land of Goshen, which Joseph had given to his brothers because it was then reputed to be the best grazing land. It no longer was, for centuries of overgrazing and pillage had reduced it to a desolation. Thousands of goat paths twined like dismal draperies around the barren hills.

We crossed the Suez Canal by ferry, and once again were warned by officials against crossing the Sinai. We felt that if the Lord got the great multitudes of Israelites and their flocks through, He would get our small party and one automobile through safely. We found that the border station had been blown up and we became anxious when we passed some Bedouins, as we'd heard that travelers could lose everything if stopped by them. We kept up a steady pace of driving, but Billy pointed toward a valley running parallel to our road. "There's a man on a camel racing at top speed in the same direction we are going. Maybe the men we saw were too surprised to rob us when we drove through, so they're rushing a man ahead to tell others to catch us further on."

Walter speeded up. Fortunately the ridges of drifted sand lying across our road had been stabilized by heavy rains which had drenched the desert the night before, making it possible for our car to outdistance the racer camel and safely reach the next British-Arab control station which was still manned and undamaged. The astonished soldiers gave us a secure night's lodging in the station guest house. On a crystal clear morning, we set off in earnest into the vast wasteland of Sinai.

The youngsters were thrilled by imagining that we were traveling with the Children of Israel. The rest of us got into the spirit of it and Walter spotted a lava cone on the horizon that could have been an active volcano in Bible times and talked about the "cloud by day and the pillar of fire by night" which guided the Israelites in the right direction on their flight from Egypt. Beside the road he showed us a small bush oozing white drops that hardened with a sweetish taste a little like molasses. This might have been the manna miraculously provided to stay their hunger.

We read in the Bible that when the Israelites tired of eating manna, the Lord sent them quail. I had read that the normal annual quail migration route crossed the Mediterranean directly north-south from Europe to Africa. But occasionally the quail fly diagonally, on a much longer flight, so that they fall exhausted on the shores of the Sinai. We actually saw that phenomenon just before our route left the sea. Arabs were catching them in nets by the thousands. So the Sinai Desert was far from empty. Besides the wildlife and the Bedouin tribes, the very air we breathed seemed to bring us closer to the people of the Bible who wandered there for forty years.

The roads were bad, but we made the crossing of Sinai in two days instead of the forty years it took the Children of Israel. Bill, Westher and Elizabeth wrote in their diaries: "We have beaten the speed record of the Children of Israel by thirty-nine years and 363 days."

Adjoining the Sinai Desert was Palestine. Like most people, we had always thought of this area in terms of the Bible and Biblical events. But politically it was a part of the territory mandated to Great Britain by the League of Nations in 1923 "to facilitate in the establishment of a Jewish National Homeland," as Britain's Lord Balfour had said it.

The British soldiers manning the outpost at the tiny, sandy, Biblical village of Beersheba were so shocked to see an automobile coming out of the Sinai, especially one carrying women and children, that they forgot to stamp our passports. (Officials in Jerusalem were to say that we must have come down from the skies, for we carried no evidence of having entered Palestine by land.)

We already felt acquainted with the Holy Land because since childhood we had known the description of it in Deuteronomy (8:7-9):

> For the Lord thy God bringeth thee to a good
> land, a land of brooks of water, of fountains and
> depths that spring out of the valleys and hills; a
> land of wheat and barley, and vines and fig

trees and pomegranates; a land of olive oil and
honey; a land wherein thou shalt eat bread
without scarceness, thou shalt not lack anything
in it. A land whose stones are iron and out of
whose hills thou mayest dig brass copper .

In the Books of Exodus, Leviticus and Numbers, the Bible
described Palestine as a land of milk and honey, which meant
to me that there were fertile grazing lands and abundant
flowering trees and plants. What a wonderful place to have
as our headquarters for our eight months in that part of the
world! Of course I knew about the wilderness where John the
Baptist had preached, but was unprepared to see what man
had done to the beautiful land described in the Bible. I was
shocked. We traveled north through what appeared almost
empty territory. Everywhere was evidence of centuries of
destruction, exploitation and neglect: ruins, broken-down
Roman aqueducts, devastated lands and wrecked ports.

The few people we saw were desperately poor and their
spirits were probably not improved by the political situation.
They were ruled from fortress-like British police stations at
intervals throughout the territory. The rumble of British
military trucks loaded with "tommies" and "tommy-guns" was
common. Interurban buses were of armored plate with
window slits at the top.

It was February, 1939, and the Mediterranean was
chocolate-color to the horizon with soil washed out to sea by
the winter rains. The heavy sands were being sorted by the
waves and deposited along the coast. We jolted along on a
muddy road past sand dunes and swamps and poor villages,
both Arab and Jewish, and began the ascent to Jerusalem
through rocky, barren hills. Each ravine had some soil at the
bottom, but all there was above such a small strip was glaring
white limestone bedrock.

"What a sickening sight," Walter exclaimed. "Not a tree
anywhere!"

Upon arriving in the stone city of Jerusalem we found our
way to the American School of Oriental Research on Saladin

Road through streets lined with sand bags, with barbed wire or cement barricades at every exit or crossroad. At the school we were greeted by its director and head of American archaeology, the famous Dr. Nelson Glueck, who had been notified of our expedition by Washington. He was a tall, Midwesterner with a catching smile. He and Mrs. Glueck welcomed us to comfortable quarters provided for our party near their own in the school compound. Walter would work closely with archaeologists because it was they who uncovered proof of the ancient agriculture--tools, pipelines, granaries, mills, olive and grape presses, irrigation systems and even records of production and trade--in the remains of vanished civilizations.

Walter was delighted with the welcome he received from the officials in forestry and land development, both British and Palestinian. They were not only glad to help him to see things, but to have a man of his experience and personality in their midst. Soon he was spending so much time at meetings and luncheons that I laughingly accused him of becoming a social butterfly.

The government furnished an armored truck manned by standing tommies and bristling with machine guns and rifles, to travel with us out of town and in dangerous areas because of rising unrest between Arabs and Jews, both of whom were agitating against British rule. We began getting acquainted with Jerusalem and soon learned to expect to show our passes whenever we moved about and to be searched before entering all public buildings; even the Post Office. The movie houses had all been closed when an explosive placed under a seat in one caused many casualties. City bus windows had been fitted with iron screens to prevent bombs and stones being thrown in.

"This holy city," I wrote in my diary, "is a savage place even after thousands of years of civilization."

Inside the Old City dwelled the various ancient communities of Christians, Moslems and Jews in their age-old styles of dress and behavior, strictly separated from each other despite their close quarters. We went through narrow

streets and alleys to see the Wailing Wall--the western wall
of the Herodian Temple on the site of Solomon's Temple--holy
to Jews the world over. Between its enormous stones were
inserted thousands of little pieces of paper containing the
prayers of those who had come to mourn the fate of their
people since the destruction of their capital and their temple
in the year 70 A.D., and to pray for better days.

We found the Old City a living museum of history, but it
was unsanitary, cold, overcrowded, and full of beggars and
sickly looking children. Everywhere, especially among the
Arabs, we saw the lame, the blind, and the poor. As a
Christian, I was shamed by reminders of the Crusaders who,
we learned, had butchered the inhabitants in 1099. I also felt
that the ostentatious ornamentation of some of the churches
missed the true message of Jesus.

The New City consisted chiefly of nondescript shops and
buildings spilling out from the ancient walls, over the hills
and new (less than 100 years old) institutions and residential
areas of mixed architecture and size, but all of golden-hued
limestone. These had been built mostly by Jews, but some
were owned by wealthy Arabs and foreigners.

Inside the School of Oriental Research, which was not far
from Herod's Gate, we became a part of the harmonious
community of archaeologists and their wives with whom we
had much in common. They brought ancient and modern
history to life for us, especially Sir Flinders Petrie, who was a
walking encyclopedia on Egypt and Palestine. Sir Flinders
was a courtly, white-haired British intellectual who devoted
his lifetime studies to this area of the world, and had time to
stop and talk with us when we met him on his afternoon
strolls.

One warm winter afternoon we sat on the terrace talking
about this ancient land. He told me that Palestine came from
the word Philistine, the name of an advanced group of people
from the Aegean area at about 1100 B.C. Although Palestine
was at the crossroad of Europe and Asia, it never had been
honored by a proper name since the dispersal of the Jews in
69 A.D. because it had never again been a sovereign state. It

was a Roman and Byzantine Province from 63 B.C. until the Arab conquest in the A.D. 600's, whose rule lasted 400 years. From that point on the land was controlled by an often changing series of conquerors--the Seljuk Turks, the Crusaders in the 1200's, the Mamelukes of Egypt, and finally the Ottoman Turks in 1517 A.D.

The Arab conquests of the seventh and eleventh centuries brought overgrazing with nomadic herds. The Ottoman Turks (1517-1917) degraded both the land and the people by outrageous exploitation and cruelty. The result was the wilderness of denuded hills and malarial swamps we were seeing now.

As each afternoon wore on, a golden glow appeared on the hills above the great rift valley of the Dead Sea, and on the ancient walls of Jerusalem. Then the sun went down, leaving for a few moments a last purple accent on the far off mountains of Moab. As we gathered for dinner, Walter began to tell us about the land as he was studying it.

"We've seen in North Africa how the agriculture and even the traditions of agriculture have been destroyed," he said. "Here in Palestine conditions seem even worse. Erosion has swept the Galilean and Judean Hills clean of soil, leaving only stones and boulders. A tragedy for this historic land.

"There is ample evidence that this was a fertile, productive land in Biblical times, supporting a large population that even exported excess food. When I retire, what I would most like to do is to come back here and put the Holy Land into contour farming to stop erosion, reforest the hills, and make Palestine more productive: to renew this ancient land."

Captain Philip L. O. Guy was Director of the British School of Archaeology. He had traveled and studied the land and what had happened to it and its peoples, and took us on several fascinating trips, generously sharing his knowledge and time.

He was a Christian, but he had married the daughter of Jewish pioneer scholar Eliezer Ben Yehuda who is credited with making ancient Hebrew into Israel's modern language. In a British accent softened by years of living in Palestine, he answered our questions. Elizabeth wanted to know just what the term Zionism meant.

"Zion is a Biblical name for Jerusalem," he explained, "the Jewish capital and the site of the Temple. Since the Jews were cast out by the Romans in 69 A.D. and their temple destroyed, the city has been an object of longing by the Jewish people. So, the movement to achieve freedom by regaining their homeland is called Zionism. Many want to come back from wherever they have been dispersed."

Captain Guy told us of the phenomenal Jewish devotion to this land over the centuries. Even when Jews were scattered across the globe, a few managed to stay on this soil, and each year all pledged to "next year in Jerusalem." In the 1880s, after centuries of exile, Jews began trickling in from Spain, Iraq, Syria, Persia, Yemen, Russia, and Poland. They came on foot, by oxcart, by camel and by boat, back to the land of their forefathers. Their standard of living wasn't much different from the Arabs in those days--desperately poor. But after 1900 Jews from Europe and America began introducing new ideas. They started small industries and plantations. Arabs from surrounding impoverished lands started flocking in for jobs.

"That should have brought the Arabs and Jews together," Elizabeth said.

"No," he told her with a sardonic smile. "Our British 'divide and conquer' policy encourages separation of the communities, so civilian unrest is on the rise."

"It seems to me," Elizabeth said, "the Jews are something like our American founding fathers. They are coming from different places and backgrounds to find freedom in a land of their own, even though it looks like a wilderness."

We were to see the changes in people and land by traveling altogether 2,000 miles within tiny Palestine and an additional 1,000 miles in TransJordan over three months. Occasionally we met other foreign Christians, some of whom amazed us by their ignorance of the Bible. For instance, near the headwaters of the River Jordan an American woman spoke to us:

"I'm so glad to find that Dan and Beersheba are the names of cities and not husband and wife, like Sodom and Gomorrha."

To the lady's dismay, we all burst out laughing, because even Westher, the youngest, knew that Sodom and Gomorrah were the two wicked cities which God destroyed.

We stood on the hillside where Jesus preached His Sermon on the Mount and pronounced the Beatitudes to the crowds eager for His words of hope. Our whole party--the family and Mac and the British Tommies assigned to guard us--ate our lunch on the seashore at the site of old Capernaum, with a dozen rifles stacked beside the walls. It was incongruous.

We passed the Good Samaritan Inn on the road to Jericho and descended 1,700 feet through desert canyons to the Dead Sea, more than 1,000 feet below sea level. We soon were climbing over the remains of the walls of Jericho. I suddenly stumbled over a chunk of earth and it rolled aside, revealing some charred wheat! Archaeologist Guy, who was accompanying us, said "the wheat probably belonged to some poor soul whose house fell in when the city collapsed and burned in Biblical times."

When our family first saw the Jordan River, it was a disappointing, muddy stream, but it was, after all, THE Jordan. As we looked across the water it occurred to the children that the only member of our party who had never been baptized was our dog, Mektube, who by then had traveled with us for 10,000 miles. His sins of commission had been many, especially in hotels, so we all gathered around for a baptism to wash them away, and Westher dipped him in. The current was swifter than we thought, and almost swept him away. Luckily he was saved!

We saw Gaza where Samson carried away the great city gates, and the fields of the Philistines which he burned by tying firebrands to the tails of foxes. We saw the ravine where David killed the giant Goliath with his sling. In Bethlehem we looked out over the field where the shepherds watched their flocks when the angels announced the birth of a Savior who would call for "peace on earth, good will toward men."

We climbed Mt. Carmel and passed through Tyre and Sidon on the Lebanese coast, where the famous cedars of Lebanon were shipped for the Temple at Jerusalem. In such a small area of the world, so much history had been made, marvelled the children. They were an impressionable 14 and 11, and impressed to see, high on a cliff at Dog River, the graffiti of passing conquerors of this battleground of history-- graffiti telling of success from Nebuchadnezzer to Alexander the Great to Napoleon.

We discovered that there was a fine school for American children in connection with the American University at Beirut in Lebanon, just over an hour's drive from Jerusalem. We enrolled Bill and Westher and moved them into nearby American homes. I could thus give more of my time to Walter's work and they would benefit from regular classes. They were happy to be with other children after seven months and I could tell that, especially with Bill's accordion, they would make friends quickly. Westher was living with two other girls in Beirut, but she spent some of the coming months with us in Israel. Elizabeth remained with us and kept up with the cataloging of Walter's photographs. (We were getting good delivery on prints made locally, and she had plenty to keep her busy.)

We were meeting modern Jews in their own historic setting. It was a new and wonderful experience. I had always felt a strong relationship to Jews as the people of the Bible, but had never really known any except one very quiet young Jewish convert who was working in China.

Two Jewish officials were assigned to show us develop- ments in forestry and agriculture. Amihud and Assaf Grasovsky were two sons of Yehuda Grasovsky, pioneer writer of the country's finest dictionaries and of many of the textbooks for the Jewish children of Palestine. The two wiry, good-looking young men were highly intelligent and cultured, both Palestinian-born, with American university degrees. Their competence was freely acknowledged by the British officials.

The Mandate government was doing some reforestation, but much more was being accomplished by the Jewish National Fund, a land reclamation agency. We soon became familiar with settlements on land which had been purchased largely with coins saved in little blue boxes that were in Jewish homes around the world. On this land they had already planted 2 1/2 million trees. The major forest was named after Lord Balfour who had pledged British support for a Jewish homeland in Palestine.

"The saplings grow beautifully if they are planted between the rocks so that their roots seek out the soil pockets in the limestone," Dr. Amihud Goor, a forester, explained.

Amihud took us to Haifa and put us up in a small inn on Mount Carmel. He proudly showed us a small forest he had planted recently where the husky saplings were doing well. He had fenced them in to protect them from the innumerable, ravenous goats. Outside the fence the land was as barren as though it had been shaved with a razor.

He also showed us a new settlement below Jerusalem. Here, five Jewish boys who were out planting trees before breakfast were ambushed by Arabs and killed. One boy, before he died, wrote in his forestry notebook: "Dying is not so bad when it is done for one's own country."

We learned from Amihud's brother Assaf that by 1939, with private purchases and through the Jewish National Fund, the Jews had bought six percent of Palestine.

"Regarding Arab land," Assaf told us, "we usually had to pay twice, first to the absentee land owners, and then to the tenant farmers who demanded to be compensated before they would move off."

However, he said, most of the land purchased had been untenanted malarial swamps, sand dunes and rocky desert, which the Jews drained and cleared before they planted crops. Walter was astonished at the high prices they had paid, especially for sand dunes. But they had no choice. They had to have land to build their towns and farms which would feed their people.

Although the Jews occupied just six percent of the land and did all the reclamation at their own expense, the British levied taxes against them which amounted to more than half of the taxes for the entire country. It reminded me of British policy in China.

The most progressive agriculture in the country was practiced by cooperatives of two types: the kibbutz and the moshav. In the kibbutzim, the people shared their lives, property and work, even the duties of child rearing in the separate children's houses. In the moshavim, families lived separately in their own houses, but they shared the machinery, some of the land, and marketing facilities. There were also some good private citrus plantations and vineyards on the coastal plain and Mt. Carmel.

Walter and I noticed that idealism was high among the Jews who had come to Palestine years before. Many had given up higher education in Europe to put their ideals into practice in Palestine. They were intelligent and quick to learn. For many years they had braved economic hardship-- natural disasters, famine and disease, attacks by hostile neighbors, and ruthless exploitation by unsympathetic governments.

New settlers--refugees from the rise of Hitler in Europe- -were also taking up farming. Walter was eager to see how they were farming with so little experience and equipment. We arranged to visit Hanita, a settlement that had been built literally a few nights before on a dry, boulder-strewn hillside near the Lebanese border.

"But how did you do it?" Walter asked in astonishment. Our young host replied simply, "The British ruled against any more Jewish settlements and Arab terrorism is widespread, but we bought this land and are determined to settle. So, we secretly made all our preparations in other kibbutzim. We precut the lumber for our buildings, got together our livestock and equipment and assembled everything necessary for our defense, even the tower with a huge revolving search light. In one night, we brought everything to our new location and completed all the work before daylight. When the local

Arabs awakened they saw the village complete. The British officials were angry, but they had not succeeded in catching us at work, and by law a settlement that exists can remain. They could do nothing."

Walter spent all that first day at Hanita on the hillside, watching the seventy young kibbutznicks picking up rocks and rebuilding the terraces that had been broken down by hungry goats centuries ago. They found the decayed stumps of huge trees cut close to the ground which convinced Walter that very large trees had once flourished there and might do so again. He loved working along with the young people and encouraging them, for they were fulfilling a part of his own life's dream. To me it was prophecy come true:

> And I will bring again...my people of Israel, and
> they shall rebuild the waste cities and inhabit
> them; and they shall plant vineyards and drink
> the wine thereof; they shall also make gardens
> and eat the fruit of them. And I will plant them
> upon their land, and they shall no more be
> pulled up out of their land which I have given
> them, saith the Lord thy God.   Amos 9:14-15.

Meantime, I spent most of the day atop the lookout tower with the young man assigned to keep watch. He spoke English quite well. I felt like weeping as I looked down upon these splendid young idealists laboring and sweating carrying rocks in the hot sun.

"How can you _ever_ make this place self-supporting?" I asked him. They owned a few acres at the foot of the slope on which they planned to grow bananas and vegetables, but I confess it all looked pretty hopeless to me.

"It will not be easy," he answered. "But we will do it. We will restore this land and raise our families here as our ancestors did. There will be one place where Jewish children can play in freedom among their own people."

Traveling among the Jewish villages, we discovered they had improved the skinny Syrian cow, common to Palestine, by breeding it with stronger, more productive types until at last they produced an animal able to endure the dry, hot climate and to produce milk in quantity. A number of Jewish doctors who had come as refugees from Germany and Poland and found no medical jobs open at the time, settled down to poultry farming and put their fine minds to work on developing a hearty "Jewish hen" which would do well in Palestine. Their determination brought to my mind the story of the artist. A woman asked him, "With what do you mix your paints?" He replied, "With brains, Madam, with brains."

Walter was so impressed by the courage and resourcefulness of these young pioneers that he said, "Here in Palestine they are doing the finest reclamation of old lands that I have seen on four continents, and the most successful agricultural settlement of modern times."

Yet, not everyone appreciated their remarkable accomplishments. At every social event we attended we heard complaints by Europeans, especially British, that Jewish activities were "spoiling" the picturesque look of Palestine with their modern improvements. In the poor Arab villages many were illiterate and sickly, but the English seemed to resent Jews giving Arabs even medical help. At a dinner at the beautiful Jerusalem YMCA, I was indignant to hear the American director reflect this attitude, and I found myself speaking out against this unfairness. At that time, the children were back with us for another weekend and it embarrassed them to see their mother provoking arguments.

"Mother," said our fourteen year-old Bill one day, "If you don't stop fighting for the Jews in public, I am not going to any more dinner parties with you."

I tried to explain to him that it is natural for us to respond to the Jews. "They are like us. We have the same God. They have the same democratic ideals as we Americans have. They are people with respect for the past. They share our enthusiasm for the present and our ambition for the future."

The more we saw of Jewish development the more enthusiastic we became, and we made no secret of it. Our outspoken admiration seemed of some comfort to those who were trying so desperately to save the remnant of their people but were meeting with resistance everywhere.

Captain and Mrs. Guy took us on the most fascinating trip of our entire year and a half in Old Roman lands: to the rose-red, rock-carved city of Petra in TransJordan, capital of the former lands of Moab and Edom.

"Petra is the city known in the Old Testament as 'Sela', meaning 'rock'," Philip Guy told us. "It was built by the Nabateans as their capital, but it was lost to the world for centuries."

To reach it we drove south from Amman through an area dotted with the remains of hundreds of ancient farms and farming terraces and dams. We crossed and recrossed the well-built Roman roads, with the ancient chariot ruts still visible in the stones. Finally, after traveling for a time through a dreary wilderness we came to the Spring of Moses, a glorious little stream gushing out of a large rock. Tradition says Moses struck this rock with his staff 3,200 years before to produce water for the Israelites in the desert. Having had no good water all day, we drank of it freely and were grateful for it, as the ancient Jews must have been. Mektube ran in, then cooled us off with a shower as he shook himself off with enthusiasm.

The Spring of Moses led us to the village of Eliji, where we mounted horses and acquired a guard of Arabs carrying a small arsenal to accompany us. Besides a camera and personal paraphernalia, I had to carry our excited pup in my arms. It was like doing acrobatics to keep both of us on the horse. Our last two hours of riding were on a descent through canyons in the dark. The deep, black gorge we took into Petra was several miles long and sometimes only twenty feet wide, with walls so high that only occasional shafts of the full moon's bright light found their way through the crevice overhead. Suddenly it widened, and before us in the moonlight gleamed the gorgeous Temple of Isis, carved out of solid red sandstone cliffs over 2,500 years ago. We passed temples and homes, and hundreds of tombs, all carved from the deeply-colored rock, their windows yawning blackly in the canyon walls.

We slept in some of the tombs carved in the walls at different levels, with stone steps leading from chamber to chamber. They were clean, for long ago the departed souls had flown and their ashes had blown away with the centuries.

Petra once flourished as a commercial and agricultural center, complete even to a rock-hewn ampitheater seating 3,500 spectators built by its Roman captors. As we looked around us the next morning, however, all was desolate except for the marvelous, everlastingly still carvings. Oleander in bloom and scurrying lizards were the only evidence of life. Lines from Shelley's sonnet "Ozymandias" sprung to mind: "Look on my works, ye mighty, and despair."

From Petra we traveled south to Aqaba. Archaeologist Nelson Glueck was excavating King Solomon's seaport, Ezion Geber, near Aqaba on the Red Sea. The Jews were anxious to find out all they could about the land of their ancestors.

On the day Walter and I and our party visited him there, the dust of long unused lands was blowing in swirls as it probably had done for centuries. About sixty workmen were busy clearing away the soil that had buried the remains of ancient houses, streets and factories. Glueck told us the Jews planned to rebuild Solomon's old port one day, and with the glorious beaches, fabulous sea life and hot, dry climate, I envisioned a marvelous thriving winter resort there.

While Walter went off to see the diggings with Dr. Glueck, the rest of us went for a glorious sailboat ride in a spanking breeze on the Red Sea. Dr. Glueck gave us a five-gallon bucket with a glass bottom so we could see the aquatic life better. Then we returned to the sleepy Jordanian town of Aqaba for a swim in the company of tropical fish flashing their colors in the transparent waters.

"It's great fun," Elizabeth lamented, "until you step on a blooming bouquet of coral. That punctures your foot as well as your enthusiasm."

On the way back to Jerusalem, through the Negev Desert, we carried a five-gallon can of water in the car so that we could wet our clothes and keep moist handkerchiefs tied over our noses in order to breathe better in the terribly dry air. The temperature was over 120 F.

As we neared Jerusalem, Walter stopped in an Arab village so he could take pictures and try his talents at winnowing grain with the men. I started passing out candy to the children who crowded around our car. When Captain and Mrs. Guy discovered that our car was not behind theirs, they rushed back and insisted Walter get back into the car immediately and drive on.

"These villagers are well known for their mistreatment of foreigners," they later told us. "They recently killed several people who stopped there." Although we frequently traveled through Arab villages we had never had a problem.

That year an American Jewish women's organization, Hadassah, dedicated its new hospital on Jerusalem's Mount Scopus. The British Governor General and dignitaries of the various communities were invited and I toured its up-to-date facilities with the head nurse. In the maternity clinic, Arab, Druze, Samaritan, and European women mingled with Jewish women from various backgrounds and their costumes made the place very colorful.

"A baby carriage has been promised for the first baby born here," the nurse told me. "Several women are already in the hospital competing for the prize!"

I met Hadassah's founder, a Baltimore woman named Henrietta Szold, and learned of her work in the rehabilitation of orphans she and her co-workers were managing to rescue from Nazi Germany. Here the horrors of the Nazi crimes came to me first hand, as I saw mutilated victims of the concentration camps who had escaped to tell the story.

In May of 1939 Britain published her "White Paper," a pronouncement that no more Jews could enter Palestine because there was "no further economic absorptive capacity" for Jewish immigration. We saw the demoralizing effect this document had on the Jews: they looked crushed. They had put their life's blood into restoring their ancestral home and creating a viable refuge for their dispossessed and tortured brethren.   But now, when that refuge was needed most, Britain had closed the gates in her zeal to win Arab loyalty in case of war.   Although some Arab leaders were Nazi sympathizers, Britain needed Arab support against Germany and Arab oil to keep her navy afloat.   Obviously she considered her promise to the Jewish people and to the League of Nations expendable.

It seemed that Walter's was the lone Christian voice in Government raised in protest.

"The White Paper is absurd!" he exclaimed.   "Let the Jews come in by the tens of thousands.   They will bring their own absorbtive capacity with them.   They can drain the swamps and de-stone the soil.   They can rebuild the broken-down terraces and plant orchards, vineyards and forests."

Walter backed up this challenge by suggesting a practical proposal--a little "TVA" for the Jordan that would benefit Arabs and Jews alike.   He had seen the good rainfall and abundant rivers of the north flowing down into the Dead Sea and evaporating there--water that was doing no one any good.

He recommended that water from the overwatered north be brought down to the dry, fertile lands of the northern Negev Desert region around Beersheba by canal and conduit. "With irrigation" he said, "Jews and Arabs can get two or three assured good crops annually, instead of the present one good crop every four or five years."

I was stirred by this prospect and recalled the words of Isaiah:

> Behold, I will do a new thing; now it shall spring forth; shall ye not know it? I will even make a way in the wilderness and rivers in the desert... to give drink to my people, my chosen.
>   Isaiah 43:19-20

And in Ezekial 36:33-35:

> ...I will also cause you to dwell in the cities, and the wastes shall be builded. And the desolate

land shall be tilled, whereas it lay desolate in
the sight of all that passed by. And they shall
say, this land that was desolate is become like
the Garden of Eden; and the waste and desolate
and ruined cities are become fenced and are
inhabited.

Walter knew of work already underway to exploit the
mineral wealth of the Dead Sea through an evaporation
system. Now he suggested that conduits and tunnels could
take salt sea water from the Mediterranean and drop it 1,200
feet into the Dead Sea through twin power plants. "This
would maintain the Dead Sea waters at any chosen level," he
said. I estimate that it would produce about one-third the
power of America's Boulder Dam."

Walter's wonderful proposals fell on deaf ears. Arab
leaders loudly refused to cooperate with anything that might
help Jewish development. Walter continued to maintain that,
even without this hydroelectric project, with modern agriculture alone, Palestine could be made to support several million
more Jews. This irritated the British officials to the extent
that they began publicly calling him "that Damned
Lowdermilk."

As our time in Palestine drew to a close, Walter prepared
to continue our study mission in Babylon and Nineva, Syria
and Lebanon, and I worked on his Palestine report. I felt
miserable with sandfly fever, but I took Walter's daily field
notes and read all the literature he brought back from the
places and projects he had visited, and worked constantly,
whether I felt like it or not, organizing his thoughts and
ideas. I also had access to Nelson Glueck's fine archaeol-
ogical library. The report grew and grew until finally I had
typed fifty pages to give to Walter's secretary, Mac. When he
brought me back a beautiful, clean copy, I put the report on
Walter's desk.

"Here is your report," I said wearily. "I don't suppose
anyone will ever read it."

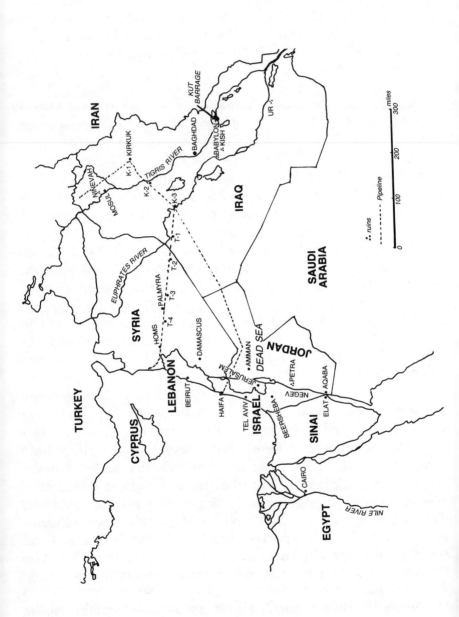

CHAPTER 14
EXPLORING ANCIENT CULTURES

Our plans included studies in the entire "Fertile Crescent" which extends from the coastal areas of Palestine and Lebanon across the Syrian desert and the Euphrates River, which traverses it, northward into Turkey and south into the "land between two rivers," or Mesopotamia of ancient Babylon. Walter, Mac, Elizabeth and I set out on the same 650 mile journey across the desolate Syrian desert that was traveled some 2,800 years ago by the ancient Hebrews after the Babylonians conquered the land of Israel and took the Jews in captivity to Babylon, where they "wept beside the waters."

First we crossed over the Lebanon mountains to Damascus. The city was in the midst of riots. Ten people had been shot outside our hotel that day, but swarms of soldiers were keeping the night quiet. As we were leaving Damascus, very early in the morning, soldiers were stacking sandbags to barricade the main square. But we had no difficulty in going eastward to Palmyra and beyond.

The Syrian desert is absolutely flat from horizon to horizon. During the long, dry summers it is a blazing oven from which the dreaded <u>khamsin</u> or choking dust storms sweep westward to the Mediterranean. During the winter rainy season, however, it is covered by a cool green carpet of grass and patches of lovely wildflowers. The soils become muddy and cars which dare to venture forth bog down, as we learned from exasperating experience. We expected to find real roads in 1939, but there were none. Dirt tracks ran along the oil pipelines which extended from the Iraqi oil fields to the Mediterranean coast at Tripoli and Haifa. There were no accommodations for travelers, but fortunately Walter's status as a U.S. Government official enabled us to be guests at the pipeline facilities from Lebanon to Iraq.

When we were well into the Syrian desert a dark winter cloud crept over the heavens and soon it emptied its contents onto our lonely auto. By four-o'clock in the afternoon we were stuck in the mud, still several hours from our only refuge--an oil pumping station resthouse. Walter took to the shovel while the rest of us searched the desert for rocks to set under the wheels. We worked for over an hour before the mud released us. Darkness came early and the car tracks were obliterated. We followed the pipeline, doing our best to avoid puddles and bogs, sometimes in old tracks but more often making new ones.

We were relieved to see a dim light on the horizon behind us. When we stopped to direct our flashlight in that direction, our car again settled heavily down into a bog, which gripped it like a vise.

The oncoming car had seen our flashing light and was coming to help. When it pulled up to investigate the trouble, it also sank into the sticky mire. A load of white-robed Arabs swarmed from the car, but neither their engine nor shovels nor even their supplications to Allah could extricate their car from the mud. Finally they released it using our jack, but the effort broke the jack. The Arabs continued trying to pull our car until our tow rope was torn to shreds. We had no language in common, so when they finally left us, we hoped they were going to get help from the pipeline station, K-3. We watched their lights dip over the horizon in the cold darkness of the vast desert. Then we waited.

Four hours passed, and there we sat with our headlights on so that our whereabouts could be seen. Eventually, three ill-fated trucks from the British pipeline station were sent out to rescue us. One had a puncture, one became lost, and one got stuck in the mud. The truck with the puncture changed wheels and finally reached our light and pulled the car out of the mud. The one that was lost eventually picked up the light of the one stuck in the mud and rescued it. They traveled in circles until their light was seen by the rest of us, finally leading us all to a happy reunion. They had brought along whiskey to revive us, but we didn't need it. By this time, we were in a hilarious mood, enjoying the humor of it all. Long after midnight, we reached Pumping Station K-3, where a hot dinner and comfortable beds awaited us. No one need ever tell me that the Syrian Desert is only hot and dry!

The following day we literally slid into the Euphrates Valley. We had been through three Iraqi customs check stations, the last being by the Euphrates. Our car wound its way through puddles, chuck holes and slithery tracks toward the broad river, flowing rapidly in a gorge lined with palm trees. We followed the Euphrates on a paved road to Baghdad, crossing the Tigris River on a pontoon bridge along with goats, sheep, camels, water buffalo, new and decrepit cars. Baghdad, the capital of modern Iraq, is the successor to Babylon and Babylonia.

The great cities of Babylon, including the palace where Belshazzar saw the "handwriting on the wall" as recounted by Daniel in anticipation of the destruction of the Chaldean empire by the Persians, are now--2,600 years later--mere hovels or tents occupied by ragged, illiterate natives. We stopped at the once-great city of Kish which the Bible tells us was the first capital to rise after the Great Flood. A forty-inch layer of silt (visible in cross-section) was undoubtedly laid down by a great deluge. The artifacts found above and below this stratum show entirely different levels of civilization. The generous hospitality of a local bedouin was dimmed by the myriad flies exploring in and out of eyes, noses, mouths, food, and tents. Human populations may have decreased, but not the fly population!

Walter took wonderful pictures of these ruins and of the remains of the mighty city of Babylon, the greatest center of culture and learning known to the ancient world. The great ruins gave us the feeling of being at a funeral. The only evidence of life we saw in this once teeming city was a lean, grey wolf, shaking his head as though annoyed by a tick in his ear. Casting furtive glances our way, he loped to his lair among the heaps and piles of all that remained of the "Hanging Gardens of Babylon," one of the Seven Wonders of the Ancient World.

How well the predictions of the prophet Jeremiah have been fulfilled: "And Babylon shall became a heap, a dwelling place for jackals,...without an inhabitant" Jeremiah 51:37 . The Hebrew prophets of the Captivity thundered their denunciations, warning that the cities of Babylon would become "...a desolation, a dry land and a wilderness, a land wherein no man dwelleth....and wild beasts shall cry in their desolate houses and jackals in the pleasant palaces" Isaiah 13:22 .

For three weeks in Mesopotamia we visited the debris left by the eleven civilizations that rose and fell in the past 7,000 years. As we explored that ancient Garden of Eden in the vicinity of Baghdad, there was a great national celebration marking completion of the Kut Barrage south of Baghdad. The Barrage dammed the Tigris River so that some of the lands irrigated in ancient times could be brought back into production, eventually 900,000 acres. The king had invited 300 special guests to feast and we received an invitation. Shortly before the event, however, the United States Consul sent word to us that Elizabeth and I had been invited only as a courtesy to my husband. As women in a Moslem land, we were not supposed to attend. While Walter and Mac sailed forth to dine with the king, we stayed in our stuffy little Baghdad hotel room. Upon his return Walter described it all to us.

"Sure enough, there was not a woman there. The feast consisted of barbecued camels inside of which were barbecued sheep, inside of which were barbecued chickens, inside of which were hardcooked eggs. The king's representatives and 300 guests ate first. When they had finished, lesser officials attacked the barbecued animals, and when they finished, it was an open race for anyone to get whatever was left. You missed a novel experience, all right!"

Walter said that after the feast a rich sheik proudly invited them and the American consulate staff across the river to his new home which boasted a movie theater, a tiled bathroom, and other modern luxuries unique to the area. As they sat in a small boat, the consular chauffeur drew the Americans' attention to several heavily veiled women sitting on the mud bank near the house.

"There are the wives of this powerful sheik." he told them. "They are anxious to see the guests coming to their home and the only way is to leave the house and see them from a distance." I felt that this attitude toward women made the country like a crippled bird trying to fly with only one wing.

The word that France had allowed Turkey to annex the most northwesterly seashore (including Antioch) of Syria under their mandate reached Baghdad as we were to leave. In sympathy with the Syrians, the unpaved streets were crowded and mobs were slashing themselves with chains to draw blood. Our hotel was on a half circle driveway with both entry and exit on the main street. The doorman warned us against trying to go through the crowds with British license plates, but our car was packed and we were ready to go. A number of times Walter tried to move forward, but could not do it. From their glowering expressions, the people indicated that if we so much as touched one of their garments with our car, they would tear us to pieces. We all stayed outwardly calm and stoical and kept quiet so as not to draw attention to ourselves, trusting in the Lord and in Walter's good judgment to bring us through safely.

Luckily, a high official in an Iraqi government car came to pick up someone at our hotel. Walter quickly maneuvered our car so that when the official car started up, our hood was practically touching its bumper and none of the crowd would wedge between us. Breathing the car's exhaust, we reached the main road, got through the crowds and onto a country

lane going toward the pipeline road, this time breathing a sigh
of relief and gratefulness for our safety.

Arriving at the pipeline headquarters several hours later,
we were greeted by an engineer who told us, "We just heard
over the wireless that the mob in Baghdad grabbed a load of
Frenchmen off their truck and pulled out all their hair. It
must have been about the time you left Baghdad. I say, you
were lucky."

As in Palestine, the fever of nationalism was running high
in the Old Ottoman Empire. The League of Nations gave the
mandate of Syria to France, who separated Lebanon as an
entity in 1926, and effectively kept the mandate until 1946
when the last French troops left. The mandate of Iraq by
Britain lasted until 1931 when Iraq became a monarchy.
Desires for independence could arouse violent reactions.

We continued driving north beside the Tigris River to
ancient Ninevah, now Mosul, where the Bible tells us Jonah
urged the people to stop their wickedness. When we arrived,
a conference was in progress and the only place where we
could secure lodging had a leaky roof that poured water down
on the entrance, which had no door. The condition of the
furniture and the lack of sanitation were distressing. I took
one look at the dirty, used bed sheets and demanded clean
ones. When we returned they had been changed, but these
were only a little less soiled than the first ones.

"We must have clean sheets and I will put them on the
beds myself," I told the white-robed manager.

When the hotel boy brought them he said, "Here, madam,
smell these. They're clean." Well, I certainly didn't find them
clean, but they were less dirty than the others.

Travel conditions were extremely difficult. All roads in
the north along the Turkish foothills to Aleppo were impass-
able. The only paved road open led far off our course southeast along the Kurdistan Steppe to Kirkuk and the oil field
headquarters. The unbridged Tigris and Euphrates Rivers
would both then be between us and our intended destination,
Beirut. But the paved road was too attractive to resist.

At Pumping Station K-1 in the great oil field at Kirkuk we were delighted to find a beautiful rest house, interesting engineers to talk with and good food. Under this area, we were told by British engineers, lies one of the largest pools of oil yet known.

Kirkuk was one of the highlights of our trip to this cradle of our civilization, for there were so many Old Testament associations. Here were Daniel's tomb and, still on fire after 3,000 years, the escaping natural gas that both the Bible and tradition claim to be the "fiery furnace" into which Daniel's three friends were thrown without harm. The gas spurts out in fiery jets through crevices even today, and I was able to gather my skirts about me and walk among the flames as the Bible characters probably did. However, during riots while we were there, two Jews were murdered in Kirkuk and were not saved as were Daniel's compatriots.

Escorted by a powerful mail truck, we began our trek from Kirkuk to Pumping Station K-3 at Haditha on the Euphrates River following our earlier steps across the Syrian desert. The Euphrates was still in flood from the copious rain. When we reached the river, an engineer directed our car onto a small platform attached to cables spanning the water. We were raised high into the air before being dipped downward over the water and pulled up by another cable onto the opposite bank. I stepped out of the car and was standing between the back bumper and the heavy iron chain across the rear of the platform. An instant before we were pulled toward the tower on the opposite bank, some impulse made me step aside. The platform suddenly jerked upward and the peg holding the rods blocking the car slipped out, letting the car crash against the chain. Had I not moved three seconds earlier, I would have been crushed and dropped into the muddy flood waters. My guardian angel was still protecting me.

Greeting us at the big double pumping station K-3, sending oil to both Tripoli and Haifa, was an engineer who told us that the Iraqi king was killed when he wrapped his automobile around a telegraph pole. It was providential we left Mosul when we did rather than wait for a cessation of the rain, as a foreign agitator started the rumor that the British has killed the King Ghazi, Iraq's second king. In Mosul, a mob stoned the British consul to death and burned the consulate. We had been about the only other foreigners in the city, and our car had British license plates.

We got as far westward as pumping station T-2 when the rains stopped us again and we had to wait three days for clearing weather. Normally only up to 4" of rain falls a year on this desert, but during our trip more rain had fallen than anytime in 22 years. While we were waiting in the desert Walter wrote "Reflections of an American Conservationist on the Rise and Fall of Civilizations in the Discarded Cradle of Mankind," published in American Forests Magazine (August, 1941). He said that the great Tigris-Euphrates alluvial plain can be a desert or a garden, dependent entirely upon the condition of the irrigation canals. Throughout history, wars have been fought and slaves brought by the tens of thousands for the endless task of clearing the canals' silt washed down from the mountains.

Alongside the canals we saw thousands of miniature mountain ranges with tooth-like peaks, as high as forty feet, created over the centuries by piling up this silt higher and higher. When these became too high, the old canals dispersing irrigation water were abandoned and new ones built beside them. Once our road passed through eleven of these huge canals with twenty-two ranges of silt banks.

The riches of each of the eleven Mesopotamian civilizations were related to how its people handled their watersheds and irrigation systems. In ancient times the Iraqi system supported populations of thirty to fifty million compared with some eight million in Iraq in 1939. The land became more productive as flood control and irrigation works developed, and its inhabitants and civilizations grew powerful. Ultimately they became corrupted by luxurious living. Then they became prey for their covetous and hungry neighbors, the nomads from the surrounding grasslands in Persia, the Caucasus and Arabia.

However, all the nomads' conquering, killing and pillaging alone could never have eradicated such vast populations. The erosion and silt from mountains to the north completed the devastation. In times of war or invasions, the social organization would break down, the canals were neglected and they would clog. When the water system failed, the agriculture failed and the cities perished. Walter wrote: "It fills one with consternation to contemplate this graveyard of cities, empires and civilizations now housing a meager, mostly illiterate, population."

"Out of the injustices, sorrows, broken spirits and ashes of vast populations and vanished civilizations," he wrote, "let us extract that which will give us the greatest assurance of longevity to our nation and our culture. 'Where there is no vision, the people perish' is as true today as when proclaimed by the prophets of old. Conservation of our national resources, both physical and human, including the individual initiative of our people, should become our vision and our goal. Since older civilizations have been brought to ignominious ends by exploitation and destruction which wiped out both physical and spiritual values and the glories and works of multitudes of people, let us seek an objective of conservation instead of destruction."

Our trip through Mesopotamia had profoundly impressed upon Walter the paramount need for formulation of a world plan for land conservation.*

After a largely uneventful desert crossing, we reported to the Tripoli oil station and said goodbye to the kind, friendly engineers, and drove south to Beirut, the capital of Lebanon. Beirut was an international city of Christians and Moslems under French mandate. It also had a delightful community of American professors and their families connected with the American University who reminded us of our happy days in

---

* In 1980, the United Nations sponsored, and the U.S. was among the nations that signed the World Conservation Strategy, the first international recognition of the soil as a public resource--Editor.

Nanking. We settled into a pleasant hotel and had a happy reunion with the children after a month's separation. The American University generously gave Walter an office on campus and provided him with archeological information about the famous Cedars of Lebanon (Cedrus libani). No other trees in human history have been so bound up with the development of ancient civilizations than these magnificent trees, and none so frequently mentioned in ancient literature. Its importance is commemorated on Lebanon's flag.

"I've made a list of ancient records regarding the use of cedar wood," Walter told us one evening. "The Bible mentions it many times. The Phoenicians are known to have exchanged cargoes of cedar for bronze articles produced by the Egyptians before 3000 B.C. Egyptian records at Karnak tell of the arrival of forty shiploads of cedar in the Third Dynasty, before 2900 B.C. Palaces and temples of the ancient world from the Nile to the Tigris and Euphrates, were adorned with cedar from Lebanon. Records dating from 2000 B.C. show its use in Babylonia."

"King David imported it for his palace. King Solomon made a contract for the cedar with Hiram, King of Tyre, and provided 80,000 'hewers of wood' and 70,000 'bearers of burdens' working in relays year after year in the mountains of Lebanon. Cedar was used extensively in Solomon's Temple, both for construction and for beauty. King Solomon used it to build his fleet and Egypt had cedar floated down to her own shipyards. The Cedars of Lebanon were a valuable commodity in the ancient world. In Roman days there were actually forest conservators to protect the trees from wanton exploitation.   But great empires came and went, and the forest suffered the mortal blows of those greedy for timber--armies and navies anxious to obtain logs for their war machines and ships, and towns and villages needing fuel."

"With the felling of the trees, the mountainsides lost their protectors and erosion laid them bare," Walter said. "Agriculture suffered while civilization went into a continual decline. Only a few groves of the glorious cedars remain to remind mankind of his squandering of one of God's great gifts. The cedars could be replanted and regrown, but it may take a generation to two to reach harvest. Still, in the history of a civilization, what is a generation?"

We saw Baalbek, "City of the Gods," said to be the best preserved and most massive of all Roman ruins. Earthquakes and vandalism had taken their toll. Huge fragments of stone tumbled about like children's playing blocks. The gigantic, towering pillars--which still stood--were astonishing. They had been floated on rafts down the Nile and along the Mediterranean to Lebanon, then rolled over the mountains before being placed upright in Baalbek.

In Lebanon, Walter studied the famous rock wall terraces which the Phoenicians began building 5,000 years ago, the forerunners of those we had seen in France. Some mountains had been terraced up to an altitude of 3,000 feet with stone benches running in and out of canyons. Some terraces had broken down over the ages, but others had been maintained as a permanent agricultural feature. About 2,000 hamlets were hooked onto these steep slopes of the Lebanon mountains. Walter wanted to experience the difficulties such farmers had in growing their food, so, much to the enjoyment of the villagers, he would often take up a scythe or a plow or put his shoulder to a well wheel. Once, in a Lebanese village, we all shrieked with laughter seeing him struggle with a primitive plow pulled by two cows on an unterraced hillside so steep that one cow was several feet higher than the other.

The French-built roads were good, but difficult to negotiate because of the livestock, primitive carts and pedestrians. We all appreciated Walter's excellent driving, especially at night, because we were confronted at many curves with dozens of tiny "headlights"--the eyes of animals shining in the darkness--before we could make out what they were. When suddenly we would approach the goats from the rear, however, their lack of "tail lights" required quick reflexes and good brakes to avoid accidents.

In Lebanon we had glimpses into Arab life as it was meeting the modern world. Some of the educated Arabs in the region, both men and women (the latter from Beirut schools), were fiercely nationalistic and strongly opposed to European domination of that part of the world. For this I could scarcely blame them, but at that time they appeared to have little idea of sacrifice or service to uplift their own people and wasted their time blaming other nations for all their problems.

In June, we made a trip back to Jerusalem for Walter to deliver a radio talk entitled "Gone With the Rain," in which he explained what erosion had done to the Holy Land. While he was preparing the talk I urged him to end it with the "Eleventh Commandment" he had composed as we crossed the Sinai. He feared that it might offend the Jews if he appeared to be adding to holy writ. But I felt it could be very effective, so I urged him to take a chance.

"Give it just this once, Walter," I begged, "and if it offends them, never give it again."

I sat in the Glueck living room with Dr. and Mrs. Nelson Glueck and others as Walter's voice came over the air telling of the tragedy of land despoliation and consequent dead civilizations he had seen in North Africa and in Mesopotamia which had made Walter appreciate the work of Palestine's Jewish pioneers all the more. He closed his talk with the "Eleventh Commandment" and he dedicated it to them. When he had finished, Dr. Glueck exclaimed, "Lord, but that's good!"

After that, Walter closed every talk he gave with this "commandment," dramatizing it with color slides taken on our trip through Roman lands showing vividly the results of man's abuse of his natural resources. He would say, "I found in the midst of a general and long decline of land productivity, the good work of Jewish settlers in Palestine. This is a new thing under the sun. It is a building back, a restoration of a man-made desert....I dedicate what might have been the 'Eleventh Commandment' to them:

> Thou shalt inherit the Holy Earth as a faithful
> steward, conserving its resources and producti-
> vity from generation to generation. Thou shalt

safeguard thy fields from soil erosion, thy living
waters from drying up, thy forests from desolation and protect the hills from overgrazing by
thy herds, that thy descendants may have
abundance forever. If any shall fail in this good
stewardship of the earth, thy fruitful fields
shall become sterile, stony ground, or wasting
gullies, and thy descendents shall decrease and
live in poverty or perish from off the face of
the earth.

*****

During the summer of 1939 we went to the Lebanese
mountains to escape the heat and to complete what was to be
Walter's final report. War clouds were looming in Europe and
it did not seem we would be able to complete our trip through
the Balkans, Russia and Germany. While in the mountains, I
read in the paper that the port at Beirut had received an SOS
from a tiny, old one-funnel Greek freighter loaded with 655
Czechoslovakian Jews. I'd heard rumors that at least two
thousand Jewish refugees, mostly from Poland and Czechoslovakia, were floating just over the horizon from the coast
of Palestine trying to get to their Promised Land, but the
British would not let them land. As soon as England and
France had dismembered Czechoslovakia, I had heard of the
frantic exodus of Jews to escape Hitler. Now I wanted to
find out first-hand what it was all about.

I learned that the port authorities had gone on board to
verify conditions and I began asking questions. I found out
that the ship was without coal, water, or food; that the
passengers sometimes could not close their eyes in sleep
without risk of attack by hungry rats; that the authorities
feared a plague of typhus might break out and some desperate
passengers might swim ashore bringing it with them. Thus
they had taken all the passengers off the ship at the Beirut
quarantine station to exterminate the rats on the ship.

Since Walter had taken our car to see the cedars, I decided to take a bus down the mountain from our summer vacation hotel to Beirut to see for myself the conditions of these refugees. I saw the ship first. It was tiny! I could not believe that 655 human beings, along with the twenty-three crew members, could ever have been crammed into it. Seeing them dispersed in the yard made it look even more impossible. Our U.S. Consul got me permission to go into the quarantine area with an interpreter. Word spread quickly among the refugees that I was the wife of an American official, and they crowded around to tell me their stories.

Many spoke English. I learned of their incredible fortitude in the face of starvation and unbelievable misery. They had been afloat for eleven weeks packed into four cargo holds, two of which were below water level, in foul air, semidarkness, and stifling heat. The two holds above water level had no portholes and the summer sun turned them into ovens. Only a third of the passengers could stand on deck at any one time and no shade was provided against the blistering sun. During rainy or stormy weather, they were forced to remain below in near suffocation. When I spoke to the women they would recoil at the mere mention of the filthy conditions. Their daily diet had consisted of a meager helping of beans or lentils. Morning and evening they had only reboiled tea leaves and moldy hardtack. They were all undernourished. The children were pale and showed signs of scurvy from lack of fresh fruit and vegetables.

Among them were forty lawyers, forty-two engineers, six journalists, and twenty-six physicians and surgeons, of whom six were young women graduates of University of Prague Medical School. There were seven pharmacists and eight professional musicians, including a grand opera star and the director of the second largest symphony orchestra in Czechoslovakia. Also in the group were two staff officers and sixty officers of the regular Czech army. Two hundred were women and children.

I could scarcely believe that human beings could endure such hardships, but these people had sustained their morale for eleven terrible weeks. Despite the lack of proper medical facilities the physicians had cared for the sick and no one had died. The musicians had given concerts daily with what instruments they had. Some had brought Scrolls of the Law, and had held daily religious services. Others had taught Hebrew songs in anticipation of the happy day they would arrive in Palestine.

On my first visit I saw the army officers organizing the camp and setting aside one portion of it for boy scout recreation! That evening the entire company sat down on the ground as a group. For the first time since they had left Europe they were not packed like cargo into separate holds. The symphony director, despite his weakened condition, was able to go through an entire opera on his accordian, assisted by other musicians and the opera star.

One of the French quarantine officers said to me, "Never have I seen people stretch out and enjoy sun and air like this pathetic group."

During subsequent visits I heard of their last days in Europe. Some of the men had been in concentration camps merely because they had belonged to the National Czech Army. In one small town, Jews had been brought to the square where the police ordered them to start running and keep running. Anyone who stopped or looked back was shot, especially the older ones who dropped from exhaustion. The few who escaped were on this ship. Other Jews had left the country by going down into the coal mines and passing under the Polish border to the other side.

The old cargo boat they had engaged packed 160 persons into each hold on wooden shelves with straw bedding running six high around the sides of the hold. It was impossible to sit up or to move. There were no stairways into the holds and no electric lights, so it was very dangerous to scramble in and out, particularly for women trying to look after their children. They finally persuaded the captain to install some toilets, but all water for flushing, bathing or washing clothing had to be pulled up in buckets because he would not run his engines to pump sea water. These buckets soon became almost unusably damaged or were lost overboard.

The captain had finally installed a large cooking vat for them to use for both preparing the one daily meal and for boiling the tea leaves. Now on land, conditions changed for the better. I could have wept when I saw the mothers' joy as they prepared salads from the cucumbers and green beans, lettuce and tomatoes brought to them by the Jews of Beirut for their emaciated children. They were so happy with so little.

After one day among the refugees I said to Walter, "What is happening to the Jewish people is terrible. It is long past due for the Christians to give the Jews a new deal. When we get back to the States I am going to tell everyone who will listen what Hitler is doing to the Jews of Europe, and how the British are aiding him by padlocking the doors of their ancestral homeland."

I had acquired the strong feeling that these people were _my_ refugees, _my_ responsibility. I dropped all work on our reports and devoted myself to doing whatever possible to help and encourage them. I went to several Lebanese mountain resorts and collected as much clothing and money as possible from the European and American guests. I was shocked to find some were indifferent. One day I asked the well-to-do widow of a former president of the American University at Beirut for anything she could give. The woman's reply was, "No, I don't care to give. They are only Jews, anyway."

The next act of this tragedy seemed the most inhumane of all. The local Jewish community and their friends offered to feed the refugees while they rested in the quarantine station, but the port officer failed to report this. The French High Commissioner, who heard that it was costing $200 a day to feed the refugees, suddenly ordered them all back on board. Small boats plied back and forth carrying the victims to the ship until 9:00 p.m. Some of the women were almost hysterical. Several had already told me they would rather jump overboard with their children than go out again into that misery on the sea. But in this dark hour, their wise leaders urged calm obedience. The ship had not been refueled. The engines were not running and there were no lights or drinking water. Furthermore, the thousands of dead rats had not been cleaned out and live rats were eating them.

Beirut's Jewish leaders sought frantically to locate the French authorities to assure them they would pay the food costs, but they had retreated to the cool mountains for the weekend. Not until the next morning did word reach the Commissioner. He allowed the refugees back ashore--and he forced the local Jews to pay the $300 cost of needlessly transporting the victims back and forth!

While this was happening, Germany and Russia declared war on Poland, commencing World War II. The French military wanted to be able to use the quarantine station in anticipation of different needs, perhaps of eventual quarantine of Germans. (Our resident German "spy" returned to Germany the day before the war broke out with his collection of easily transportable diamonds.) The refugees would have to go.

Each night, back at our hotel, I described all this to Walter, and he said bitterly, "Now, the sell-out at Munich has prevented the members of the National Czech Army who are on board your little vessel from fighting Hitler. This experience must be worse for them than death on the battlefield. Here they are eager to fight on the side of the Allies, sixty-two officers, almost 200 potential soldiers and more than thirty doctors. Yet, because of British fear of Arab displeasure, these highly-trained, staunchly-democratic people have again been cast adrift on the Mediterranean, with nothing but the supplies which you and the local Jews have been able to collect."

The next morning I looked down on the port from our mountain guest house and saw that my one-funnel ship was gone. I hurriedly dressed and went down to the port. Sure enough, all my precious human cargo had been reloaded and put out to sea. I was beside myself with anxiety, but I sensed that the local Jews were not nearly as disturbed as I was. Walter concluded that they knew something we did not know.

I found out what had happened a little later when I spoke to some visitors from Palestine. During their brief time

ashore the passengers had established radio contact, something impossible when aboard their tiny ship. They learned
that a group of 700 Jews from Poland, anticipating Hitler's
march into their country, had escaped with enough money to
purchase a small Greek ship for $10,000. They hired a crew
who would take them to Palestine and leave the ship just
before they reached the coast.

At sea again, the Czech met the Polish ship, and the 700
Polish refugees crowded the 655 Czechs onto their even
smaller boat, though there was scarcely standing room from
the engine rooms to the decks. Now, with 1,355 souls and
crew on board, men and boys were dangling from the masts
and rigging. Before taking off in a launch, the crew explained
to engineers among the refugees how to beach the ship.

As they neared the shore at full speed, a British Coast
Guard cutter signaled them to stop. Not knowing the mari-
time signals, they did not reply. After two more unanswered
signals, the cutter's guns fired into this mass of humanity,
killing and wounding a number of the refugees, but the ship
ploughed forward until it ran aground. They all scrambled off
the ship with their tiny bundles of possessions. Those who
could swim helped the others to reach the shore.

At last, after more than three months of unbelievable
misery and discouragement, the refugees had reached their
"Promised Land." Many wept for joy; some knelt and kissed
the sand; others removed their shoes before they stepped
reverently upon the sacred earth of Palestine.

The British could not put the refugees back aboard a
wrecked, crewless ship, nor did they want to feed them
indefinitely in concentration camps. So after a few days of
registration and fingerprinting, and having their number
deducted from the small legitimate quota of entrants, the
victims were turned over to the Jewish settlers, who welcomed them with open arms.

We had put Bill and Elizabeth on a ship from Beirut to
America with several sons of American university professors
returning to school. Before they reached Gibralter, World
War II broke out. Because the many Americans in Europe

were frantic to leave, the ship took on an overload of passengers in France. Bill and the other boys were asked to work
in the kitchen and live in the crew's quarters of the ship,
relinquishing their cabins to desperate women with children.

This was a good experience for Bill, who at fifteen felt
quite important to be able to work and receive a refund on his
ticket to New York. Upon arrival in America he and
Elizabeth went directly to my sisters' home in Pasadena,
where Bill could enter school. Meanwhile, Westher remained
with us in Lebanon.

With the advent of war we had to abandon the planned
itinerary for Turkey and the Balkans. Besides the welfare of
the family, my growing awareness of the refugee problem
made me anxious to get back home and make others aware of
it, but we encountered difficulties. We tried to sell our car,
but no one would buy it, knowing it would be confiscated by
the military and gas was severely rationed. The usual return
fare for taking it home by ship was $132, but all the regula-
tions and red tape jumped the price to $400. Our funds were
in Paris, but export of money from there was prohibited. It
took many cables and much negotiating to get enough for our
ship tickets. We got them just in time, for shortly it became
practically impossible to send cables or make phone calls.
Everything was censored.

With its oil pipelines and refineries and its important
ports, this coastal region would be an important target for
Hitler's forces. All of Lebanon was blacked out at night. A
string of submarines patrolled the harbor and mines were laid
so that departing ships had to be escorted out into the
Mediterranean. Our route from the mountains to the port
was clogged with tens of thousands of French soldiers arriving
with masses of military equipment and boatloads of ammunition to be stored in the mountain caves. The French expected
the Germans to make a bee-line for Beirut.

Transportation was difficult because we could only buy a
few pints of gasoline at a time, and then only with special
permission, ration coupons, and two to three hours wait. In
fact, there were interminable delays for almost everything.

Finally we could do almost nothing except wait for our ship. To relieve the frustration, I wrote a summary of our year-and-a-half's activities and read it to Mac, Westher, and Walter at dinner.

"We have traveled more than 37,000 miles by car, over some of the world's worst roads and tracks, sometimes ten to seventeen hours a day. We have slept in 148 different beds of every description. We have met with more than 120 scientists, agriculturalists, archaeologists and government officials in conferences and many more informally. We have carried on a correspondence of over five hundred letters in connection with Walter's survey at 124 areas in fourteen different countries. My husband has taken 3,500 still pictures or slides and shot 3,000 feet of movie film. He has given seventeen public addresses and a radio talk, and written twenty-six special articles for publication. His reports will show our government the reasons why most of the old Roman lands, which at one time had a flourishing agriculture that supported great populations, are now largely man-made deserts."

At last, early one morning in November the four of us and the Buick were taken aboard the American passenger-freighter Excambian. Sadly, we were obliged to put Mektube to sleep, as we could find no home for him, and he was not permitted on shipboard.

To avoid mines and enemy submarines, our captain first steered a northerly course, then turned south to Alexandria, where our ship was to pick up a huge cargo of cotton for America. The trip was short, but miserable with heavy winds. When I saw the huge heaps of cotton bales awaiting us on the dock I was sure that our cargo was bigger than our ship, but it was bound to make the ship more stable.

Eighty miles out of Gibraltar we saw several lifeboats at a distance, their distress signals up. Passengers all gathered on deck to watch as our captain changed course and headed for them. But we found the boats empty. For a half mile around, the sea was strewn with debris and cargo from the British ship Ledbury which we learned had been torpedoed only a few hours before. On the horizon a British destroyer was picking up survivors from still another ship that had been sunk by a German submarine.

A few minutes after we had left the floating debris of the Ledbury, a periscope appeared above the water close by and looked at us twice from different directions. These were tense moments, but since the United States had not entered the war the huge American flags painted on the sides of our ship evidently saved us from attack. The periscope disappeared, and there was no torpedo. As we sailed on, Walter and I remained on the deck for a while. He took my hand and we stood there thoughtfully, and soon young Westher came looking for us and squeezed in between, and we all watched the foam of the ship's wake. We were grateful to be Americans headed for home in a free country.

CHAPTER 15
BACK TO WASHINGTON AND WAR (1940)

We arrived in New York harbor one cold morning in November, 1939, eager to leave the ship and start for Washington. The crew was slow unloading our car, however, so we waited in the ship's lounge, which I had been unable to enjoy because of my old susceptibility to mal-de-mer on rough seas. Then we put Westher on a plane for Pasadena where she would enter school with Bill. It was a great comfort to us that my capable, loving sisters were again ready to care for our children when there was need. It would be some time before we could be settled as a family because we did not have a Washington house.

The second day after arrival in Washington, Walter created a sensation in the Department of Agriculture by appearing in Arab garb we had bought him. He had let a goatee grow during the year and a half we'd been gone and he looked distinguished wearing the baggy trousers under a long silk overgarment and silk jacket. A crushed silk sash held the usual curved dagger in its silver inlaid sheath and the white flowing headdress was held in place by the twisted black wool eagl. The next day, however, he got into his business suit and plunged into his customary rigorous schedule.

Milton Eisenhower had received Walter's many reports in the Public Relations Department and greeted him: "You look well, so I know you ate. But when did you sleep?"

We had not trusted the last of Walter's reports to the war-time mails, but brought them back so he could deliver them safely himself. Secretary of Agriculture Henry Wallace asked the Soil Conservation Service to send Walter's Palestine report over to him right away, since he had promised to pass it on to Justice Brandeis of the United States Supreme Court. Being Jewish, the Justice had been concerned by the British White Paper excluding Jewish refugees from Palestine.

"If Lowdermilk agrees with the White Paper," Secretary Wallace reported Justice Brandeis to have said, "I will have to give up my dream--the restoration of the Jewish Homeland."

Wallace read the fifty pages, called a taxi, went personally to Justice Brandeis and, handing it to him, said, "This is the best statement for Zionism that I have ever read." Justice Brandeis was delighted with Walter's observations and his strong recommendation that "Jews be allowed to enter Palestine by the tens of thousands, for they would bring their own absorptive capacity with them." The report also contained an outline of the plan to use the waters from northern Palestine to irrigate the fertile lands of the Negev around Beersheba and thus increase the cultivable lands and potential food supply for future immigrants.

The following Sunday Justice Brandeis invited us to a small reception at his home. Several other Supreme Court Justices were there. I remember enthusiastically telling radio commentator Martin Agronsky what I had seen of Jewish achievements in Palestine, such as the restoration of the land and the work of Henrietta Szold and the Hadassah Medical Organization, then of my dismay at the unspeakable treatment of "my" shipload of Czech refugees in Beirut. Our host was at my side drinking in every word. Obviously Americans, even Jewish Americans, were not yet fully aware of what was happening in the Mediterranean.

"I think our people should hear you tell these things," Justice Brandeis said. "If Jews said what you are telling us, it would be called propaganda; but if you, a Christian, tell them what you have just told Martin Agronsky, your words will have much weight. Would you be willing to give some talks?"

I did not need a second invitation. I should have been uneasy, since I didn't know what I was getting into, but that was exactly the opportunity I wanted. The agonies of the Jewish refugees had not left my mind for a day since I encountered them.

The following week, introduced by Mrs. Brandeis, I spoke at a meeting of Hadassah and Youth Aliyah, an organization dedicated to the rescue of Jewish orphans from Nazi Europe. Ten days later, we attended Hadassah's annual "Donor" fundraising dinner at the Mayflower Hotel with 1,500 guests. Hadassah's president had told me a few days earlier that if Rabbi Heller, the first speaker, did not exceed his forty-five minutes they would like me to take the microphone for fifteen minutes.

The broadcasting experience I'd had giving talks for the Department of Agriculture in Washington had taught me that fifteen minutes means <u>fourteen</u> minutes, to allow for announcing and a thank you. I had carefully prepared my talk, starting off with an amusing incident to be followed by information calculated to bring some laughter and yes--tears, for the refugee situation was uppermost in my mind and heart.

The rabbi was well into an hour-and-a-half when I whispered to Walter, "I'm rather glad I won't have to speak," as I was just recovering from the flu. I relaxed and looked over the vast audience at the tables. With my poor hearing I didn't notice when the rabbi finished and the president was on her feet again. Anyway, I wasn't really listening.

Suddenly Walter's elbow gave me a dig and he whispered, "They're introducing you."

I jumped to the microphone so excited that I gave my speech in twelve minutes instead of fourteen. It was followed by absolute silence, as though the audience were trying to recover themselves, before they burst into applause. My message had affected many, but I still wondered if I could make any real headway in making Americans understand what was going on in Europe and the Middle East.

Then Mrs. Paul Muni, the wife of the actor, who was on the platform also, asked me, "Would you come to California?"

When I told her I planned to spend the summer in Pasadena with the children while Walter went on a lecture tour, she asked me to speak at Hollywood's Coconut Grove where 700 guests were expected to raise funds for Youth Aliyah. I gladly agreed. The longer we were back from abroad the more I realized how few Americans really had any concept of the disastrous events Hitler was bringing about, or how Christian nations such as Britain and France were adding to the loss of Jewish lives.

Before our travels, I had been almost unaware of the problems Jews had been forced to contend with throughout the centuries. Walter and I had almost no Jewish contacts in our personal lives until meeting the Jewish pioneers of Palestine. When we realized what a contribution they were making to the land and to the human race in general, besides rescuing their own people and keeping their age-old covenant with their God, we saw how very close to them we should be.

At summer's end, 1940, I returned to Washington, and to Walter. Hadassah called a meeting in New York for all the women in charge of raising money for Youth Aliyah in the larger cities. By this time, although many Americans did not want to believe it, it was clear to Jewish leaders that Hitler was in the process of wiping out the Jews of Eastern Europe. As members of the organization closest to the rescue operation in Palestine, the Hadassah women felt that if the Jewish children of Europe could be saved from the death camps, the Jewish people could have some hope. They were desperately raising money for Youth Aliyah in the larger cities and asked me to speak. They knew I had seen youngsters come ashore at Haifa, with their sad faces, ragged clothing and drooping shoulders. I could tell them I had seen the Hadassah women take these orphans into loving arms, bathe them and put them in new clothes; and the doctors examine them carefully. I had also seen these same children after they had been rehabilitated, with their heads lifted, their dejected expressions fallen away. They were well fed and they laughed and played, for they were <u>home.</u>

At the end of the New York meeting, Mrs. Brodie, the chairman of Hadassah's speakers' bureau, said, "We have had seventeen requests today to have you speak in the same number of cities. Of course we don't ask you to do this without a generous honorarium. Just set the amount you want."

"Mrs. Brodie," I answered. "I could not think of taking one dollar from those orphans. I will speak and raise money to the limit of my time and ability, but I want it known ahead of time every place I go that I am not accepting money for my work. I don't want anyone to say, 'Oh, she's a Christian and you can depend upon it, she's getting well paid!' They must know I speak from my heart and not for money."

Walter was very supportive of my work and even appeared with me whenever he could, but he was being sent on one speaking trip after another by the Soil Conservation Service.

Walter's wonderful personality came through when he was speaking on an informal basis, but as a scientist he was accustomed to reading papers at conferences. He started out by reading his talks when he spoke to farm groups. Of course, his lectures sounded dull to the farmers. Knowing that few men will take lessons from their wives, I finally persuaded him to take speaking lessons from a woman in Washington who had taught some Congressmen and Senators to improve their public speaking. She insisted that Walter discard his reading material, work out his outline, and try to memorize it in a general way. Then he should get up before an audience and talk to them, looking at their faces, not at a paper. The idea terrified him but he did what he was told. The first time he tried this method he left out much of his material, but he was more successful with his audience than he had ever been before. Never again did he read a speech. From that time on he was able to hold the attention of any audience.

During this period there had been some shifts in personnel at the Soil Conservation Service which had disturbed Walter. At first I thought it was good that his tour would take him away from Washington to be among the farmers and stockmen he so enjoyed. Also, he was eager to bring to them the conservation lessons learned from the study of ancient lands, and to observe at the same time the progress of various Soil Conservation Districts formed as the result of his recommendations before his year-and-a-half abroad. Yet, when I looked at his trip itinerary, I was concerned that it seemed unusually strenuous, and I objected. Nevertheless, Walter was determined to carry out his department's expectations, regardless.

With both of us traveling so much, it was pointless to rent a house when we would seldom be there, so we made our headquarters in rented rooms in a large Washington home. With the children at school and well cared for, we decided to use our own car so that I could go with Walter on his tours that fall. Often I would take part by taking the first ten minutes of the program for what I called an "ice breaker"-- telling some funny travel experiences and giving information that would not be in my husband's serious talk. By then the audience would be warmed up and Walter would give them the "meat" of the program.

We presented what we had learned around his general theme, "Conquest of the Land Through 7,000 Years"* and used the dramatically beautiful slides Walter had taken in Old Roman Lands. He did a wonderful job with these presentations and, typically, drove himself relentlessly to keep up with his speaking schedules. Twice we went seventy days at a stretch, without a pause between cities. At each stop, we were confronted with a new group of farmers and farm officials, all eager to tell Walter their problems and seek his advice.

Newsmen always trailed along with us and their reports appeared everywhere in the local papers. American farmers and stockmen now realized the importance of saving our

---

*"Conquest of the Land Through 7,000 Years" was later made into a Department of Agriculture Bulletin reprinted for the third time in 1974 and 3½ million copies have been distributed.

natural resources and Walter's illustrated lectures of what had happened to agriculture in North Africa and the Near East helped them to see it as even more urgent.

Our two strenuous trips--in addition to his administrative duties in Washington--were obviously taking their toll on my husband's health, and I insisted he have a medical examination. Our doctor urged him to take three months' rest, but Walter felt that the work was too important and he kept going.

Several months later, when we were back in Washington, Walter experienced a severe pain in his chest at three o'clock one morning. I thought it was congestion from being chilled at a garden party the evening before, but putting on a hot poultice did not help. Next I tried an osteopathic massage treatment on his back, but the pain worsened. He became restless and wanted to get up and walk, but as he sat on the edge of the bed, he said to me suddenly, "The pain is reaching my throat. I think it must be my heart."

I dashed downstairs to phone for a doctor, but my eyes were too blurred to see. I called to our landlady to come and get a doctor. She knew one only a block away. The doctor scarcely took time to dress before arriving. He listened to Walter's heart for one moment and gave him a big dose of morphine. Then he went downstairs and called for an ambulance. By the time it arrived Walter was comfortable, enjoying the strong cup of coffee the doctor had ordered. The attendants carried him downstairs, and I went along. They drove without sirens, for it was just about daybreak and the traffic was light.

It was a relief to learn that the doctor in charge of the cardiac section at the Veterans' Hospital in Washington was a personal friend from our Hamline Methodist Church. After he had examined Walter, he called me aside. "I think you should know that your husband's life may go out like the flicker of a candle, at any moment," he said. "But try to keep his spirits up."

I was stunned. I pretended to be cheerful with Walter, but inside I was praying desperately. I told the Lord that

Walter hadn't finished his life work, that at 53 he was too young to die, and prayed that if the Lord would only save him, Walter would have more important work to do.

About dusk I left the hospital and went home for the night. I flung myself across the bed sobbing, dreading a future without Walter. This seemed hopeless. How could I manage? We were helping our fathers financially. Our children were only thirteen and sixteen, with all their expensive schooling ahead. We had saved little since being wiped out at Nanking and struggling through the Depression. To top if off, a girl we had promised Westher to sponsor--Lennie Holenkoff, a Beirut schoolmate of Westher's who was a White Russian refugee--was at this moment on the high seas to stay with us for the duration of the war.

I saw on a table our unopened mail which had piled up during our last speaking trip. My sister Beatrice had forwarded a letter from the Veterans Administration saying Walter's insurance policy had lapsed and enclosed a notice for reinstatement requiring a doctor's signature that he was in as good physical condition as two weeks previously when the insurance had lapsed. This was the last straw. Beatrice had taken care of our business affairs while we had been traveling but thought that now we were back in Washington I had taken over payment of the bills.

Suddenly I forgot about my problems for the moment as I realized how Beatrice might be blaming herself for the lapsed insurance now that Walter was so sick. I jumped up and sent her a telegram telling her not to worry, I was sure everything would be all right.

Then, actually, my burden suddenly lifted. A presence seemed to surround me, assuring me that it truly would be all right, that it would work out for the best and Walter would recover. I felt at peace.

For nine weeks I stayed at Walter's bedside. I kept fresh flowers in his room and helped the nurses in every way I could to keep him calm so that he could have the rest he needed. I fed him, which at first he could not do for himself, and read books and letters to him.

In about seven weeks Walter was sitting up and wanting to go home. Having the family all together was now more important to him than anything else. But we had no home. Walter started going through the papers each day looking for something to rent, but nothing seemed suitable. It seemed best to buy, and with the return of the money paid into insurance we had enough for a down payment, so he picked out houses for me to investigate. The activity seemed to cheer him up. The thought of having a home and the family together gave Walter an added incentive to get well, and we called my sisters to tell them to send the children. It was difficult to make a decision when Walter could not see the houses, but I finally picked one in Chevy Chase, with lovely trees in the backyard and a glassed-in porch where Walter could enjoy looking out on nature as he continued to regain his strength.

The children and I were settled in the new house by the time Walter was released from the hospital. Walter was enjoying Bill and Westher and her refugee sister Lennie and the garden. It was not long before he was able to have visitors and was looking forward to going back to work.

One Sunday afternoon when we had guests visiting, we were all listening to music over the radio when suddenly we heard the sound of bombs falling and an excited newscaster shouting, "We're being bombed. Bombs are falling all around in the harbor, too!" It was the attack on Pearl Harbor, December 7, 1941. The war we had predicted had come, and in the way we anticipated.

Walter asked me to get a letter from his files which he had written to the <u>New York Times</u> six years previously, when so much scrap iron, oil and planes were being sent to Japan. The letter declared we were building Japan up to be a Frankenstein who, when ready, would spring a surprise attack on us. We were supplying all the trappings of war to Japan except the manpower. Once they got started we might not be able to defeat them. American business, however, was finding the trade with Japan very lucrative. The letter was returned unpublished.

The following morning Walter took the letter with him to the Department of Agriculture and read it to some of his colleagues. "Why didn't you make this information known publicly before?" they wanted to know. He showed them the date--March 3, 1935.

Now we were predicting and warning again, this time about the Middle East. Outside the Jewish population, people seemed reluctant to recognize what was happening.

Palestine Jews had been staunch supporters of the Allied cause in two wars and, despite Britain's broken promises to them, had already joined the Allied forces in great numbers by the time the United States entered the war. I now regarded my efforts on their behalf not only my Christian duty but my patriotic duty, as well. With Walter well again I resumed speaking for the Hadassah Organization and Christian groups.

During those war years I addressed audiences large and small, using a model speech which could be enlarged or shortened according to the time allowed, and which was augmented by many personal experiences. Called "Eight Reasons Why I as a Christian Believe There Should Be a Jewish Palestine," it was based on these points:

1. Because God gave it to the Jews (Genesis 13:14-17)

2. Because prophecy is being fulfilled in Palestine today. (Amos, 9:14-15) "And I will bring again...my people of Israel, and they shall build the waste cities, and inhabit them; and they shall plant vineyards, and drink the wine thereof; they shall also make gardens, and eat the fruit of them. And I will plant them upon their land, and they shall no more be pulled out of their land which I have given them, saith the Lord."

3. Because the British promised it to them through the Balfour Declaration and the League of Nations gave Britain the Mandate to facilitate it.

4. Because the Jews have earned it by their remarkable work on the land--the finest job of reclamation Walter had seen on four continents.

5. Because the Jews can make it a viable productive state and a bastion of democracy so important to the free world.

6.   Because of its strategic location at the crossroads of air and land routes between the continents of Africa, Europe and Asia, and its proximity to the great oil reserves.

7.   Because the Arab people need help so badly--their downtrodden masses need the stimulation of a modern, democratic nation in their region.

8.   Because the Jewish people need it. The tragedy of European Jewry calls loudly for humanity to permit them a refuge in the ancestral homeland from which they were driven.

Everywhere I went I was overwhelmed by Jewish women who saw me as a Christian trying to help save the remnant of their people.   As I became acquainted with more Jewish people and heard more of the story of Hitler's genocide, I learned of the agony the Jews had endured.   Even American Jews had not realized how bad things were.   It was just then being revealed, how the British had padlocked the doors of Palestine against survivors.   Since most American Jews had relatives in Europe, virtually every one of my audiences was affected personally by the catastrophe.

The most painful part of my own experience was realizing that Christian charity had its limitations in the minds of my fellow Americans.   To me, the Jews were people suffering and dying unnecessarily and my Christian upbringing made me do what I could without hesitation.   I was shocked by my experiences with the few Christian audiences who could be persuaded to listen to me.   For example, when I told a group at a New England YWCA how British guns were firing on Jewish refugee ships, one woman stood up and denounced me:

"Mrs. Lowdermilk should not be allowed to speak in public," she declared, "because she is being critical of our allies."

There were other individuals like Walter and me both here and in Britain, but we were few and far between.   It was simply unpopular to speak on behalf of Jews.   We heard from a reliable source that the State Department spokesman had even approached the great Rabbi Stephen Wise asking him not to make public what was happening to his people for fear we should have friction with the British. True, we were at war and everyone had difficulties, but the callousness of those "Christians" toward the Jewish people was devastating to discover. Even President Roosevelt, who showed unusual concern for the poor of America, reflected what was probably an inherited, subconscious attitude toward Jews as old as the church itself. I wondered how the Jew, Jesus, would be met if He should come among us then.

I introduced Eddie Cantor at an enormous public gathering sponsored by Jews in San Francisco where he announced that he was appealing to the United States government to admit 20,000 orphans fleeing the Nazis, and that he would be personally responsible for them.

"They will be taken immediately into homes," he promised, "and they will not cost the nation or any state, county, or city one single dollar."

How could our government or any person object to such a life-saving, magnanimous proposal? But the United States had a strict quota system on immigration, so the matter had to be taken before the President. He refused. His wife, Eleanor, eventually persuaded him to admit 10,000 children-- half those Mr. Cantor had pleaded with him to save. Many of the other 10,000 were destined to perish in death camps.

I sometimes wept with shame at the injustice done to the Jewish people, and I spent hours in prayer trying to understand the Lord's purpose in all this. I threw myself into the Jewish refugee cause so wholeheartedly that once Westher had to phone me at a hotel to say that I had forgotten to pay the electric bill and the service was about to be cut off!

It seemed that Walter and I were voices crying in a Christian wilderness, but sometimes others did respond. Dr. Carl Hermann Voss, Secretary of the Church Peace Union, heard me speak in New York City. "The leading clergy should hear about this," he said, and he arranged for me to speak at the Ministerial Association the following week.

The ministers did not understand what was happening to the Jews. I explained it to them. Their Christian consciences were stirred and, on that day in 1942, the American Christian

Palestine Committee was born--an organization that was to include leading clergy and lay Christians from across the United States. Its purpose was to support the Jewish aspirations for a haven and homeland in Palestine.

I also spoke in many Sunday Schools on behalf of the American Christian Palestine Committee's Children Memorial Forest in Palestine, honoring the one million Jewish children murdered by Hitler. Christian children poured out their piggy banks and small earnings for this.

A short time later, a group of us went to the British Ambassador in Washington with a petition signed by leading American Christians reminding the British of their promise to the Jewish people and urging them to allow 100,000 refugees to enter Palestine. The Ambassador's exact words were: "There are times when moral obligations must give way to political expediency." This cynical attitude summed up Britain's policy in handling the Palestine problem.

During 1942 and 1943, more and more of our friends and their children were leaving every day for war service of some kind. The war finally came close to our home when Bill volunteered for the Army Air Force. It seemed such a short time ago that he was a little boy. We were proud of his spirit, but seeing him in uniform in wartime united us with parents the world over who were facing the same heartrending situation.

CHAPTER 16
THE WAR YEARS (1941-45)

The war had given Americans added incentive to increase food production for our population at home, for our combat troops abroad, and for some of our allies under seige. The armies in Europe were engaged in fierce fighting, while in the Far East the Japanese already controlled most of Southeast Asia, including much of China. The Allies were taking terrible losses in the South Pacific and they desperately needed more Chinese manpower to fight the Japanese. West China was still free, but the resistance forces had to be fed.

Chinese officials, remembering Walter's effective work there, urgently requested that the U.S. State Department send him to rally the farmers of West China to produce the maximum of food. Walter seemed well, but we were concerned about the travel requirements. He would have to be flown into Yunnan from Burma over the Hump in the Himalayas. High altitudes in planes without pressurization or oxygen alone would endanger the life of a man who had suffered a massive heart attack. Yet Walter was eager to help and I realized his powerful need to do the work to which he felt he was called. I knew that it would take a great deal of faith and prayer on the part of the whole family. Bill came home on a pass and we all talked about it. We understood that he should go. From the moment we made the decision I never doubted that Walter would do his work well and return safely to us.

While we were busily preparing for Walter's departure, Justice Brandeis and others began urging that Walter enlarge his fifty-page report on Palestine. At that time, Walter felt he couldn't, and shouldn't, accept additional obligations. But then the Struma--an old vessel carrying 700 Jews fleeing Hitler and denied permission to land anywhere--sank while floating off the coast of Palestine. Everyone on board drowned. A mass memorial meeting was organized in New York and I was asked to speak about my experiences with the shipload of Czech refugees. Dr. Emmanual Newmann, of the Zionist Emergency Council, arranged for me to have dinner with him beforehand.

"Mrs. Lowdermilk," he said, "I have heard you say that you would do anything possible to help victims of the tragedy taking place in Europe. Now we want you to live up that promise." He asked me to pursuade Walter to enlarge his report on Palestine into a book so the facts he documented could be set before the world.

"There are many Jews better informed who could do it," I protested, wanting to protect Walter's time and limited energy.

"No," he insisted. "It should be done by your husband, a non-Jew and an international authority on land reclamation and water development. His work has proven that Palestine is capable of settling all the Jewish regugees who can reach its shores."

Reluctantly, I told Walter about Neumann's request, even though it meant giving up the family vacation we had promised ourselves to take before Walter left for China and Bill was transferred overseas. For the next several weeks Walter went to his office only one or two days a week. The other days--our "vacation" days--we labored on the book from morning until night. To escape the summer heat we worked in our basement, putting our bare feet on the cool, concrete floor. We both did research and we both wrote, spreading the material out on the ping pong table. By Walter's departure date, the book was largely completed and I was left to get it published.

The Allied Command scheduled Walter to fly across the Atlantic and straight through the Middle East to his destination, Chungking. However, escalation of the North African campaign suddenly cancelled that route. Instead, Walter was put on one of three small munition ships leaving in a convoy from Charleston, South Carolina. Their indirect route took him down through the Caribbean Sea, through the Panama Canal, then down the west coast of South America, around Cape Horn and up the South Atlantic to Capetown, South Africa.

Walter faithfully recorded his entire journey in a daily diary of letters, the first of which he mailed to me after reaching Capetown. We were shocked to learn that on the way a German submarine sank the ship in front of Walter's and the one behind it. He wrote, "I was not worried, as I knew if we were hit there would be only one loud explosion."

From South Africa Walter flew the length of Africa to Karachi, to India and east to Burma. Going into China over the Hump in an unpressurized plane, he wrote me, he tried to minimize the danger to his heart by leaning back and breathing carefully and fully and keeping an ammonia capsule handy. By the time he reached Chungking, he said, he experienced a strong feeling that the Lord had taken care of him.

At this time, the U.S. government was making public appeals to citizens to open their homes to the thousands of girls who were coming to the capital to play their part in the war effort as secretaries in government and military offices. Housing was desperately short. With Walter and Bill away, Westher and I and the "extra daughter" we had expected—Lennie Holenkoff from Beirut who had arrived to be with us for five years—had extra rooms. We were among the first to respond and House Beautiful did a feature about us and our young renters hoping to encourage others to take the girls in. We developed a fine rapport with our four young women; they shared with me their homesickness and other personal problems, and I rejoiced with them in their fun and romances. The house was full again to overflowing.

Westher was doing her part to help the war effort by going with her accordian band to U.S.O. shows at camps and hospitals nearby. Though still a teenager, she took charge of our household and kept things running smoothly whenever I was away speaking or working on Walter's book. Each time I went down to Walter's office to type, I met with discouragement. Always someone there would say to me, "You can't print that book. They won't let you publish it."

Finally I asked, "Who is this _they_ you are talking about? Make an appointment for me here in the office for me to meet "them" and talk it over."

Three days later "they" arrived in the form of a tall, handsome State Department official.   His manner was cordial, but it was obvious he was thinking, "I can settle things with this woman in a hurry."

He began with flattery and went on to persuasion. He told me that he--as a writer in World War I--could have made money writing on certain subjects, but he published nothing so as to avoid offending certain people important to the safety of our boys overseas.

"And I am _sure_ you would not want to harm our war effort by disturbing the Arabs with this book of yours," he said.

"Why it would do no such thing," I insisted. "This is a constructive book that would benefit both Arabs and Jews." We argued for an hour or so. "This book was not written for personal gain, but to contribute something beneficial to the people of the Middle East," I finally told him.

At this he clapped his hands in apparent joy and said, "Oh, Mrs. Lowdermilk, that is just splendid. If the book was not done for profit, then what you should do is give the manuscript to us at the State Department. Then, when the war is over, we will have it on hand and will know what to do about it."

I was indignant. "Yes," I replied, "and then you would put it away in a pigeonhole and our hands would be tied. No, I will do nothing of the kind. My husband wrote this under pressure before leaving for China because he felt it would point to a way of solving land and water problems to benefit those fleeing Hitler and poor Arab peasants, as well." By this time I was flushed with exasperation and almost in tears. It was obvious that this man's intention was to see that our book would not be published.

Realizing he could not influence me, he rose and said, "Will you promise me one thing?"

"What is it?"

"Tell no one of this interview," he asked. Then he closed our meeting by warning me again not to publish the book. "In any case," he emphasized, "you could never get all the necessary okays. You would need approval from the Soil Conservation Service, the Department of Agriculture, and the State Department before you got through to the Office of War Information. So you see, it would be best not to try."

This situation seemed hopeless, but I had seen my mother's faith in action and experienced much of God's help in my life, so I prayed. My miracle soon came, carried in a red convertible.

A few days after the interview a beautiful Texas girl named Faye Ivy came to live with us. Often, a man in a red convertible dropped her off after work.

"Who is your boyfriend?" I asked her.

"George Barnes," she replied. "He's my boss, first assistant to Elmer Davis, head of the Office of War Information."

This looked like my answer. "Why don't you invite him to dinner?" I suggested, elated at the idea of making a friend in the War Office.

When George came to dinner I lost little time in giving him a background of my husband's work. Over a home-cooked meal I told him about Walter's efforts in land and water conservation in the United States and other countries. He seemed pleased to be invited back again the following Sunday. This time I told him the details of a master water plan for irrigation and a little TVA for the River Jordan that would enable Palestine to support several million more people. I "innocently" added that because my husband had

been sent to China by our State Department, this constructive plan was left with me to get published.

"Is there some way whereby the Office of War
Information could give me an OK to get this book published
without my going through the red tape of obtaining approval
from all the other departments?" I asked him.

George Barnes thought for awhile. Then he said. "Yes,
one way, but first you must delete all criticism of England or
any other Allies." Then he dictated to me what had to go on
the frontispiece:

> The author wishes to make clear that this book
> was written from the viewpoint of a land
> conservationist, whose life work has been to
> study the relation of peoples to their lands. The
> opinions expressed here are personal and
> unofficial. They do not necessarily represent
> the point of view of the U.S. Soil Conservation
> Service, of which the author is the Assistant
> Chief, or of any other government department.

I now had permission from the highest and final authority
to publish the book. But it still wasn't clear sailing. When
Hugh Bennett, Soil Conservation Chief, learned that I was
publishing the book he phoned me, virtually shouting, "You
can't publish that book."

Perhaps his anger was a reflection of the discomfort he
had always shown whenever Walter was in the public eye. I
read him my authorization from the Office of War
Information and he had no answer. Later, the State
Department man who had interviewed me phoned again to
remind me of his instructions. I happily read him the same
statement from the Office of War Information. He, too,
could respond only with silence.

Financially, however, I could not handle the next step--
the big deposit required from the publishers, Harper Brothers.
I asked Dr. Neumann to make it, and promised to give the
Zionist Emergency Council half the royalties. He and his

group stepped in and did a marvelous job of publicity and distribution. When the book came out the New York Times and the Washington Post had double-page spreads in the Sunday editions with Walter's picture and a map showing his master water plan for Palestine and proving that millions more people could live there.

When Walter arrived home from China in 1944, he was honored with a large, well-advertised dinner in Washington. Many leading Americans attended. A nationwide radio broadcast carried Walter's message to millions of Americans, describing his water and land reclamation project and its potential for good. When President Roosevelt died, Walter's book, Palestine, Land of Promise, was found open on his desk, about halfway read.

Just before the issue of partition came before the United Nations, a copy of the book was given to every Congressman, Senator, each United Nations delegation, and to leading Americans across the nation. Its impact was such that England had to give up her main propaganda argument of "no further economic absorptive capacity" for Jewish immigration into Palestine. Britain then changed her line to claim that the powerful Arab League (a straw man built up by the British) was demanding that Jewish settlement be stopped.

George Barnes told us later that this book enabled world leaders to see that, through proper planning, a viable Jewish state could exist and would also bring economic advancement to the Arabs. The book exerted considerable influence on the U.N.'s decision to partition Palestine so that Jewish and Arab Palestinians could each have a state, but with economic union.

*****

1945--the war was over. The young ladies who lived with us for the duration went their ways and I happily prepared the house for the reunion of the family. Walter returned after one and a half years in China and Bill was discharged from the Army Air Corps. We were a fortunate family, safe and together again.

Before long the Secretary of Agriculture sent Walter to Puerto Rico to see about improving the lot of its farmers. Once again, on American territory Walter found disgraceful poverty because of advanced erosion on farmlands. He also found a native grass so tough that it could be used to hold the soil in place. He advised the farmers to reinforce the outer edges of their terraces on sloping lands by growing a border of this grass. The dirt within could then be cultivated and the grass would hold the embankment. It proved effective and for a long time was known as the "Lowdermilk Terrace."

In the spring of 1945, the National Research Council requested Walter's services. A volcano--Paricutin--had burst out of a corn field in central Mexico. NRC wanted to know the effects of ashfall and erosion on land use. This intrigued Walter. The American Geophysical Union, of which he was president, would have the first chance to study a new volcano on the North American continent. In Mexico they would study the effect of rainfall on volcanic ash and learn more about erosion in one week than they could normally learn in a year.

We decided it would be a wonderful experience for Westher, so father and daughter spent the whole summer together in close companionship with an active volcano, working and studying, by car, horseback and on foot.

Westher had decided to enroll in Oberlin College in the fall. Bill chose the University of California at Berkeley. We sold our house in Chevy Chase and I moved back into our Berkeley house to make a home for Bill, at least during his first college term. Walter made his temporary headquarters, once more, at the Cosmos Club in Washington.

After speaking to so many Hadassah chapters east of the Mississippi and from Texas to Canada, I was shocked to find there was none in my own hometown. With the cooperation of the Oakland Hadassah chapter, I invited the president and her fourteen Berkeley members to my own home and organized a new chapter. Today that chapter has over 800 members and has won many national awards.

Walter phoned to say he had invited a long-time Chinese friend and colleague to stay with Bill and me. Dean Djang, from the University of Nanking, was returning to China with his wife after an American visit, departing from San Francisco. But a shipping strike idled all ships on the Pacific coast, so the couple remained our houseguests for the next two weeks.

Just before the strike however, Feng Y-Hsiang, a Chinese dignitary known as the "Christian General," arrived with his wife in San Francisco by ship. Apparently his popularity had displeased General Chiang Kai-shek who, we learned, had Feng removed from the scene giving him $100,000 ($60,000 for himself and $40,000 for four others) for a study of American dams and irrigation works. Our government asked Walter to work out a schedule for the group. He called me from Washington to tell me to arrange a reception at our home, since the general had given one for him while he was at Chungking during wartime.

On a Friday afternoon I sent Dean Djang across the Bay to ask the general whether he would accept such an invitation. He replied that, yes, he would like to have the reception the next Monday! I immediately got on the telephone. I called one of the university professors, who agreed to invite at least six others with the wives, and I asked an Oakland Methodist minister to bring six other clergy with their wives. Then I hurriedly called several government men and all of Walter's friends that I could reach.

We had a wonderful turnout of Californians to welcome Feng, his wife and colleagues. The weather was beautiful and the house and garden were full of September flowers. The general and his wife were delighted. One of Feng's engineers had been on the six-month expedition Walter led during the war to the western end of the Great Wall of China, to Lake Koko-Nor and to several Tibetan cities.

General Feng and his wife wanted to remain for a time in the Bay region before starting on the U.S. tour. But at their San Francisco hotel they observed behavior offensive to old-style Chinese, such as women smoking and couples dancing cheek-to-cheek in the dining room. Typical Chinese courtesy requires that one not ask for a favor directly because a refusal would break the friendship. So, the general sent word through Dean Djang that they were so pleased with our neighborhood he wondered whether I knew anyone who might be willing to rent them rooms for two months. Of course their meaning was clear to anyone who knew the Chinese: they wanted to stay in our home.

At first I could not imagine how Bill and I could manage. Our refrigerator, on order since the war, had not arrived. Feeding everyone would mean shopping daily in addition to all the other extra tasks needed to host guests. I couldn't expect to get any help because in those days educated Chinese did no manual labor. However, knowing that Walter would want me to do it, I agreed. I found rooms for the general's entourage with neighboring professors' families and took the Fengs in with us.

I explained to them all that in America it was honorable for everyone to work and, under the circumstances, it was necessary for us all to cooperate. I assigned everyone a specific task. Bill and another student were to do the dishes. One of the Chinese was to help me cook, another was to set the table, and so on with each one. Once they got the swing of things they really enjoyed it. When we sat down for a meal, the general, at the head of the table, asked God's blessing on the food.

Walter came out from Washington and together we took our guests on a tour of the Grand Canyon and Boulder Dam. Once, as Walter was explaining the great turbines, an American lady came up to Walter and asked, "Is the water any good after all the electricity is taken out of it?" Everyone laughed.

Meanwhile, the general was writing a regular column on U.S. water projects for the Chinese newspapers, but it turned out that he focused as much attention on the intelligence and industry of American faculty wives. One night after I had prepared their dinner, I put on a long dress and went to a banquet at the City Women's Club where I lectured and

showed slides on our trip to the Old Roman Lands. The
general and his party were amazed. They could hardly
believe the way faculty wives worked and adjusted themselves to tight schedules and to different kinds of tasks. All
their American hostesses cared for the children, did their own
housework, most of the gardening, and were active in church
and civic affairs.

I listened in whenever my guests talked about China,
always hoping to hear news of my friends there. Although
Chiang Kai-shek had been appointed United Nations
Commander-in-Chief of the Chinese theater of war in 1942,
the Communists had emerged from World War II strengthened
by the Soviet takeover of industrial Manchuria. There were
rumors of corruption in Chiang's government, as his
Kuomintang was in a death struggle to remain in power on the
mainland.

It didn't surprise me when General Feng announced he
intended to find a house of his own in the San Francisco Bay
Area. He did, and stayed there for several years! (Later we
learned that he had died mysteriously in a fire on shipboard
returning to China.)

At the end of his first school term, Bill decided that he
wanted to make films to help with technical assistance to
developing countries. My alma mater, the University of
Southern California, offered the degree he wanted, so he left
for Los Angeles. Once more I rented our Berkeley house,
took one last wistful look at our panoramic view, and joined
Walter in Washington. We took rooms in a home near the
Capitol.

Walter had been working with the U.S. Soil Conservation
Service for fifteen years by 1947. In addition to the strain of
the many long trips with their killing schedules, Walter was
distressed by the friction developing between two top men in
the department. His chief, in fact, seemed increasingly
resentful of Walter's achievements. He would display anger
for which nobody could understand the cause. Walter met
these onslaughts with dignity, but clearly the situation was
becoming destructive. I was increasingly concerned about his
health.

One Friday evening before his 59th birthday, which would come on Monday, I said to him, "Walter, do you think you could continue to carry on under these circumstances until you are at full retirement age--another three years--without having another heart attack?"

He thought carefully a moment and then said, "No, I doubt if I could."

"Next Monday morning will be July first, the end of the fiscal year," I said. "You already have an appointment with the Chief at nine o'clock. I hope you will immediately announce your retirement as of nine A.M., July 1, 1947."

Walter agreed, and I felt as though a big burden was lifted from us. Early retirement increased Walter's chances of finding new work of his own choice. We had long dreamed of returning to Berkeley. Now at last we could go home.

Our university and church friends gave us a warm welcome. Our house and garden became a central meeting place for friends we had met in many countries, including missionaries and Chinese friends from Szechuan. At one of those gatherings I was to learn at last the fate of my beloved Chinese "little sister," Rachel Pen Sih-ru.

All foreign missionaries had been forced to leave and Rachel, who had been made head of the large Methodist Training School at Tzechow, was doing a magnificent job directing all the Methodist women's work, the girls' schools for the province, and managing all the funds from America. When the communists took over, their policy was either to convert or liquidate Chinese leaders, especially those known to advocate democracy, Christianity or friendship for America. Many were eliminated immediately, but Rachel was so well-known and beloved by so many that the communists believed she could be more useful alive if forced to repudiate her beliefs. She became a "must" target, courted as a potential communist leader. But she steadfastly refused their blandishments. Then the harassment began. The Training School was taken over as Communist headquarters and Rachel was held prisoner in a small room on the top floor. Then came long weeks of brainwashing.

Rachel must have thought often of her grandfather's words, "You can kill my body, but you cannot kill my soul." Somehow, I learned, she managed to get a note smuggled out to a friend which read, in part, "I will never repudiate my God, my religion or what I have tried to do for my country. Neither can I turn against America and the friends who have made my life work possible. The Communists will try to torture me into saying words which are not mine. Instead, I make this final protest by this declaration of my faith. Tell my friends why I died."

The only thing in the room which Rachel could use to carry out her resolve was the small pail of water for drinking and washing. This she conserved until night. Then she lay down across her cot, lowered her head into the pail and held her face under water until her unpolluted soul joined that of her martyred grandfather. Someone told me it is impossible to commit suicide this way, but knowing Rachel's willpower, I believe she did. By her death, Rachel gave one last glorious testimony of her unconquerable soul and her belief in Shang Ti, her "Heaven Father." I feel she is with me yet.

I also heard the horrible story of what happened to the three girls who spread Rachel's message that was smuggled from the prison. They were tortured, then drowned in pits of "ripening" human excrement. I remembered other young Chinese girls who were my students and friends--how dear and beautiful and gentle they were--and my heart ached for those three brave heroines.

Because Walter was susceptible to flu and pneumonia, we began to think of a winter home for sometime in the future. We considered the homestead land the U.S. Government was opening up in the Southern California desert. My widowed sister Beatrice wrote us about her burst of pioneer spirit and how she acquired a five-acre tract in Morongo Valley about twenty-five miles from Palm Springs. We caught her excitement and acquired a tract the same size next to hers and my sister Winifred acquired one adjoining. It had been forty-three years since we sisters had pioneered with our parents in Arizona, and now we were together again.

What memories came back from earlier years! We found that once again we were living with rattlesnakes. Once, when my sisters and I were alone, we saw a huge rattler climbing our cholla cactus trying to reach the nest of our dear little cactus wren and her babies. It must have looked funny--three elderly ladies, Beatrice with a shovel, Winifred with a hoe and me with some rocks--rushing to the rescue. One of my stones knocked the snake down and Beatrice rushed at it with her shovel while Winifred clawed at the air with her hoe trying to keep it from getting away. The snake's head was moving rapidly back and forth, showing its fangs. Finally Beatrice pinned down its head with her shovel and with great effort, ground it off. It was half an hour before we buried it, yet its decapitated head was still wildly biting at the air. We appreciated the ecological value of the rattlers, but surely Morongo Valley was overpopulated.

The magnificent scenery and the sense of freedom in the desert made up for those occasional frights. Year by year, with hard work, our place became more of a joy and a haven of rest and introspection.

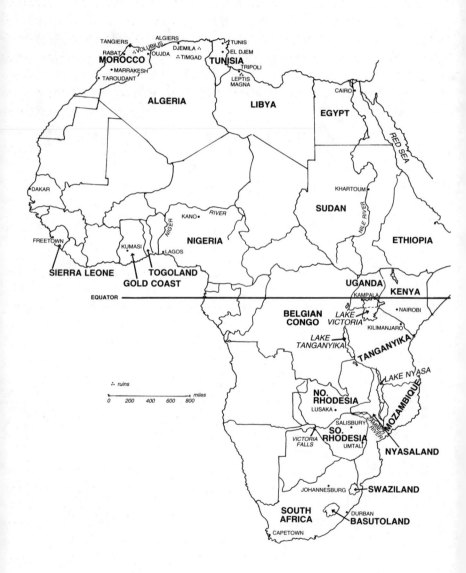

CHAPTER 17
TAKING ON THE CONTINENT OF AFRICA (1948-50)

We had been at home for just a few months when the French Colonial Government discovered that Walter was available. They asked him to return to North Africa early in 1948 to deal with some water problems in Morocco and Algeria. Walter, of course, agreed to go. We invited Westher, who was 19 and a college junior, to join us. She and I drove across the country in February to join Walter, and shipped our car to Morocco ahead of us.

En route to Morocco we stopped over in the British Isles. Some friends in England had suggested to Lord Janner, a leading British Jew, that we be asked to make speeches in England on behalf of the Zionist cause. At that time, there was fierce fighting in Palestine between the Jewish settlers and the British mandate forces and feeling in England was running high against the Jews.

Despite the prevalent anti-Semitism, some audiences were persuaded to hear us. Walter spoke to the larger audiences and I went to church and club groups in England and Scotland. British sentiment became clear to me after I finished a talk at one Methodist group. The chairlady rose and condescendingly told the audience: "Mrs. Lowdermilk means well, but remember, she is not informed." In spite of inward anger, I tried to reply with information and not emotion.

On another occasion, an American friend took me to a luncheon at which I was astounded to hear the prime minister's wife, Mrs. Ernest Bevin, say, "If my Ernie had his way, the bloody Jews would all be driven into the sea." How could I sit quietly in the face of this injustice?

I felt revolted to hear such an attitude expressed by the wife of the highest authority in Britain, a Christian country. More and more I sympathized with the peoples under British rule, and I felt a kinship with my forebears who freed our thirteen colonies.

At an elegant luncheon, I spoke to a group of young British businessmen and politicians. During my talk several of them interjected sneering remarks about the Jews in Palestine. I countered by asking, "How can you have such an attitude when your own great Winston Churchill has said that it is a breach of the honor of Great Britain to support the White Paper and its refusal to allow Jews to enter Palestine?"

Apparently, their British good sportsmanship got the better of them. To my surprise, the audience rose and cheered me.

From England we flew to Rabat, Morocco. Walter tackled the land problems with his usual zest. He consulted with government officials and members of GETIM (Groupement pour L'Etude de Travaux d'Irrigation au Maroc), and later went into the field for research.

Accompanied by French officials from the Ministry of Agriculture and Forestry, we drove up and down the fertile coastal plain between the ocean and the Sahara Desert, and over the seriously deforested Atlas mountains toward the desert. The variety of history and landscape was striking. Portuguese fortresses flanked the coast with guns facing inland and Roman ruins lay wasting. We saw Arabs on the plains and Berbers in the mountains, Bedouins of the desert and Blacks from the South, all of whose cultures were overlaid by French influence.

Walter commended the French for doing a good job of building dams for irrigation and power. They were trying to preserve the land they had brought into farming by ripping out the thick growth of <u>Chamelops,</u> a scubby palm tree, and encouraging the <u>Argania</u> tree, which produces oil, fodder and wood. I watched Walter standing in the ruins of Roman towns such as Volubilis and near Taroudant, thoughtfully listening to his guides and taking notes, searching in the sand and rocks and examining the pieces of broken pipe or the olive and grape presses or grinding stones which indicated a previous abundant agriculture. As usual, Walter generously shared his advice and encouragement.

In Walter's studies, he always tried to find local farmers, who by trial and error had hit upon solutions to their problems, which with scientific principles be more effective and used for demonstrations and pilot projects to show, rather than tell, other farmers. An early and amazing discovery in the Middle East centries ago was being used in Morocco (and modernized by the French) is that of the rhetara (or foggaras). These connecting wells dug from mountain ground water in a gently-sloping underground channel delivered the water on the plain where desired for irrigation and watering thirsty people and flocks.

Through our Moroccan tour, we drove in a convoy of two to four cars, sharing ours with some officials who spoke no English. I did not understand or speak French and so, for several months, I was very nearly mute. Westher, however, improved her French sufficiently to translate for me. Much later, I heard a woman's voice speaking English at our hotel. Excited, I dashed out into the hall and embraced her as we both spoke rapidly and happily. She was visiting her in-laws, who spoke no English, and felt the same frustration with silence as I had suffered.

After the field research, Walter, Westher and I proceeded to Algiers. We witnessed improvements since 1939, when we first had seen the Berber people farming the mountainous regions of Algeria. Walter had observed then that because of careless agriculture and overgrazing, erosion had left almost no topsoil to cultivate. He had advised the French Colonial Office after World War II to ask for U.S. Marshall Plan aid for earth-moving machinery so they could properly terrace more of the mountain slopes. The request was made, but the Americans in charge of the Marshall Plan office in Paris would not recognize that Algeria had a sufficiently demanding erosion problem. Walter convinced the Marshall Plan Director of Algeria's desperate need and, soon afterward, 250 bulldozers were sent to Algiers. Several years later, the officials sent Walter pictures of whole mountainsides with contoured terraces and flourishing plantings of trees and grain, showing Walter his suggestions had also flourished.

"These lands used to be worth only 7,000 francs a hectare (2 1/2 acres)," the officials wrote Walter. "The people were so poor that one olive tree might be owned by several families. But when fruit production began after three years with your new system, the lands were valued at 110,000 francs per hectare, and the peasants' income significantly raised their standard of living."

The U.S. fleet was in port and there were American sailors and officers everywhere, especially at our magnificent Arabian-style hotel. Located on the hills above Algiers, the St. George Hotel had beautiful mosaic tiles and gardens that attracted many visitors.

When we took our car out, I would offer a ride back to the city to any American Navy men about the lobby. Usually one or more would come along. One day an officer got into the back seat and I began spouting at some length about some American policies of which I disapproved. Intent upon the subject, I paid no attention to our passenger's uniform.

"Here is where we turn to go to town," I said when we came within two blocks of the port, "so we will let you out at this corner." That left him two blocks to walk in the sun down to the docks.

"Thank you very much, ladies," he said, closing the door. "I would like you to be my special guests at our ship's open house tomorrow at two. Just ask for me upon your arrival," and he gave us his name.

Westher and I thought the event would be enjoyable, and looked forward to associating with Americans again, so we decided to go. It was a swanky affair. Sailors in starched whites bowed to us from the wharf entrance, escorted us to the ship, and assisted us safely up the step ladder to the deck. I gave the name of our passenger from the day before, and was horrified to learn that the man I had regaled with complaints about our Government policy and dumped out of the car in the broiling sun was the Admiral of the United States Mediterranean Flagship! I apologized profusely--he graciously accepted--and the afternoon proved to be delightful.

Sharing these Algerian experiences with us was a young 19-year old Moroccan girl we hired as a seamstress to make up some local cloth and the beautiful woolens we had acquired in England. We decided to hire a seamstress who spoke French to give Westher a chance to further improve her French. Since she had arrived without a veil and her name was Marguerite Cohen, I knew she was Jewish. Her father was a rabbi who had followed the Biblical injunction to "be fruitful and replenish the earth." He had seven living children and two in heaven. Marguerite was the eldest daughter.

From Marguerite we learned the story of her family and also about life in Morocco. Originally the family had farmed a small plot in the country but local Arabs had taken the livestock, beaten the father, and driven them out. They fled to the rabbit warren-like slums of Tangiers where they lived in three rooms with dirt floors. The nearest water was a quarter mile away. Rabbi Cohen, who had been unemployed for a long time, was then running a small second hand furniture store.

The general standard of living in Morocco was very low by our standards. But it was doubly hard for minority people, like the Jews, to make a living. Furthermore, it was the philosophy of North African Jews not to profit from religion, so the rabbi gave many hours to the synagogue without pay. All the Cohen children who were old enough were working at every little job they could get.

In November, 1947, the United Nations had made the decision to partition Palestine into a Jewish and an Arab state with economic union. The Arab leaders were so enraged by this proposal that the lives and property of Jews in all Islamic countries were in danger. Although Marguerite had completed only six months of schooling before being apprenticed to a dressmaker, she knew four languages and commenced learning English rapidly. I recognized that in this bright, young girl lay my opportunity to do something for the Jews in a personal way.

When Walter and I were to revisit Algeria for a month after the Moroccan study, we obtained permission from Marguerite's parents to take her with us as a "helper." We were able to get her a passport stating she could go to Algeria and then return to Morocco. We felt a serious responsibility for her, since the week before, at Oujda, Arab mobs had killed ninety Jews and looted all their shops. Even though we could not speak much together, her large brown eyes, so full of laughter, completely won me over. Marguerite fit into our family beautifully, and Westher and she became good friends.

In the U.S. we had managed to keep up with events in the Middle East through the media and the many personal contacts we had made in those countries. In North Africa we picked up the European papers every day. Early in 1948, Britain withdrew from Palestine at the request of the United Nations, disarming the Jewish settlers, and arming Arab agitators before leaving. As Britain evacuated, she allowed Egyptian troops into the south, Lebanese into the north, and Syrian, Iraqi and Transjordanian troops to enter from the east, to take over military installations. When the State of Israel was born in May, 1948, six foreign Arab armies converged on her immediately and she was in a battle for her life.

The big powers who had recognized the Jews' right to independence stood by while the invaders set out to drive the new nation into the sea. Hundreds of thousands of Palestinian Arabs and Jews were displaced. The attack wrecked the chance for peaceful partition which would give the Palestinian Arabs the area allocated them by the United Nations.

At first the Arabs, outnumbering the Jews in arms and military personnel, were victorious. But the tide turned and the Jews began to win. Just as Israel was hours away from reaching the Jordan River, Britain demanded that the United Nations call a ceasefire. Had this ceasefire occurred later, the Jewish settlements in the West Bank would not have been destroyed. There would have been no Arab refugee problem, for the Jews begged the Palestinian Arabs to remain safely in their villages until the war was over and they could work together for the common good. Many did remain, but others followed the invaders' instructions to flee.

In spite of its violent beginning, the Jews had their homeland once again and were welcoming homeless refugees, Holocaust survivors, and other Jews who wanted to come from every part of the globe. We offered to help Marguerite to get to Israel.

"No," she replied. "I can try to use my passport to get a boat to Marseilles later. But please," she begged, "help my brother, Mark. When a Jewish boy tries to leave, they are afraid he'll fight for Israel, so they imprison or kill him. If you can get him a passport and take him with you, nobody will suspect anything and he can get away."

When Walter's assignment in Algieria was complete, we went to Tangiers, met Mark for the first time and were impressed with him. Mark was eager to go with us. I took him to the passport office where I told the official that we needed him to take care of our car on our trip through Spain and France. Upon seeing the name Cohen, he refused to grant the passport.

"We have many fine young Arab men who could do the job better," he told me.

"We want only Mark," I insisted. "We know him, he knows our car."

We waited in the passport office for a long time, but nothing happened. Unwilling to give up, I decided that if I had to do things their way, I would. I spoke again to the Arab passport official, but this time I slipped a bribe into his hand. It worked. Within a half hour Mark had his passport

allowing him to accompany us through Spain into France, then
return to Tangiers.

Unexpectedly, Walter had the opportunity to sell our car
for a good price, so we traveled by air instead. As the plane
took off, Mark looked back through the window, deeply
moved: "I never want to go into an Arab country again as
long as I live."

In France we gave him some money and a ticket to
Marseilles, along with a note to the Jewish Agency people,
asking them to help him and his sister Marguerite get to
Israel.

Later, in Paris, we asked the Israel Consul what had
happened to him. We were stunned to hear that, instead of
going to Israel, Mark had gone back to Tangiers! We felt
there must be some mistake. But in time we learned the
story: when the Jewish Agency representative had read my
husband's request to get Mark and Marguerite to Israel, he
said, "If you can get your family here we'll see that they all
get to Israel."

Spurred by the hope of getting his entire family to Israel,
Mark decided to return to Tangiers. He borrowed money
from his employer for tickets and passports to get his family
to Marseilles. In exchange, he bonded himself for three years
of work.

Mark's frail mother was still nursing her six month old
baby. Mark and his sister Miriam found a doctor who would
certify that she must go to France for medical treatment.
Her husband was allowed to go along to care for her, bringing
the two little boys and the baby. Later, by overcoming the
endless red tape and bribing officials, young Marguerite and
fourteen-year-old Semadar joined them in Marseilles. Mark's
seventeen-year-old brother, Albert, looked very much like
Mark on the passport photo, so Mark gave Albert his own
precious passport and remained behind. Had the authorities
found what they had done, it would have cost Mark his life.

Albert, who was better educated, spoke six languages:
Arabic, Spanish, French, Hebrew, Italian and English. The
Jewish Agency kept him in Marseilles for seven months to

interview other Jewish refugees on their way to Israel. The rest of the family were sent directly to Israel. I later learned that Albert joined the Israeli army and saved the men of his unit by catching an enemy grenade that was thrown into their shelter and tossing it back before it exploded.

Returning to America at the end of summer, we thought our African travel was over; Westher would enter the University of California and we would be together in Berkeley. But another surprise awaited us. Shortly after our ship docked in New York we met Dean Reisner, head of the Methodist Missionary Board, whom we had known in China. He had followed Walter's work and he knew that other areas of Africa needed his advice. Reisner offered us a new and exciting assignment, financed by the Carnegie Corporation and sponsored by the British colonial government and the British and American Missionary Association. This time Walter was asked to spend 18 months assessing the condition of the lands of British Colonial Africa and explain to Africans--officials and citizens of all walks of life--that while Africa was doubling her population every twenty-five years, she was continuing to practice an agriculture that could not feed the increase.

"Mankind is in a race with famine," Walter had said long ago, "and the outcome is in doubt." Africa might well be the first crucible.

After studying North Africa from the Atlantic to the Sinai in 1939 and 1948, we looked forward to seeing the regions south of the Sahara. We left London one very cold day and a four-motored "sky bird" whirled us over the heart of the great Sahara Desert to the tropical "hot house of the world" at the bottom of the great Western continental bulge (then known as British West Africa). The total blackness of the desert night faded with the first rays of dawn, and we saw great bare mountains with occasional game trails leading to waterholes, miniature <u>kraals</u> with mushroom-like huts, and the ancient Nigerian city of Kano, where the landscape was covered with little farms. As we circled over the city it appeared to be still sleeping under the early morning sun.

Here was a famous crossroads of ancient civilization which, along with neighboring Timbuktu and Lake Chad on the Niger River, had always intrigued me.

Our plane came down slowly onto the runway, and we stepped out into the glaring heat. It was like an open furnace. Fortunately, we were able to get out of the intense heat by flying almost immediately down to Lagos, Nigeria's capital tempered by the ocean. From the plane we watched the mighty Niger River slowly unrolling itself across the land, meandering from one side of the horizon to the other. The river begins only 150 miles from the Atlantic but, finding no way down to the sea, it wanders northward along the edges of the Sahara, then southwest to the Gulf of Guinea near Lagos, a course of 2,500 miles. Because of the summer cloudbank, our plane flew low giving us a superb view of forests, swamps, and clusters of thatched mud huts in the clearing.

This area is called the "hot house" of Africa because there are two kinds of weather: hot and dry, and hot and wet. The precipitation can reach 200 inches in the mountains, and vast amounts fall everywhere except the deserts. We were treated to a dramatic demonstration of this tropical rainfall soon after we arrived at the Governor's residence in Lagos. The heavens opened with great noise and suddenly earth and sky were joined by falling sheets of water.

"This rain forest is a paradise to look upon," the Governor told us, "but it is a green hell to fight one's way through. Jungles can threaten man more seriously than seas or deserts."

Obviously, food production was very limited in such an area, but more than an erosion problem, it was a matter of leaching tropical rains and rampant growth draining the soil of its nutritive properties.

For a few days we enjoyed the luxury of the Governor's mansion while Walter was briefed by British officials on the general situation of African agriculture and the problems with the land. We were to travel near the coast as well as to the northern territories. Sometimes a day's ride over those roads was like riding a bucking bronco. We thought our car axles would break. In some areas the soils were a flat, red color and Walter would return from field trips with his hair red from the dust. Seldom was there anything to bathe in but a little tin tub, and all the water had to be carried in on top of servants' heads.

Wherever we went we were entertained by local British officials. The nightly dinner parties clearly illustrated the differences between the British Colonials and the people they ruled. At first I felt it rather ostentatious for foreign women to wear long dresses at every dinner, and I had brought only two with me. However, an experience I had soon afterward caused me to change my mind.

Although there was an abundance of insects in West Africa, the British did not install screens on their windows. They believed, we were told, that screens were an unnecessary expense and would hinder air circulation. In such a climate we certainly needed every possible breath of air, but we also needed some protection from insects.

Once we returned late from a field trip and didn't have time to change before being taken to a large dinner party. The guests were already seated at a very large round table. The women wore long dresses and the men, too, were well-covered, from their ankle boots right up to their necks.

From the moment we sat down, hordes of mosquitoes made a beeline for an American dinner--my legs--an easy mark through my thin nylon stockings. All through the meal I had to smile and be jolly, suppressing a desperate urge to reach under the table and scratch. The next day I bought some material and had more long dresses made.

The insects were not the only uninvited visitors at these parties. At one elegant party, the dining room was brilliantly lit by a couple of gas-burning lamps attached to the wall, which naturally attracted swarms of insects. Pink lizards, from six to twelve inches long, ran everywhere. Periodically they would zoom up the walls toward the lamps and gorge themselves. I could actually hear them chewing! When they were stuffed, they would drop to the floor with a thud, while other lizards competed for their places. All this was so commonplace to the other guests that they paid no attention, but the incongruity of swarms of pests amid such elegance tickled my sense of humor.

In the "hot house" countries--Sierra Leone, Ghana, Togoland and Nigeria--the British claimed, for the Crown, all the wealth, including minerals and diamonds. The Africans lived on their own lands without interference from the Europeans, following their tribal ways, including the agriculture of their ancestors. British colonial officials, who appeared to be trying to modernize them, found themselves hampered by ancient prejudices and taboos.

Western progress had hardly affected these countries. Some native peoples had no written language, practiced human sacrifice, and were dominated by a belief in juju or witchcraft. Former great African cultures seemed to have long since disappeared, almost as though they had never existed. There were no foundations upon which modern Africans could build unlike the long traditions and national disciplines in China and India.

Yet by 1949, British West Africa was changing at a fast rate. Although there was a great need for education, colonial officials had soon discovered it was expensive to employ teachers from England and Europeans were reluctant to go to Africa because of health hazards. As a result, the schools had been turned over to the missionaries who were already devotedly serving there. The British subsidized these mission schools and children were taught to speak English.

From the start, the white man set a bad example by never performing any manual labor. Educated Africans felt that they, too, should avoid labor and hire others to do it for them. This troubled Walter, who was asked to speak in schools wherever we went. He would ask the students what they wanted to do in life.

"How many of you want to be clerks?" he would ask. Many hands would be raised.

"How many want to be teachers? Politicians? Doctors?" Many hands would go up for each of these choices, but nobody wanted to be a farmer, a builder, a carpenter, an engineer or anything else that required manual labor. They especially looked down on agriculture. Only the women, using the most primitive methods, did the growing and harvesting.

Walter kept asking the students, "How can you have the self-government you demand if no one can do anything or make anything but paperwork?"

In Freetown, Walter took my picture under a giant kapok tree which was formerly the landmark for slaving ships to come ashore. There, captives were held in chains to be auctioned and taken away to America and the slave marts of the New World. Today this great tree, once a monument of injustice, shelters the imposing edifice of the Court of Justice.

The Gold Coast (now Ghana) was dotted with some thirty European castles. One of the most important castles during slavery days was Elmina, the departure point for hundreds of thousands of slaves. I peered into some of the dark, damp dungeons and pictured the Africans, from the open life of the forest, dying like flies in those cages while they waited for shipment. To my African guide I expressed horror at this example of man's inhumanity to man. His reply was simple.

"Ah, yes, but now you have your atom bomb and can kill a hundred thousand at one time. Is that progress?"

Walter traveled everywhere, tirelessly preaching his gospel of land conservation to officials, farmers, missionary workers and students, many of whom were eager to learn from him. The Reverend Amissa, President of Wesley College and director of all the Methodist programs among the Ashanti tribes of the Gold Coast, organized what was later described as the most elegant affair ever held there. It was in honor of Walter, and a British official came to escort us. On the way he insisted on stopping for a drink at a wayside bar.

"Africans are always late," he assured us. "Let's have some beer and enjoy the shade."

As he continued drinking, I became more and more uneasy, then finally insisted that we go. When we arrived, we found that some three thousand people had awaited us for over an hour, standing in the broiling sun. We were told that this was the greatest event the people of that region had ever put on and no one had wanted to miss it. I was terribly embarrassed, but I put my feelings aside to enjoy the program the people had prepared.

We were escorted to the center of a great football field where there was a palm-covered dais and someone carrying a huge red umbrella. On one side of the dais over one thousand guests sat under an immense roof. On the other side, standing patiently in the direct sunlight, were about 1200 students from the lowest grades to college level. Black African women, who seemed to participate joyously in almost everything, made up a good part of the audience.

To the accompaniment of drums and horns, we were taken across the field under our great red umbrella to shake hands with some fifty chiefs and elders, then returned to our dais. Then the great spectacle began. The Chief-of-All-Chiefs led the others to us across the field. Retainers sheltered them with huge, colorful umbrellas as they walked. Their streaming, bright-hued robes, heavy with gold decorations, were held up by courtiers. The chiefs' "sacred bodies" were also supported so that they would not stumble, and to preserve their precious energies, courtiers supported their arms when they shook hands with us. One chief, we were told, had eleven wives and forty-five children. I wondered how far "conserving their precious energies" went!

A marvelous performance of tribal dancing and singing followed. Then, on signal, the chiefs' servants presented us with gifts of turkeys, eggs, yams and many other foodstuffs (which we later left with Reverend Amissa, our host).

The celebration didn't end that day. Other events took place, and the climax of the festivities was at Kumasi, the inland capital of the Ashanti tribes. It consisted of a great reception and dinner at the missionary college. Walter sat beside the Chief-of-All-Chiefs, who was resplendent in feathers and gold. I sat beside the Queen Mother, whose ample figure was handsomely garbed in brilliant red turban and dress of blue and yellow handblocked cotton. Among the guests were well over 100 Europeans and educated Africans, including representatives of government and the missions, with many Protestant clergy and Catholic priests and nuns. The college art department had combined African and European art styles to decorate the dining hall.

The exuberance of the whole affair showed that the African people recognized the importance of agriculture for their survival and were paying tribute to Walter as a man who would help them to improve it.

Our itinerary took us from the Gold Coast back to Nigeria, to the agricultural station at Asaba supported by Canadian Christians. Kenneth Prior, an agricultural expert, and his wife, Pearl, a nurse, ran the station. They were an inspiring couple wholly dedicated to helping Africans achieve a better life mentally, physically and spiritually. Kenneth was assigned by the government to conduct our tours in the surrounding region.

When Pearl Prior led me into their guest bedroom, the first thing I noticed was that the thatched roof came down close over the far side of my bed. Memories of previous experiences with rats, bats, snakes and insects dropping out of the thatch made me grimace. Noticing this, Pearl spoke up.

"Oh, don't worry about 'little creatures' in the thatch," she said cheerily. "The natural 'exterminators' have already been here. Only a short time ago, we saw a stream of driver ants heading our way, so we packed our suitcases and left for a couple of days. Millions of ants came through our house going through everything, never missing a crack or a straw, and ate every living thing."

Pearl, the only source of medical care in the region, was trying to educate people who had no notion of their need. As an example, she told me how, a few days just before our arrival, she had looked out of the window and had seen two men carrying someone in a hammock. They stopped at the gate and a pregnant woman got out. Just as Pearl was going to see what they wanted, there was a wail and a black baby dropped from the mother onto the road. She picked up her

sterile scissors and went to help. Pearl cut the cord and
gently carried the new little one into the house to bathe and
wrap it in a blanket. When she took it back outside to the
mother, she found the entire group gone! Once over her
surprise, Pearl had sent a young Canadian from the station
after the mother on his bicycle, with the bundled baby
dangling from the handlebars.

He overtook the group about two miles away and called
out to the woman, "You forgot something!" The mother had
birthed a twin, but she took the abandoned infant back.
Twins were considered unlucky in that part of the world, so
parents preferred to let one of the babies die. Pearl didn't
know what would happen to it.

The Priors had worked at Asaba for many years under
considerable hardship. Because of the perpetual heat, living
without a refrigerator was a major problem. American
missionaries commonly had refrigerators operated by bottled
gas lamps, but the Priors never had ice, a cold drink or a cool
salad. No food could be kept overnight without growing green
mold, so the cook had to bicycle six miles to market each
day.

"Why haven't you asked your Canadian supporters to send
a refigerator?" I wanted to know.

"They would feel it was an unnecessary expenditure,"
Kenneth replied.

The Prior's salary was so small they could not afford to
purchase a refrigerator on their own, let alone pay the high
tax required to import one. I thought Pearl deserved to have
a refrigerator and I promised the Priors I would do something
about it.

Soon we set out with Kenneth Prior to inspect the
agriculture of the region and analyze the condition of the
soils. Wherever we went we heard of driver ants--the Prior's
'natural exterminators.' They formed an army, with squad-
rons, scouts, temporary field headquarters, and a whole
organization to feed their multitudes in the ant city. We
were told they eat everything in their paths, even tethered
live animals, leaving only the bones.

"White ants" or termites were common, too. A Methodist missionary near Lagos told us how millions of termites had turned a wall of his living room into a honey-comb. He discovered them when a chunk of the wall fell out into the room. He was just wondering whether he would have to tear down the whole wall when he saw his African helper disappear into the bush. While the missionary still pondered the wall, the helper returned with four or five driver ant scouts which he put through the hole in the wall. This seemed no more than a futile gesture to the missionary, who dismissed the problem for the moment and left to attend a meeting.

When he returned home, he found a black river of ants, twelve feet wide, streaming out of the bush and converging at his door. It crossed the living room and crowded through the hole in the wall. Then the tide turned; in a few hours the driver ants had eaten their fill. Each ant reappeared carrying a white termite in its powerful jaws. Last of all came those carrying portions of the queen termite--shapeless blobs of white fat. By morning there was not a single termite to be seen. The wall was still clean of them when we arrived two years later.

Not all problems were so easily solved. One Sunday we were the guests of Dr. and Mrs. McDonald at the Itu Leper Colony. I was frightened of this horrible disease, and had tried to think of some excuse for not going. Finally I decided that if the McDonalds could live and work with lepers, I could at least pay them a brief visit.

That day turned out to be the most deeply stirring of our whole year in Africa. Our tour began at the huge church, which had been built entirely by the lepers out of mud, timbers and thatch. Walter and I sat on the church platform and looked out on almost three thousand lepers, packed tightly in the pews. No one had foreseen that the colony would grow so fast. In the crowd it was not evident that many lacked limbs or had other disfigurements. Anyway, it was not long before we simply looked at them as people, no different from ourselves. An eighteen-piece all-leper orchestra carried the congregational singing, played an offertory and led the youth choir. Each leper put a coin on the collection plate when it passed.

"Walter", I whispered as soon as the service was over, "this is so fascinating I can scarcely wait till lunch time to hear the story of this project. Here is Christianity in action as I have never seen it anywhere!"

At luncheon we learned that Dr. and Mrs. McDonald had been sent by their church in Scotland to Nigeria. When they arrived, Dr. McDonald had been appalled at the great number of lepers, tragic outcasts, wandering about aimlessly, begging and totally neglected. He requested and received permission from the British authorities to develop an unused swamp into a colony for them. The officials had been skeptical, but the McDonald's great determination and enthusiasm overcame their reluctance.

"There was no problem getting lepers to come," Mrs. McDonald said. "Word spread rapidly on the leper grapevine that there was a missionary at Itu who wanted and needed them, who would treat them, give them homes and teach them a trade. There was little money to make a start, but these people had an overwhelming faith and hope. We planned everything on a cooperative basis, and the work grew by leaps and bounds. Only the doctors and the treasurer are Europeans. The entire African staff are lepers. Today, the colony covers three square miles and it is practically self-supporting."

The McDonalds described how they had built canals to drain the swamp land and establish farms. Each family built its own home out of local materials. Those who wished could have their own plots of ground to cultivate. Those too weak to work could fish in the canals. Each person contributed according to his or her own strength. Babies of infectious mothers were lovingly cared for until the women were no longer contagious.

Model villages with small industries grew up near the farms, all run by cooperatives but allowing individual expression. Dr. McDonald had collected discarded parts of old engines and made their first steam engine. Forty men continuously felled timber and prepared it for their carpenter shop where windows, doors, and furniture were made for the houses. They extracted and marketed palm oil and even manufactured some chaulmugra oil then used for the treatment of leprosy.

The colony had its own transport and sanitary systems, dairy, cinema and library, music and sports. Police, judges, jury and a chief justice were all elected from among the lepers. There was also a big central market, so dear to the hearts of all Africans, where products and gossip were exchanged. Community kitchens and special care units provided for the needs of those too ill to work.

"The afflicted ones arrive at this colony as outcasts" Dr. McDonald related as we were winding up our tour. "They are dirty, hungry and apathetic. But those who have been cured leave with heads erect, clean, self-sufficient and better educated than most unafflicted inhabitants of the villages to which they return. They have the added prestige of being trained to be useful in society. Each year we hold a 'valedictory service' where those leaving us are given diplomas declaring them free of disease and wishing them God's speed." The successes of these people working together was truly a Christian inspiration.

Kenneth Prior took us near the ancient city of Zaria in northern Nigeria to visit another missionary couple. The day before, one of the dreaded spitting cobras had shed its skin in their living room, leaving its discarded wardrobe on the floor. They found signs that the snake had been living in the mud wall of the room. Where there is one cobra, there usually is a mate and perhaps even a brood of slithering little ones, almost impossible to catch. They practically tore out the wall looking for the second cobra, but she was not to be found. I had the uncomfortable feeling that there were snakes all around me. I even jumped at the common lizards running freely in every unscreened house. Walter refused to condemn the lizards. He said they were excellent pest controllers.

After my experience with malaria in China, I was even more terrified of infected mosquitos in the hot house of Africa than I was of snakes. We took five grains of quinine regularly every day. If we thought we had been infected we jumped the dose to thirty grains, then tapered to twenty-five the next day and so on back to five grains. How I hated the sight of those pills! I sometimes felt I would ooze bitter quinine juice if someone squeezed me, but we never caught malaria.

Our three-and-a-half month tour of British West Africa was coming to an end. When I was completing the typing of Walter's notes on the Prior's guest room table, I realized that words could not begin to tell how much it had meant to us. Nor can they explain how crucial were the land and food problems of this part of the world. Soils were depleted both in tropical and interior dry areas. Walter was especially concerned about Nigeria and he told its leaders so.

"This country would have had famine years ago had not oil been discovered which provided the dollars to purchase food from abroad. When the oil gives out, where will food be found? Nigeria cannot produce it, nor will she have money to buy it, and at the current rate of growth, in another hundred years she'll have four times the present number of people."

It was difficult to get the message across, but it did not always fall on deaf ears. Once, when Walter was addressing a conference of clergy on the subject, a Nigerian minister rose and said, "Now we realize for the first time why hunger done already catch us."

We bade a reluctant farewell to Kenneth Prior, our escort for the Nigerian tour. To us, he and Pearl truly symbolized the white hand outstretched to the black one in brotherhood.

I hadn't forgotten my promise. "Don't be surprised," I said to Kenneth, "if you receive a refrigerator one day."

His expression said, "You're just an American woman making talk."

Walter had already told me we couldn't afford it, but I still was determined that the Priors should have their refrigerator. I sent in the order that very day and told him that I proposed to earn the money to pay for it. I soon found a way.

Walter had been asked to write an article for the South African <u>Farmer's Weekly</u>. He was about to refuse it for lack of time when it occurred to me that since I knew most of his material almost by heart, I could write it in the car while he was off in the fields with farmers and officials. The article turned out to be much longer than the <u>Farmer's Weekly</u> had requested, but there was no time to cut and retype it, so we just turned it in under Walter's name. The editor was delighted. He printed it in two installments, one week apart. That paid for the refrigerator, but there remained the problem of the high import duty.

We had become friendly with Mr. Foote, the British High Commissioner in Nigeria. I knew that he was very interested in the Priors' agricultural station, so I wrote to ask him if there was some way the government could pay the duty. He answered that there was and soon the refrigerator was on its way to the Priors. Later we heard from Pearl that the gift had changed their lives in more ways than one.

"First of all," she wrote, "it has brought a constant stream of Africans through the house who want to see and taste ice for the first time in their lives--so many, in fact, that we had to move the refrigerator out of the kitchen into the front room. Secondly, we can have ice cream daily. At every meal we tinkle the ice in our glasses and say, 'God bless the Lowdermilks.'"

CHAPTER 18
BELOW THE EQUATOR (1949)

We left Lagos and the British West African colonies for those of the southern hemisphere, flying first across Africa to Kenya, and then on to Johannesburg, South Africa. Our tours would radiate from there.

As we settled ourselves on the plane for the last leg of the flight, the pilot asked me if I would please visit with his elderly mother-in-law, who also was on board.

Then he added something exciting: "I promised her that if today is one of the rare times when Mt. Kilimanjaro is not shrouded in clouds, we will fly over and around it."

After chatting awhile with the woman I returned to my own seat. Glancing out the window I shouted to Walter, "Look! Quick! We are over Kilimanjaro!"

There was no doubt about it. We were peering into a large crater. Inside we could see clearly a forest of great, elongated icicles. The famous extinct volcano is the highest mountain in Africa. Walter grabbed for his camera and got two fine pictures. Then, to his disgust, he ran out of film. The pilot circled the entire rim of the mountain, so close at times that our wing tip seemed to touch it.

We landed in Johannesburg and traveled by car across South Africa's open lowland countryside to our first assignment, Swaziland, a tiny country in the hills to the east. Walter showed immediate concern at the poor condition of

the land resulting from overgrazing.   Cattle were everywhere.

We were intrigued to learn that Swazi cattle primarily
were used not for meat or milk, but as a measure of wealth
and for the buying of wives!   Swazi wives were the labor
force; they worked the land and bore the children.   The more
wives a man had the richer and more influential he was.   The
first four wives were taxed, the rest came tax-free.   Then,
the going rate for a wife was from two to thirty cows,
according to her strength, youth, good looks and family
prestige.   A chief's daughter, for instance, was very desirable,
especially if she was strong and handsome.   But of paramount
importance were the number of years of work a man could
expect from her and the number of children she might bear.

My sixtieth birthday happened to fall while we were
there.   Rather proud of my health and energy at that age, I
asked an English-speaking native how many cows a woman my
age would be worth in Swaziland.   He hesitated, looked
embarrassed and refused to answer.   After I insisted, however, he finally replied, "Madam, at your age you would not
be worth even one cow. You would only be worth two goats."

Now, over thirty years later, my worth to a Swazi man
would probably not be a dozen eggs--scrambled!

Although the British had planted some beautiful forests
and attempted to protect them, overgrazing had resulted in
innumerable dongas--deep gullies which were eating away the
land like a great cancer.   Not surprisingly, it rained out of
season while we were there and Walter was able to show the
Swazis just how the soil was being washed away.   He urgently
advised them to plant fast-growing shrubs on the bottoms and
sides of the dongas and to limit grazing on surrounding
areas.   But it was a difficult and frustrating task for the
British colonial officials to convince the Swazis to change
their treatment of the land.   Their widespread belief in juju
kept them clinging superstitiously to their old ways.

We learned firsthand about juju through a very fine young
Swazi, mission trained, who wanted to farm his father's land
according to modern methods.   When the rains and weather

were just right he put in his crop by the new system. But he had made a mistake--he dared to plant before the local chief had plowed his own fields. This was taboo. The young man received a series of threats and ultimately the witch doctor put a curse on him. An official later told us that "They got him." His death was a tragic loss.

Juju was also practiced in Basutoland (Lesotho). According to British officials there were 250 ritual murders that year. When the witch doctor put a curse on a man, he died or was killed and his organs were used for magical concoctions. Although Basutoland had great open spaces and magnificent mountains, its people were poor. Even the white settlers were having a difficult time. Large areas were overgrazed and erosion was spreading rapidly.

We flew to Southern Rhodesia, today's Zimbabwe. Salisbury, the capital, was a beautiful city designed by the country's founder, Cecil Rhodes. The streets--wide enough for a team of forty horses with huge wagon loads to turn around--were lined with jacaranda trees which shed a carpet of bright blue petals. Walter and I fell in love with the country and became so friendly with some of the officials who traveled with us that we corresponded with them for many years.

The government provided us with a seven-passenger touring car so that as many officials as possible could discuss land problems with Walter while they traveled. Because there was one official too many for the car, I insisted he take my place so as not to miss out on the discussion. I followed in his small car with his driver. The roads through the fertile Saba Valley were so bumpy that the little low car seemed to be scraping bottom the whole way. The heat was almost intolerable. We passed many giant baobab trees. Natives hollowed out small caves in their 10-30-foot diameter trunks in order to get out of the sun, and women working in the fields placed their babies there to sleep. We were told that the heart of David Livingston was buried in a huge baobab tree.

At higher elevations the rains came in the summer while the winters were sunny and mild. The soils were excellent and there was abundant water for irrigation. Walter became very excited about the enormous potential of Rhodesia if people would only avail themselves of scientific methods of agriculture.

Walter visited the tomb of Cecil Rhodes, through whose generosity he had enjoyed three years' study at Oxford. In the nineteenth century the country was very sparsely populated and Rhodes had given large tracts to white farmers and cattlemen. He also allotted 20,000 to 40,000 acre tracts to missionaries who would accept responsibility for developing and cultivating the land and educating the Africans. The American mission station at Umtali was the best we found in all of Southern Rhodesia, with well-trained agricultural missionary working on water diversion schemes.

Walter was personally as well as professionally pleased to meet Emory Alvord, a Mormon from Utah. Like Walter, he labored right along with the African farmers in the fields. Alvord had been successful in getting them to adopt new farming practices where the British officials had failed, and was eventually made Minister of Agriculture.

Alvord got each farmer to set aside a certain plot of land for "modern conservation farming." On these plots the farmers built compost piles, sowed high-grade seed he obtained for them, and kept careful records of their crop production. Those who participated in this scheme were called "modern farmers" and every year a great fair was held where prizes and certificates were awarded to those who had increased their crops. The "modern farmers" were very proud of themselves and it soon became apparent to them that the new ways brought better results. Nevertheless, Alvord told us, unless the farmers were given constant encouragement and advice and had a white expert with them, they would quickly revert back to the old ways.

The white farmers, too, had a lot to learn. We visited many of the huge cattle ranches, sometimes a million acres in size, and observed that no hay was stacked against the dry times. The cattle had no watering places, so they died in large numbers during the dry season. Unaware of modern options, the ranchers just accepted their large losses without making any attempt to remedy the situation.

Ignorance of the effects of mismanagement was illustrated to us at a very large English mission station south of Salisbury. The missionaries who come from a country where the misty climate keeps the vegetation lush and green had no idea of erosion's devastating effect. They had allowed Africans to build huts and run their animals all over the station lands. As a result, the dongas were spreading faster than the missionaries could plant trees and bushes to hold the ground.

Walter told the English priest, "This mission may be preparing the souls of these farmers for heaven, but their soils are going to hell."

Some newspaper reporters happened to be with us on that trip, and the next day, across the entire front page of South Africa's largest paper, huge headlines read: "'SOULS TO HEAVEN, SOILS TO HELL' SAYS LOWDERMILK, AMERICAN LAND EXPERT."

In Nyasaland (Malawi), we spent Christmas in a charming hotel on the shores of Lake Nyasa. The views were marvelous, but the big crocodile population on the lake was frightening. We were told how crocodiles would lie in wait for native women washing clothes. One would sneak up behind a woman and, with a flip of the tail, toss her into the water where all the advantage was with the crocodile. In the stomachs of crocodiles that had been killed were found necklaces, bracelets and earrings. I shuddered when I saw crocodile heads pop up out of the lake with mean eyes and vicious jaws.

One afternoon as Walter and I sat out on a bench overlooking the lake, we were intrigued by a roiling black cloud on the opposite shore. It was a couple of miles long and several hundred feet high, and looked like smoke from a fire. Walter called to one of our fellow guests, an Englishman strolling nearby, and asked about it.

"It is no fire," he replied. "It is something worse, and we can be thankful it is on the other side of the lake. That 'cloud' is said to be one of the plagues that God inflicted upon the Egyptians when the Pharaoh refused to let the Children of Israel go. That cloud is made up of billions of tiny gnats which mate in the air, die, and smother every living thing in the vicinity."

We had become acquainted with mosquitos, ants, lizards, crocodiles and gnats. We met baboons on our first evening at one station with a good-sized congregation of farmers, who worked hard to grow their food. A missionary told us he had killed 7,000 baboons in and around his village during the twenty years he had been in Africa. I was horrified at first. It seemed such needless cruelty, but I changed my mind when I learned how destructive they were.

"The mango trees provide a fruit important to the baboon," the missionary told us. "At night baboons climb the trees when the fruit is still green, take a bite out of each sour fruit, and spit it out. A baboon will nibble one mango after another until the tree has been stripped and all its fruit spoiled."

It was even worse with the corn crop. He described how baboons would go down row after row of immature corn, systematically stripping off the ears of corn and putting them under their arms. Baboons can only count to two, so each time they picked a new ear they dropped one. At the end of a row each baboon had only two ears of corn, one in the hand and one under the arm. The rest lay destroyed on the ground.

Our host explained, "In some ways baboons are smart enough to outwit the native farmers. They have lookouts stationed at various points who sound a warning at the slightest suggestion of danger, so the whole group can quickly hide. The only way we can get them is with a gun. Since they can only remember two, three of us go out into the field where they might be feeding. Their lookouts sound the warning and the group instantly disappears, but of course they are peeking at us from behind the bushes. The man with the gun hides while the other two walk off nonchalantly. Thinking that all is clear, the baboons come out to resume feeding. Then the man with the gun picks a few of them off before they can all get away."

After seeing the devastation wrought by the baboons my sympathy went to the hardworking farmers.

We saw even stranger things in Nyasaland. We arrived during the "hunger season" before the big rains came. There was a beautiful lake of sweet water 200 miles long, with fertile inlets and outwash fans, so easy to use for irrigated crops. Yet, except at the American mission stations, not a single acre was under irrigation. Instead, the British were buying food and shipping it in to prevent starvation until the rains came. The Shire River emptied out of Lake Nyasa over steep, roaring waterfalls which could have supplied electric power for the whole nation. We could not understand why the British government was not developing such remarkable resources.

From Nyasaland we went to Northern Rhodesia (Zambia), which possesses some of the greatest copper mines in the world. That year, 1949, some progress was evident, but on the whole the country was still very underdeveloped. We stayed with some British officials who were trying hard to bring about some improvements but I felt, as I told the Governor, "British policy is endowing backwardness and stabilizing stagnation."

For example, it was clear that Northern Rhodesia had sufficient swampy lands to enable it to become of the world's great rice-growing areas and easily supply all the rice needed locally, for England and for many of her colonies. Yet when we were there, nothing was being done to develop this enormous potential.

One day when we were traveling through a forest, one of Walter's shoes gave out and he asked our British escort where he could get a new pair. After explaining that we were more than two days from anything that could be called a town, he finally offered directions to a little country trading post nearby. From its appearance, we thought there would be no chance of finding shoes Walter's size there, but somehow the propieter found a pair. As we were paying him, something caught my eye.

"Walter!" I cried. "Look at that! There is a little Blue Box of the Jewish National Fund." Sure enough, it was one of the small collection boxes in which Jews had saved money for the purchase and reclamation of land in Palestine, now Israel. It was like meeting an old friend. Both of us immediately emptied our change into the Blue Box, much to the amazement of the storekeeper and our British escort.

One evening as I studied the map for the next day's journey to Lusaka, I said excitedly, "Walter, do you realize that before you give your final report to the government officials at Lusaka, our route will take us along the Zambezi River near Victoria Falls? Can we stop to see them?" We agreed to speed up our schedule so that we could spend a few hours at one of the great scenic wonders of the world when we were so near.

As we approached the falls from the tree-dotted plain we heard an awesome roar. Suddenly we saw the mighty Zambezi River hurtling with earth-trembling force over a sheer precipice into the boiling depths 400 feet below. The Africans call Victoria Falls "The Smoke that Thunders" because of the clouds of spray that shoot hundreds of feet into the air and form a great mist that can be seen from miles away.

Enthralled, we lost track of time and remained at the falls long after we should have started for Lusaka. Walter had been busy taking photos and I delayed things further by insisting on having my picture taken in front of the largest baobab tree we had seen. I lost my hat when we stopped again later to photograph some giraffes nibbling the high branches of a tree. Just as Walter focused the camera, one of them leaned over the fence with his long neck and snatched my hat to taste.

Belatedly, we got on our way. Night fell suddenly, like a black curtain; there were neither stars nor moon. All the villages and farms were behind us and the dirt road we had been following took us some distance through a great swamp.

Suddenly, the car began to jerk and sputter, gave a last gasp and stopped. Walter and the driver pushed as I steered, hoping that the engine would start on a slope, but no luck. So, taking our flashlight, the driver started walking toward a mission station he estimated to be about eight miles away and left us waiting in the car.

"Sh-sh-sh-sh," suddenly Walter whispered. "Some animal is sniffing around the car." We listened breathlessly.

"What kind of animal?" I asked him in suspense.

"Keep still," he ordered.

Then to my horror, Walter--always the eager scientist-- got out and walked around the car. I pleaded with him to get back in, remembering the story of some tourists who had run out of gas in a place like this. A bunch of rambunctious "teenage" elephants had bounced their car around with all of them in it, then picked it up and dropped it with a bang, before dragging it off into the bush.

"Walter, what is it?" I asked. "Could it be a lion? And what about crocodiles, or a hippo! If a stream of driver ants caught us here," I wailed, "there would be nothing left of us by morning except bones."

Walter was annoyed. "Must you talk about every animal in the Ark? Besides, hippos eat only vegetation, so stop worrying." We never found out who our nocturnal visitor was, but I worried all night long.

Our spirits rose just before daybreak, when a glow of light appeared in the distance slowly coming toward us. Our driver had reached the mission station only to learn that the missionary had gone, with his car, to a conference. But his wife awakened her houseboy and sent him with our driver through the forest to the home of a white farmer who hurriedly dressed, jumped into his pickup truck and came for us.

Never were we so glad to meet a stranger. We put our baggage in his truck and he drove us through the swamp to a junction on the main road to Lusaka. We found a restaurant, had a hurried breakfast, and I asked whether anyone would give us a ride. Fortunately a friendly family squeezed us into their already overcrowded car and sped us on our way toward Lusaka.

We could hardly believe it, but Walter entered the capitol building at exactly 10 am--the hour he was expected. He gave his report to a roomful of awaiting officials. Despite his lack of sleep, Walter did exceedingly well and the audience obviously appreciated his insight and observations.

We stopped again in Southern Rhodesia while on our way back to Johannesburg. There we were faced with one of the most difficult decisions in our lives. An American named Kapnek, who had read about Walter's work, urged us to visit Frogmore, his estate near Salisbury. Frogmore turned out to be one of the most beautiful farms we had ever seen--13,000 acres of rich land in a region where summer rains and sunny winters were perfect for crops. A stream had been dammed to form a lake for irrigation and there was a source of inexpensive labor nearby. There were hundreds of acres of orchards, as well as tobacco and other field crops, and still more land than the owner cared to plant. Kapnek and his wife were childless; the "Frogmore" estate was his baby. He was very impressed by Walter's background and after a few days of getting acquainted and hearing Walter's ideas, he made us an offer.

"Come here and stay for nine months of the year," he told Walter. "Give us the benefit of your experience at Frogmore, and I will make you rich. Choose any 80 acres you wish. I will give you a deed with permanent water rights and a house built to your own specifications and a seat on the Frogmore Board of Directors." In addition, he offered to put Walter on the boards of South Africa's largest flour mill, its biggest brewery (which he also owned), and to give us an interest in his diamond mine. "I will make you rich," he repeated. "Go to America or anywhere you wish for three months of the year, but you must devote yourself to Frogmore for the other nine."

What a dilemma! Walter was retired from the U.S. Department of Agriculture so we were free to do whatever we wanted. We had both had a financial struggle since we were very young and it seemed this multi-millionaire was offering us the sort of life one dreams of. Tentatively we chose our 80 acres and made a sketch of the house we would like, overlooking the lake. I imagined the garden parties we would have under the huge trees in the front yard.

"It would be wonderful," Walter said, "to have space, beautiful scenery, and ample help. Guests from Salisbury, tourists from America and old friends could visit us." We would be so rich we could afford to send them tickets to come! Yet we hesitated to give Kapnek an answer.

We had two or three weeks before we had to leave South Africa, and had committed ourselves to some speaking engagements. The South African Jewish community had invited us to talk about Israel in some of the big cities. In lieu of payment they wished to take us through the country of which they were obviously very proud. The Jews of South Africa were a very vital part of South African life. Many had been there for generations, and so they were interested in Walter's reports on Israel both as Jews and as pioneers and farmers.

We made a delightful tour around South Africa, speaking to interested audiences and seeing many splendid farms and wonderful, gardened cities. We visited the famous Kimberly diamond mine, and a gold mine near Johannesburg where we saw an exhibition of African tribal dances that made the earth vibrate. These dances were encouraged, we were told, to keep the workers fit and to fill their off-duty hours, since they were imported from neighboring countries and were separated from their families most of the year. The tour was a wonderful conclusion to our African odyssey, though it saddened us to realize that despite the wealth of this country, most of the benefits of democracy were enjoyed only by the white minority. The Jews of South Africa seemed to have more empathy for the blacks, perhaps because of the history of persecution their own ancestors had suffered.

Of course, Kepnek's offer to make us rich was always in the back of our minds. It was the chance of a lifetime. Life had dealt us some hard wallops, but things had turned out well whenever we asked the Lord's guidance. So we consciously made this a matter of prayer.

I had discovered many years earlier that Walter was the "don't fence me in" type. I guess I was, too. The more I thought of being so far from America, from the children and my beloved home folk, and having Walter's talents monopolized, the more uneasy about the offer I became. Walter had always wanted a farm--and this one was beyond his fondest dreams--but he, too, began to doubt. Supposing he was offered a chance to be of real service elsewhere and he was tied to Frogmore for life? The more we prayed, the more we realized we should not choose riches. In the end, we refused. This was one of the most important decisions we ever made. As a result, we were to find more happiness and satisfaction than any amount of money could have brought.

Walter's last African studies were completed, we had sent off his report, we were free and spending a few days relaxing in the temperate climate of Entebbe. Although at the equator, it is 4,500 feet above sea level. A deep desire came into our hearts as we rested. We wanted to see the new State of Israel.

We had been so thrilled reading of the achievements of the brand new little democracy, especially after our recent visits with African Jewish communities, that we decided to give ourselves the pleasure of a visit. We bought tickets on Israel's brand-new national airline, El Al.

The night before our departure I was restless. Perhaps it was only excitement, but I was uncomfortable. I had difficulty breathing and it felt like wings were brushing my face. With the first light of day we decided to get up. I looked at my husband.

"Walter!" I exclaimed. "Your face and pillow are covered with a grey film of tiny gnats!"

I couldn't talk without gnats getting into my nose and mouth. Needing a breath of fresh air, I stepped out to the veranda and suddenly skidded as if I were walking on ice. Gnats were piled up in foot-high drifts against our door! With each step I crushed thousands. So this was what is was like to be inside of the "black cloud" we had once seen at a distance across Lake Nyasa. Walter and I dressed hurriedly and dashed to the screened dining room, thinking we would be protected there from this plague.

As soon as Walter laid down his coat, it changed color to the dull grey of a layer of gnats. We tried to have a cup of coffee, but by the time we had skimmed off the gnats and lifted the cups to our lips, they were replaced by another contingent. Meanwhile, the hotel help were shoveling piles of gnats from the porch and around the doors into sacks from which--we were told--they would make gnat pudding. They were welcome to it! By the time we went out to the airport, the sun was higher and the air cleared somewhat. Finally we could breathe without competing for oxygen with gnats. It was rather a bizarre ending to our African odyssey. We had driven 30,000 miles over the years in Africa, and as many air miles.

El Al Airline had only a small plane flying between Entebbe and Lod/Tel Aviv, and its passengers had carried too much weight to allow takeoff. The crew left behind what they could, including, I believe a passenger or two. Still somewhat overloaded, the little craft lifted, barely making it off the runway. We stopped some hours later at Wadi Halfa near the Egyptian border in Sudan to refuel before crossing over the Red Sea. We ate a quick meal in the stifling heat, then were airborne again. We traveled the 500 miles across the Red Sea and the Gulf of Aqaba and over the Negev through winds so violent it seemed that the wings of our plane would be blown off. We flew into a black, stormy night, unmarked by stars. Suddenly we could see below us the first rural lights in the new State of Israel. We forgot all else in our excitement.

CHAPTER 19
THE NEW STATE OF ISRAEL (1950)

In 1949 the Jewish state was one year old. According to Israel's "Law of Return," anyone claiming to be Jewish could have automatic citizenship. This was a most dramatic change from what we had seen 10 years earlier, on our first trip to the Middle East, in 1939. Then, the land of Israel was called Palestine and the British were preventing entry to the hundreds of thousands of Jews fleeing Nazi Europe.

Israeli Government officials gave us a warm welcome to their fledgling state. We viewed some of the damage from the War of Independence; places where there had been fierce hand-to-hand fighting, where walls, pockmarked from shell-fire, had collapsed. We saw rolls of barbed wire left across some of the fields and around the government offices and on the beaches.

In the old city of Jaffa a mosque had been used as a snipers' tower to fire down upon adjoining Tel Aviv. But we noticed that, in all the battle-scarred areas, the towers of churches and mosques stood amidst the devastation, unharmed. When we asked for an explanation, we were told that Israel's forces had definite instructions to leave holy places untouched, even though this policy cost many additional Israeli lives.

While we were there, forty to fifty thousand destitute Jews were pouring in every month--Jews from Hitler's Europe and those forced to flee their ancient homes in Arab lands. We toured new agricultural settlements and saw the temporary camps hurriedly set up to handle Jewish refugees until they could be properly settled. The situation was desperate. To add to the crisis, wherever we went, we saw soil erosion. Walter was so shocked by this he visited the President, Dr. Chaim Weizmann.

"You cannot feed a fast-growing population with constantly decreasing soils and fertility. What are you going to do about it?" Walter asked.

The President shook his head sadly, "We can do nothing. We are swamped just trying to feed, house, clothe and find jobs for our newcomers. We have no one trained to do the type of work you have in mind and no money to pay an outside expert."

I knew "in my bones" that the Lord had been preparing my husband for this work and I was grateful that we had declined that tempting offer to stay in Southern Rhodesia. No one could have been more qualified than Walter with his excellent background in forestry, his work in famine prevention in China, in the U.S. Soil Conservation Service, and his studies of Africa.

That night we discussed what we could do about the crisis in Israel. The next morning Walter went back to President Weizmann and offered one year of his services to the new state--without salary, just expenses. The President gratefully accepted and Walter and I--excited about this new challenge--began to make plans. Everyday we felt more rewarded for not accepting the riches in Rhodesia.

To get reacquainted with the land we spent 18 intense days touring. Everywhere we went people had heard of Walter's book, Palestine, Land of Promise. That slim volume had helped American and United Nations leaders realize the feasibility of allowing Jews to resettle their ancestral homeland. Food and almost everything else was being rationed, but destitute though their little country was, the Israelis were enormously proud of it and wanted to show us everything. What we saw affected us deeply.

As the newcomers arrived, they were put into tiny, one-room shelters in <u>maabarot</u>--temporary immigrant camps--surrounded by winter mud. Each received blankets, a cot with a straw mattress, a small, one-burner kerosene cooking stove and some food. Government agencies helped them to learn Hebrew and to find work as soon as possible. New settlements were established almost weekly, housing more than 100,000 people.

"To those without vision such a herculean task must seem hopeless," Walter remarked. "But the Israelis are tackling their problems with the same enthusiasm and courage that won them their independence. To be with them at a difficult time like this is inspiring."

Many Jewish families celebrated the re-establishment of their country by taking Hebrew names. So it was with the Grasovsky family. In 1939 their sons had been assigned to show us around by the British Mandate Department of Agriculture. When we met them again in 1949, they had chosen the name <u>Goor</u> (lion cub). Amihud Grasovsky, of the Forestry Department, was now Dr. Amihud Y. Goor, first head of Israel's Forestry Department. He was already putting refugees to work in a variety of innovative projects to help control forest disease, to produce nursery stock, and to harvest some young forest products like fence posts which could be exported for much needed foreign currency. The other Goor brothers also headed departments within the new Ministry of Agriculture.

In each ministry and department of the new government Israel's best trained leaders worked energetically to get their jobs done with the help of all kinds of new citizens. They came from different cultures and spoke nearly 90 different languages.

The massive rehabilitation problems confronting the new state with its cruelly limited resources were overwhelming. In less than four years Israel would double her population while she struggled to bring deserts, swamps, and rocky hillsides into cultivation to feed the new arrivals. With the idealistic aim of reuniting the Jewish people as fast as possible, the highly educated were put side by side with the ignorant, and those from the East worked with those from the West. The living conditions were crowded and the people were unfamiliar with each other's ways and languages. As a result, sometimes there were painful cultural clashes.

Although they had virtually no experience with running a government, those already there tried to handle all these problems with unending patience, hard work and love. Few complained. Except for bread, almost everything of quality that was produced in Israel had to be sold abroad for foreign currency--clothing, oranges, even peanuts. Israelis had to line up for their rations of second-rate vegetables and, when and if they were available, eggs.

The leaders shared what they had with others, and performed their duties on low salaries. When I remember the pitiful rations on which the population existed, from the President on down, I marvel at their ability to carry on. Walter and I realized that we were witnessing an extraordinary human experience.

A few others recognized this, such as Bartley Crum, a founder of the United Nations and a member of the Anglo-American Commission on Palestine. Crum wrote: "When I saw what the Jews were doing in Israel, I felt that I wanted to go to my hotel and get down on my knees in humility, for they were more nearly living up to the teachings of Jesus than any Christians I know of. They are literally feeding the hungry, clothing the naked, healing the sick, sheltering the shelterless, comforting the broken hearted, and helping those that are in distress."

From time to time people who admired Walter's work contacted us to show, in different ways, their appreciation. One day we returned to our hotel in Tel Aviv and found a huge basket of Bible Land wild flowers in our room--anemones, cyclamen, lupine and wild iris--with a card signed "Rifka Aaronsohn of Zichron Yaacov." We were so touched by this gift that we decided to thank the donor in person the next time we went that way.

Zichron Yaacov, we soon discovered, lay on a low mountain overlooking the sea, halfway between Haifa and Tel Aviv. It was established by Jews in 1881 when Palestine was a remote part of the Turkish Ottoman Empire. The settlers were well-known for their good relations with their Arab neighbors. There, in a house filled with Turkish furniture, we met Rifka and her companion-housekeeper, Malka.

Rifka Aaronsohn was about my age, dainty, elegant without affectation, and warmly hospitable. Malka was earthy, hearty, rotund and bursting with fun and generosity. She had come as a child by oxcart all the way from a Russian village.

The Aaronsohn's were among the founders of Zichron Yaacov. Rifka's gifted brother, Aaron Aaronsohn, was at a young age a renowned agronomist and the first to identify the wild wheat from which our food grain of today evolved. An ardent Zionist who realized that the Turks would always thwart Jewish ambitions to develop the land, he led the Nili group which spied for the British against the Turks prior to World War I. They were caught. While being tortured, Rifka's sister--also a member--managed to slip into another room long enough to kill herself. Her parents were badly mistreated before they died, and her fiance was killed. Aaron himself died under mysterious circumstances in Europe.

Rifka returned from Europe to build a beautiful herbarium and museum on the old family property. She built this for Israel's future generations as a memorial record of her valiant family. Her neighbor, Malka, had come to help her years before and became her lifelong companion. Together, they kept alive a hope for the future of the country written in living things.

In the south of Israel we saw Eilat, the tiny new desert town on the Gulf of Aqaba near where we had visited archeologist Nelson Glueck in 1939. At that time there was nothing but a couple of huts, but now new buildings were going up. Since the Suez Canal was blocked to Israeli ships, Eilat was Israel's door to the East. We went for an exhilarating ride on an Israeli tugboat over the Red Sea, and saw some funny-looking black things sticking up out of the water. They looked like planes that had nose-dived, with their tails still in the air. Drawing nearer, we saw that they were large porpoises playing in the water. Unafraid of our boat, they swam in the fast-flowing waves alongside of us, so close that I could actually touch their backs with my hand!

During this trip I acquired a strange new name--"Mrs. Glass Bottom Boat." In 1939, near excavations of King Solomon's old seaport at Etzion Geber, we had looked at undersea life through a bucket with a glass bottom. Remembering the glass bottom boat at Southern California's Catalina Island, I thought what a wonderful tourist attraction it would be for this town. I talked glass bottom boats to everyone on that visit, even the mayor, but they all thought it would be impossible to get such a boat to Eilat over the desert or even in a ship. So I gave them a challenge: to cut out the bottom of a large rowboat, seal in a heavy strip of plate glass and put seating around the wall of the inside. "If people won't pay you a good price for a ride in that boat to see the fabulous underwater life of the Red Sea, then it won't cost you a thing. I will pay you back every penny you spend on it."

Because of my passion for the project, I earned the embarrassing nickname of "Mrs. Glass Bottom Boat". But it was worth it. (On a subsequent trip to Israel, I was delighted to find eight companies with glass bottom boats all doing a thriving business. By 1975 a permanent submerged tower had been built for viewing aquatic life.)

Before leaving the Gulf of Aqaba we revisited the site of King Solomon's copper mines, which the Israelis were reopening after 2,000 years. The manager of the modern mining operation told us that, in biblical times, thousands of slaves had worked the mines, the industrial works, and the port of Etzion Geber. Many copper articles were made there and shipped to Africa and the Mediterranean countries. I picked up some of the copper nuggets lying on the surface and thought about what a terrible life it must have been for those toiling in the awful heat.

Although our Israel tour was exciting and informative, we were anxious to get back to America. We missed the children and we needed to clear up other matters before returning to begin the year of service Walter had promised President Weizmann. Our plan was to purchase a new car as soon as we were back in the States, drive it west to see the children, and then take it back to Israel with us. But that was not what happened.

Dr. Morris L. Cooke, appointed by President Truman to head an enormous study for a U.S. water policy, reached us with word that Walter had been designated head of the Division on Basic Data of several major U.S. rivers. Dr. Cooke explained to us that the project might take the better part of a year. As usual, Walter and I talked things over and, although it was disapppointing to delay our return to Israel, we knew that his work in the U.S. would be important. We were comforted somewhat by the realization that, so soon after World War II, the heavy equipment needed for reclamation work in Israel would be hard to get. We took a room at the Martinique Hotel in Washington DC where Walter would be near the Water Policy Headquarters and he set to work on his part of the study.

At the same time, we continued with preparations for the Israel assignment. We learned that Israel's Golda Meyerson (Golda Meir) and Finance Minister Eliezer Kaplan were in New York. They has just successfully negotiated a $200 million gift to Israel from the United States Government for agricultural development. We went to New York to see them so that Walter could explain, in person, the work needed in Israel and what was required to get it done. Walter wanted to be sure that some of the U.S. gift money be allocated for three sets of earth-moving equipment--one for the Galilee, one for the coastal plain, and a third for the northern Negev. They agreed and told Walter to send a detailed equipment list to the Israel Embassy in Washington, which he did at once.

Westher had written that she had found the man of her dreams. They were planning to marry on the day of her graduation from the University of California at Berkeley.

The people renting our Berkeley house generously offered to stay in a nearby apartment so that our family could all be together in our own home for the wedding preparations and the ceremony.

On the afternoon after graduation ceremonies, Westher came down our stairway to the music of the Lohengrin wedding march and walked across the room arm in arm with her father to join Wilmot (Bill) Hess, her six-foot five-inch bridegroom. As Westher and Bill recited their vows from memory, Walter and I were thinking of our many happy years together, of Westher growing up into a woman, and seeing her begin a marriage which, like our own, seemed to be "made in heaven."

To avoid Washington's summer heat I remained in California with my sisters. When Walter returned to Washington he was asked to go to Japan to join General MacArthur's team of experts in the occupation government. Their task was to modernize and develop a water policy for that nation. During the six months that he was gone, I continued to prepare for life in Israel. Having seen the austerity there, I collected trunks of good clothing to give away, planned our own supplies very carefully, and then shipped everything ahead by sea from California.

When Walter returned from Japan, pleased with what had been accomplished there, we began our departure to Israel. More than a year-and-a half had elapsed since Walter had been promised his heavy equipment--plenty of time for it to reach Israel.

In 1951 it took twenty-six hours by El Al's propeller-driven aircraft to fly from New York to Tel Aviv. We needed an extra week for our ears to return to normal.

Although damage and debris from the war remained very much in evidence, progress was being made. Roads to the new villages were being cut across the dunes and through the rocky hills. Small apartment houses were going up everywhere in the attempt to get people out of the camps as soon as possible. We saw devastation and poverty, but we also saw hope.

The Ministry of Agriculture driver who had met us explained why so many languages were spoken in the streets: most people still had not learned Hebrew. The government's first priority was to unite the citizens through a national language. Newcomers were immediately started in ulpan--language schools. Classes were taught according to vocations or professions in order to speed up their ability to make a living.

Gas rationing was strict; there were almost no cars on the street. But one Saturday we managed to get a cab and visited the Cohen family. Marguerite had married and was living in a pitiful, crowded district on the outskirts of Tel Aviv. She took us to see the rest of the family--all except Mark--who were living near the sea in Maabara Salome. Mark was still in Tangiers paying off in labor the money he had borrowed to get the others out.

It was a happy reunion, though it hurt us to see them living in such conditions. Like everyone else in Israel, they were struggling to rebuild their lives. Marguerite traveled daily into Tel Aviv on a hot, rickety bus to the dressmaking establishment where she had found work. Albert (to whom Mark had given his passport), who had arrived in time to become a hero in Israel's War of Independence, was living in Kibbutz Oagania. The youngest boys, Benjamin and Ben Sion, did whatever they could to earn money or food. I was able to help them get full scholarships to trade schools through the Mizrachi Women's organization. Little Semadar helped her careworn mother with Miriam, now a toddler.

"Where is your father?" Walter asked when we suddenly realized that the rabbi was not going to appear. Then they told us an amazing story:

After settling in Israel, Rabbi Cohen could hardly wait to make a pilgrimage to Jerusalem. But he couldn't, because most of the Jewish holy places were in enemy territory. Jordan had annexed the rest of Palestine and denied the Jews access to their synagogues and holy places.

Although he took pride in Israel's celebration of her first year of independence, the rabbi could never get steady work and he felt useless in this hard-working society. One day he disappeared, and for three days the family heard nothing of him. Just as suddenly he returned, and they learned that, disguised as an Arab, Rabbi Cohen had crossed the enemy border and gone to see Hebron, the burial place of Abraham, Isaac and Jacob, and the mothers of Israel. He had seen the Wailing Wall in Jerusalem. Finally satisfied, he made his way back across the border into Israel.

"My dream has come true," he announced to his family. "I have seen the holy places and have seen my people living in the Promised Land. Now I can die."

A few days later while working in the hot sun in the maabara, Rabbi Cohen was stricken by a cerebral hemorrhage and died. He was just 47. Because of his great determination, he fulfilled his dream of visiting the Jewish holy places. His example helped me to understand why each of his children were so determined to make their own dreams come true too, even though all the odds were against them. I resolved to do the same.

On the first working day after our arrival in Israel, Walter reported to the Ministry of Agriculture, housed in a former German religious colony at the edge of Tel Aviv. When he came back from his meeting he looked shaken.

"What is it, Walter?" I wanted to know. "You look as though you'd had a terrible disappointment."

"There is no equipment for my work," he replied.

"That's not possible. Some of Israel's highest officials promised you would have it. It has been delayed, that's all. It will be here soon, I'm sure."

"No," he said. "It has not been delayed. It was never ordered. The money was spent on something else."

We could hardly believe it. Walter said he had learned that the person in charge of such orders at the Israel Embassy in Washington had decided other things were more important. Feeling that Israel "did not need Lowdermilk to tell them what to do," he diverted the funds to purchase irrigation pipe instead. There wasn't a single dollar left for Walter's work.

I could tell that Walter was sick at the thought of having to delay preparation of the land for food production when Israelis were enduring such privations. Why had the officials not believed his warnings? Why had they let us interrupt our lives, leave our home and country and come such a distance to do nothing? Walter began to wonder whether this was an indication that we weren't wanted there. We talked about it.

"Walter," I said, "I know your pride must be hurt. You are well known in your field and you are giving of yourself and your time. But think of the terrible experiences Jews have had with Christians. Besides, they are overwhelmed with problems and the judgment of one man should not make us go back on our word. Let's stay our year as promised. Let's show them that our friendship is real."

Walter agreed. He didn't mind that his "office" would be out on the land itself, but he could do little without equipment. He began writing letters to friends abroad asking for help. The response was wonderful. It would take time to get them, but soon he had the promise of, as I laughingly like to recount, five Christian vehicles and five Jewish ones.

Meanwhile, Walter suggested that newcomers from Yemen needing work be employed to search among cactus hedges and abandoned Arab villages for seed from ancient grasses which might have survived grazing animals. These could supply a nursery for indigenous grasses. A good area was chosen in the south for growing the seed in quantity. We were astonished at how soon this project was producing tons of seed for the range lands.

When we arrived in Israel we were given housing in the hilltop town of Tivon, fifteen miles inland from Haifa. There was no telephone or regular transportation. In the heat of the day there was almost no ventilation. There was not even enough room for either of us to work comfortably. But the tiny flat did not bother me much. After all, the refugees were living in even more limited space. But there were other problems. Walter's contacts in the government all lived either in Tel Aviv or Jerusalem, some distance away. He would have to write a letter for every appointment, wait for the uncertain mail delivery, then drive from Tivon to another city for his business. Only two families in the whole town spoke English.

Walter was getting restless. He was frustrated at not being able to do what he came to do. He was still waiting for his equipment when, to my relief, he was asked to deliver a paper at an international scientific conference in Belgium. I urged him to go.

"Walter, this is the perfect time for you to take a break. When you finish your meetings in Belgium, accept Lord Janner's invitation to come and stay with him in England. You can use the quiet of his country place to catch up on the material for the article you promised to do on Africa. By the time you get back, all your equipment will be here."

He went, and I remained in Tivon all summer, trying to make the apartment into a home for us. Daily I prayed that this experience in Israel would somehow work out beneficially.

I needed some household help and engaged a refugee woman from Germany, Janette Pessatti, for three half-days a week. Since there was no place nearby to take Hebrew lessons, I began learning words from Janette. Comically, Chinese was so imprinted in my brain as my "non-English" language that, as I tried to speak Hebrew sentences, Chinese would invariably come out. One day, when someone else heard my attempts to speak Hebrew, she said, "Oh, Mrs. Lowdermilk, Janette is teaching you Hebrew with a heavy German accent. Don't learn any more words from her." So instead, I taught Jannette English.

She was eager to learn, and soon we could understand each other quite well. Sometimes we laughed together and sometimes we cried. She told me of her terrible years in a German concentration camp. She had been taken out into a forest at dawn each day to work at one end of a saw, cutting up trees for the German army. When she fell and broke her leg, the Germans did not bother to set it but made her work as usual. Her leg bone healed crookedly.

Janette told me how, as the camp became overcrowded, SS guards periodically would make the inmates line up at daybreak and stand in the shivering cold until everyone had been accounted for. Then they would go down the long lines shooting every tenth person. She saw her sister and other relatives killed. Once, out of the corner of her eye she saw that she was to be the tenth one and she stood there frozen, unable to scream. A shot rang out and the woman beside her fell dead. To learn first-hand how these victims of Hitler's Germany had suffered was utterly heartbreaking.

In Vienna, Janette had been a concert singer and her husband had been a cantor. However accomplished the Jews may have been in Europe, all from the camps arrived in Israel destitute. On arrival they were given cots and boxes for stools and tables. I helped Janette to obtain some second-hand furniture from a departing diplomat. As soon as I unpacked my trunks, I gave Janette's husband a good suit of clothes, some shirts and an overcoat. He hurried into the other room, put them on, then rushed to the tiny, makeshift synagogue in their nearby maabara to thank the Lord. My friendship with the Pessattis has continued through the years.

That year--1951--there was a lot of excitement as preparations for Israel's second elections progressed. Israel's first elections had been in January, 1949, but the job of registering a new and fast-growing population, many in temporary housing and speaking so many different languages, was tremendous. Few of the voters were from countries with free elections, and some 300,000 Arab citizens, who had never voted in their lives, were just beginning to do so.

I asked the driver-interpreter who was working for us to take me down to the Arab quarter of Haifa. I knew this was the first time most Arab women had ever taken part in public affairs and I wanted to see what they would do. They obviously had never dreamed of such a privilege. Most of them still wore the veil and were unable to read or write, but they came in droves, and with enthusiasm. Living in a democratic state was going to make enormous changes in their lives!

After watching for some time, I heard a big commotion in the polling place. An Arab woman was, as the Chinese say, "telling the world her troubles." I sent the driver to find out what was going on. He came back smiling. The yelling had ceased.

"Those who can neither read nor write are allowed to register with their thumb prints, then sign by thumb print when they come to vote," he reported. "That woman was refused a ballot because her print was different from the one on her registration. But it turned out that she has divorced and remarried since she registered so she thought she had to use a different finger for her new name. When the officials finally figured it out they checked her thumb print and gave her a ballot. She then calmed down and voted."

People and their life stories fascinated me. I enjoyed meeting them and entertaining them at home. But Walter was in Israel to work for a limited length of time, and there was so much to do. Things were moving too slowly. I had been praying for a breakthrough for him.

Some time earlier Walter had prodded the United Nation's Food and Agriculture Organization (FAO) to provide experts to help solve Israel's erosion problems. When he returned from England his friend and former Washington colleague, agricultural economist Albert G. Black, was heading up the FAO mission in Israel.

"You can do so much more for this country if you're employed by the FAO than if you are employed by no one," Dr. Black said, frankly delighted at the idea of Walter joining his team. With Walter's assent, Black arranged for the Israeli government to request Walter's services on the FAO team not just for a year, but for an indefinite period of time.

Living in Tivon had become so impractical that we decided to move to Jerusalem, and I set out to find us a place there. In the 1948 War of Independence, Israel had lost the Old City to Jordan, and there had been much damage everywhere while Jerusalem was under siege. But the New City, outside the walls, was growing. It was my good fortune to meet Rachel Yarden, who was repairing a beautiful, but war-damaged house on Alfasi Street. She needed funds and we needed living quarters large enough for Walter to have a study and to be able to talk with groups at home. She rented us two rooms with a balcony and we shared her kitchen, dining and living rooms. In the apartment immediately below us lived Professor and Mrs. Michael Evenari, with whom we became friendly. He was a botanist deeply interested in the agriculture of ancient times. The entire neighborhood was friendly and we soon felt like Jerusalemites.

Rachel's parents had come from Poland to Palestine in the early 1900's, during the days of the Turks. She herself had gone through the 1947 siege of Jerusalem. Her brilliant mind stimulated us constantly. Together we held open house every Shabat (Saturday) afternoon, when anyone who wished to visit with Walter was welcome. Fortunately I had brought supplies for the mounds of cookies Rachel and I provided our guests. (My guest book for the next two years gathered over 2,000 names.)

One day I received a letter from an American friend, a Unitarian minister's wife named Martha Sharp. She had been in refugee work and was one of the first to enter the Hitler death camps at the close of World War II. She had told me about seeing a small, living bundle of bones there, dressed in rags. At his feet she had picked up two pieces of paper on which were drawn cruel, hideous human faces.

"Who drew these?" she asked.

"I did," the child said.

"How could you imagine such terrible faces?" she wanted to know.

"They were our SS guards," was his reply.

His name was Yehuda Bacon. He was about eleven years old, very small for his age. His smile touched her heart, and Martha saw to it that he was sent to Israel in the first group of orphans to go. When she learned that we were living in Israel, she asked me to look up Yehuda.

I found him in the Hadassah Hospital, too frail to work and ill with pneumonia contracted from wearing insufficient clothing in the winter cold. He was sitting up in bed drawing pictures of women, all with big, hollow dark eyes. I asked him why the women he drew were always like this. He replied, "This is the way they all looked in the concentration camp."

I learned that when Yehuda was rounded up with his relatives for the gas chambers, he was so small and thin that he could creep around people's legs to the back of the line and then slip away. Now he was eighteen years old and the sole living member of his family. My heart went out to him. From then on I visited him regularly, got him some warm clothing and brought dried prunes, raisins, soups--anything nourishing I could get. Even in the hospitals food was at a premium. After he left the hospital and moved to a tiny room I did whatever I could to make things easier and healthier for him.

One day he said to me, "Mrs. Lowdermilk, I think if I had some paints and brushes and a pad, perhaps I could really paint." But art supplies were not available then in Israel. God had no way to answer prayers except through some person. This time it was a man from Duluth who was visiting me. I told him the story.

"Have Yehuda send me a list of the things he needs," he said, "and I will send them here as soon as I return to the States."

When I took the longed-for package to Yehuda, he stroked each paint brush across his cheek with tenderness and looked with such love upon each tube of oil paint that tears came to my eyes.

He began to pour out his soul in pictures. Soon he had enough paintings for an exhibit which we arranged at the YMCA. That weekend a South African couple, also named Bacon, were staying in the historic King David Hotel across the street from the "Y." They went to the exhibit to see whether the artist was a relative. They found no relationship, but they were so touched by Yehuda's personality and his work that they took him and all his unsold pictures with them to South Africa. They held an exhibit in Johannesburg and enough were sold to enable Yehuda to study for two years in Paris and London.

Yehuda wrote me regularly telling of his joy in his studies and that he was beginning to sell his art and become self-supporting. Two years later, en route back to Israel, he wrote me a touching letter, thanking God for being so good to him.

"But now it is good to be going home," he wrote me. Home was Israel and the love and care that the Hadassah women had given him as a youth. He became a teacher-artist at the Bezalel Art School in Jerusalem.

The immigrants, especially those from Europe, had known much terror. Unfortunately, it was not over for them yet, even in their new state. There was continuing terrorism against civilians from across Israel's borders.

Jerusalem had been literally split in two. The Jordanians, contrary to the truce agreement, were denying the Jews access to their own buildings. Our home on Alfasi Street was very near the Jordanian line. One night three Israeli boys, totally unarmed, were sitting around a little campfire protecting stacks of building material for a construction across the street from us. We were just going to sleep when suddenly we heard a burst of gunfire outside our bedroom window, then the sound of the boys' dying groans.

"Don't turn on the lights!" Rachel called to us.

Downstairs, Dr. Evenari immediately called the police, who arrived in three or four minutes. They found the three bodies and took off in pursuit of the terrorist, who disappeared over the border a few yards away just as they caught sight of him. They found his cap where he had dropped it. It was an Israeli cap with an Arab cap inside it.

Over 600 Israeli citizens, some of them Arabs, were killed or wounded by Arab terrorists from across the borders while we lived there in the 1950s. When I remember how we Americans reacted to violations of our country's boundaries in the early days, I am amazed at the forbearance of the Israeli population. But to them, living in Israel was at the very heart of life. Even though they had lost their holiest places during the war, they at least would rebuild their nation within sight of them, on some of the land of their ancestors. The land was their great love, and that love was expressed in their passionate efforts to make it productive again.

Soon the long-awaited vehicles arrived and Walter was able to begin work which would demonstrate what needed to be done. The leaders in agriculture were mostly from European cities and had little understanding of erosion and its results. They did have an agricultural experiment station started by the British, but Walter shocked them once by telling them that on the grounds of this experiment station the soil erosion was a disgrace. They reacted in anger, but when Walter took them out to show them that the plots were ploughed up and down the hills so that the good soil was washed away by rain, Levi Eshkol made a stirring statement:

"Until now I did not understand the meaning of erosion; from now on I will see these gullies as open wounds in my own flesh."

From then on Walter received more understanding and support from the government. From the first, however, he had the keen interest of the young men assigned to work with him. He would go out into the fields with them to teach them. He emphasized that this was their land and, therefore, he would suggest no action without first discussing it with them. Before long they had made a complete inventory of all the lands of Israel. This information enabled those in charge of new settlements to make more logical, productive decisions as to what crops to grow and what forests to plant, where to put people on the land and how to train them.

Walter and his extraordinary "boys" began to demonstrate how to rebuild old stone terrace walls so that the soils left on the hillsides could be prevented from washing off. In time, the government procured earth-moving machinery and thousands of miles of broad-based terraces were built to prevent further erosion on the lower hills. When Walter arrived, the Israel Soil Conservation Department was the smallest in the government. Two and a half years later it was one of the largest. His "boys" proved so efficient that, as he so often liked to say, they worked him out of a job and were able to go ahead by themselves.

Walter encouraged the Soil Conservation Service to marshal public opinion in favor of laws regulating land usage, because he was determined that Israel should not repeat the mistakes made in the United States. At the instigation of his department, the Israeli Knesset passed a law prohibiting construction of factories, cities or towns on food-growing land. Such building was restricted to coastal sand dune areas or rocky slopes.

President Chaim Weizmann and his gracious wife were still living in their home near the Sieff Institute, which had become part of the Weizmann Institute of Science at Rehovoth. We visited them several times and renewed our acquaintance; but he was ill, and before we had been there long, he died.

Yitzaak Ben-Zvi, an early pioneer, became Israel's second President, and when Walter's work came to his attention, we were invited to their home. The presidential dwelling in Jerusalem was a modest house, rather an elaborate "pre-fab" hut. The President and his wife set the tone for the entire leadership of the country reflecting Israel's conditions. They accepted a modest salary and made the best of what they had. Open shirts for men and the simplest frocks for women were fashionable for all.

William Henry and May Victor Marks, 1893. Parents of Inez
Lowdermilk

Wilcox, Arizona, 1909. Scotch and Fuzzy on the donkey. Inez Marks, 19 years old.

Sedan chair and river junk travel. Szechuan, China, 1916-21.

Inez Marks, age 20. Chicago Training School, 1910.

Inez Marks (age 29) and her "little sister" Rachel Pen Chengtu.

Trackers' towing path on Yangtze to haul junks up river.
Photo courtesy of Dale Corson

Yangtze gorges.   Photo courtesy of Dale Corson

The family in Pasadena, California. The four Moodys: Elizabeth, Beatrice, Charlie and Miriam; the four Lowdermilks: Billy, Walter, Westher and Inez; William Henry Marks and Winifred Marks. Taken a year after the death of May Victor Marks.

Bill Lowdermilk, Elizabeth Moody, Ben Saada and Westher Lowdermilk. Tunis, 1939.

Stuck in the mud in the Syrian Desert, 1939. C.B. McKnight, Inez Lowdermilk and Elizabeth Moody in the car.

Roman ruins at Timgad, Algeria.

Terracing to control erosion on mountain farmland at Beit ed Dine in the Lebanon Mountains.

Some houseguests during World War II in Washington, D.C.
(Left to right) Lennie Holenkoff, Violet Bean, Martha Morris
and Westher Lowdermilk. On the floor, June Bright and Fay
Ivy.

1947. Walter Lowdermilk (second from left), Y.H. Djang,
General Feng-y-Hsiang and (seated) H.C. Lowdermilk, father
of Walter Lowdermilk and Inez Lowdermilk.

Walter C. and Inez Lowdermilk as a working partnership
(taken 1949 in Johannesberg).

Walter C. Lowdermilk during field work in Israel, 1955.

Inez Lowdermilk and Golda Meir, 1976

Inez Lowdermilk and Yucca bloom in the front desert garden at their home in Berkeley. The "going away" floral gift from Walter C. Lowdermilk, May 6, 1974.

Walter C. and Inez Lowdermilk, 1965, in their backyard. The Redwood tree, planted as a sapling in 1932, is in back.

A young Lebanon cedar seedling growing in the last remaining old groves with barren mountains behind. Walter C. Lowdermilk's favorite picture, taken in the Lebanon mountains. He entitled it: "The Promise of the Future Against the Degradation of the Past."

CHAPTER 20
MOUNT CARMEL (1952-7)

We had long looked forward to retirement and we were eager to return to our Berkeley home, but somehow there was always another assignment awaiting us. This time Walter was asked to help train Israelis to become agricultural engineers. Through Dr. Albert Black, the FAO was asked to extend Walter's assignment for that purpose. We were delighted. But, in this case, I decided to make one condition: I told Walter that I would agree to this assignment only if we could live on Mount Carmel in a house of our own. I missed our home in Berkeley, and the beautiful view of Haifa Bay I felt would compensate somewhat for San Francisco Bay.

Walter had often suggested that Israel train her own students rather than sending them to study in other countries where the problems were so different. This opinion was shared by Dr. Sidney Goldstein, head of Israel's Institute of Technology at Haifa, popularly called "The Technion." Dr. Goldstein asked Walter to give a series of illustrated public lectures there showing the hazards of uncontrolled soil erosion. The lectures proved so successful that the Israeli government requested Walter to develop a school of agricultural engineering. We didn't imagine then that the school would one day bear Walter's name.

Our plan was to find a Haifa home, go to Rome to deliver a talk for the FAO and then to the U.S. for a furlough before beginning the new assignment. Housing was still scarce, but over the years I had learned that if you really want something you must go after it with prayer as well as action, so I started looking for a house to rent months before we went on furlough. Someone told me that British General Orde Wingate's mother-in-law, Mrs. Patterson, an ardent Christian supporter of the Jews, had a fine house in Haifa that would be for rent in a few months. I immediately contacted her.

When I saw the home, I felt that Heaven must have prepared it just for us; it was perfect. Placed high on the hill, the front garden and entrance were at street level, but the house was three stories deep at the back. From the large balcony we had a glorious view of the gardens and golden dome of the Bahai Temple below. We could see the entire city of Haifa, the harbor and bay with the 'Arabian nights' city of Acre and the lofty Lebanon mountains beyond. Mrs. Patterson agreed to have the house ready for us when we returned from our furlough and we set off secure in the knowledge we had found such a beautiful home.

We flew first to Rome so Walter could deliver his report, in person, at FAO headquarters. In his report he declared: "Israel has demonstrated how a people with vision, courage, determination, and hard work can employ modern scientific methods of production along with conservation of its lands and waters to raise the standard of living for its increasing population. This Israel has done to the highest degree of any country in the Middle East--perhaps in the world--and she has done it under a democratic system and without the oil resources with which the Arab States are generously endowed."

"Israel has achieved this out of necessity and in her own interests, but she also has been hammering out on the anvil of adversity solutions to problems that two-thirds of mankind must face up to sooner or later. These solutions are important to all emerging nations and lesser developed countries seeking to industrialize their subsistence agrarian economies."

The report delivered, we were now free to set forth on our well-earned vacation in the U.S. and in Europe with the children. But there was a surprise for us. When we landed in New York, rumpled and tired after sitting up all night on the plane, we were met by newspaper men and representatives of the American Technion Society who had spent half the night waiting for us at the airport. After publicity pictures were taken, we had a few nights' rest and were rushed off on a nineteen-day speaking tour for the Technion. We had not expected to do this, but felt we could not refuse. Our schedule took us to New York, Philadelphia, Chicago, Houston, Milwaukee, Cleveland and Detroit. There was no rest, but being faced with a worthwhile job, we managed to forget ourselves and even seemed to acquire new strength.

Walter was convincing Jews in both Israel and America that Israel was well able to train her own experts in soil conservation and water use. Wherever we went, his description of Israel's progress was received with tremendous enthusiasm. In Detroit, for example, Mr. Sam Brody announced from the platform that he would donate $100,000 towards a building for the Technion's new Agricultural Engineering School.

Just as we finished the Technion tour, another assignment appeared. The United Nations Technical Assistance Administration urged Walter to spend the following year working out a world-wide water policy. We realized this would mean living in New York and postponing for another year the start of the new school. We discussed the matter with the Israelis who, realizing the importance of the project, agreed to delay. Technion contacted Mrs. Patterson and she promised to keep her house available for us.

Then we had a shocking disappointment: Walter was abruptly informed that he did not pass the security clearance required by our Government to work for the U.N. This was the terrible period when Joseph McCarthy headed the House Unamerican Activities Committee. If one even spoke to a relative or friend accused of being communist, knowing a communist, or having "communist leanings," one could be blackballed without ever knowing the accuser or the charges.

Walter was deeply hurt, then angered. He could not eat or sleep and paced the floor. He was sick to think that after a life of devotion to hard work and patriotism for his country, he was accused of being disloyal. He wrote to Washington time and again, but all his letters were ignored. Weeks went by. He had no job and the situation became desperate. If he could not work with the U.N. in New York, neither would he be allowed a passport to work in Israel.

I, too, was extremely distressed and made it a matter of constant prayer. Then a "postcard from heaven" told me that Walter should go to Washington to see his friend, Senator Hayden of Arizona. Walter agreed. Senator Hayden was indignant when he heard Walter's story. He found out the so-called evidence: guilt by association--with me! I had worked for Chinese relief during the Japanese 1936-8 bombings. Now that China had a communist government, anyone associated with helping China at <u>any</u> time, even for humanitarian reasons, was suspect. Also, Walter had published an article on conservation in the respected magazine <u>Pacific Affairs</u> whose editor was pro-Chinese. Senator Hayden grabbed his phone, demanded to talk to the head of the Civil Service Commission, and insisted in no uncertain terms that Walter be cleared immediately for his assignment. He would personally, he said, fully guarantee Walter's loyalty, as he had known both Walter and "his pappy" before him.

Within an hour, Walter's security clearance came through.

In New York we settled into the Beaux Arts Hotel opposite the United Nations. Walter worked with a splendid group of colleagues at the National Resources Section of the Bureau of Economic Affairs.

Before long, Arab delegates to the U.N. started to protest Walter's appointment. They opposed the program he had previously developed for the River Jordan, despite the fact that their own peasant farmers would have benefited from it as much as the Israelis. But the U.N. stood behind Walter on the grounds that his present assignment was "in the interests of the whole world," and of no political benefit to Israel.

That year, I did a good deal of speaking as well. Out in Los Angeles I met Ann Pollock, a woman of great vision and the dedicated Executive Director of the West Coast Friends of the Technion. She put me to speaking to help raise money for the new school of agricultural engineering. Ann had founded a Technion Women's Division to raise money for scholarships and the members were eager to hear all about Israel and the new Institute.

Through Ann, I again experienced the fact that "some plant so that others may harvest." She arranged a dinner invitation for Walter and me at the home of a philanthropic couple, the Harveys, so that we could tell them about the Technion. As Ann continued to cultivate their interest, they increased donations and eventually gave the sum of $1 million to endow the annual Technion Harvey Award for outstanding contributions to mankind.

After our sojourn in New York, the head of the Natural Resources Section wrote Walter a highly complimentary letter on the job he had done with the Natural Resources Section. When he had read it, I whispered to Walter my own little phrase for him: "She said 'at she did and 'at he was." This meant that she said that she did love him and that he was wonderful.

*****

With service to the U.N. at an end, we could resume our activities with Israel. On February 6, 1955, we returned to Israel to begin the Technion assignment. At Israel's Lydda Airport we were warmly welcomed by faculty members and driven to Haifa. What a thrill it was to ascend beautiful Mount Carmel up the winding streets lined with handsome, though modest, stone apartment houses, many still under construction.

The Patterson home was all ready for us and, when the welcoming party left us, Walter and I walked arm-in-arm out onto the balcony. We stood, as we so often did at our home overlooking San Francisco Bay, and contentedly gazed out over the blue Bay of Haifa and the open Mediterranean beyond. We felt completely at home.

We were excited to learn that we would be joined by family in Israel. Our son, Bill, or "Skip" as he was now called, came with his wife to work in Israel for the U.S. Agency for International Development (AID) for two years. They had been married in Israel in 1953, and this year 1955 their first baby was born in the Sharon Valley and named Sharon Vale by her grandfather.

The Technion was growing rapidly and Walter was soon busy selecting the courses and choosing the faculty for its new School of Agricultural Engineering. Technion had many important departments, but this school would always keep especially close contacts with the Israeli population since it would train personnel and do research for the optimum use of the land. Next to the people themselves, the land above all was the most precious national and personal resource.

"We must have a first-class school," Walter told the administrators and his associates, "with full equipment for measuring water action. Such an institution will not only give Israel her own engineers for future development of the land, but it can eventually contribute to the advancement of the newly independent countries of Asia and Africa, by training their people."

I had two jobs--to keep my husband comfortable, healthy and happy at home, and to create good rapport with the faculty and students. Although nearly everyone spoke English, many of the professors at Technion were originally from Europe where academic tradition kept them aloof from students. We wanted to create a different spirit, one in which the students would gain a feeling of solidarity both among one another and with their professors.

I felt our home was the best place to begin this "bridge building" experiment. First we invited faculty members and their wives for a special dinner. When they arrived, everyone was stiff and formal. Determined to encourage a more relaxed mood, I presented them with chopsticks and placed two bowls each of raisins and peanuts on the tables.

"Divide yourselves into two teams," I instructed them. "We are going to have a contest to see which group can empty all its bowls by eating the raisins and peanuts--using only chopsticks!"

They looked at me in consternation, but to be polite they went along. Soon everyone was laughing. By the time we went in to dinner all their reserve had evaporated. Next we invited students and did the same thing. The third party combined faculty and students. Before long, the barriers were dissolved, and the parties became like family get-togethers. I had tapped the fun-loving spirit of the Israelis.

I put a canvas roof over our balcony so that even in the strongest sun or stormy rain, visitors could wander outside and enjoy the superb view from Mount Carmel before we began serious discussions. Sometimes Walter gathered the whole group out on the balcony to illustrate his lectures with the land in front of them. I especially enjoy the memories of students sitting on chairs or on the floor of the balcony after dinner in the moonlight, with the lights of the city below, clapping hands and singing songs.

When the groups grew too large for our home, we held regular parties at a campus recreation hall. We invited General Dori, the new President of the Technion, to one of these affairs. He was so pleased with the camaraderie that he urged other departments to follow our example. It proved to be the start of an important Technion tradition.

Another innovation was our <u>Shabbat</u> afternoon open house. Technion people, neighbors and others from through-out the country came to socialize and to hear Walter speak. Soon the Foreign Ministry and the Government Tourist Agency were bringing us groups of foreign visitors who had entered Israel from enemy countries and were touring Galilee. They usually would arrive tired from their journey and bewildered, if not prejudiced, by the anti-Israel propaganda they had heard before crossing into Israel. Good American coffee seemed to work wonders for them, as did a piece of home-made angel food cake. Then we would make them comfortable on the balcony and Walter would talk to them.

"Now, as you go through Israel," he would say, "if you will just open your eyes to see and your ears to hear, you will find modern miracles being enacted in this wonderful little country."

People relaxed as they listened, and many went away with a clearer vision of what this new democracy in the Middle East meant to the world.

Providing refreshments for so many guests during those years of austerity took some doing! Israel was still struggling with food shortages, and rationing was so strict that, except for children, even eggs were limited to two a month per person. Fortunately I had anticipated the problem, to some degree, and had shipped cases of angel food cake mix from the States. Adding just a cup and a half of Holy Land water gave me a beautiful cake.

I had also brought cases of raisins and peanuts, both nutritious and a treat in Israel. Raisins and peanuts were among those products which Israelis were working desperately hard to produce for export in order to get foreign currency for housing and industrial development. They were not available on the domestic market. Neither was candy. I enjoyed being able to buy these with dollars and have the fun of giving the Israelis something special from their own country.

The Agricultural Engineering Department at Technion originally was housed in prefab schoolrooms on the old campus in downtown Haifa, above the port. The rooms were stifling hot in summer and so cold in winter that Walter had pneumonia once and flu twice. Then the new 300-acre campus was established high on Mount Carmel, overlooking the Mediterranean with a view of the fast-growing port and industrial center. The agricultural engineering students studied in the various buildings as they were completed, while Walter worked with the architects on plans for the building that would house his department.

President and Mrs. Ben-Zvi kept informed about the progress of the new school, and once again made us welcome in their home in Jerusalem. Rachel and I shared interests in children and in raising the status of women. Although my time was nearly all occupied now with Walter and making our home available to groups, in my small way, I was helping a few immigrant girls to improve their self-image. I had told an audience in America about the orphan girls I met in Israel who were now of marriageable age but could not afford wedding dresses. Mr. Held, owner of a Hollywood bridal shop, was in that audience. He donated a wedding dress for me to bring back to Israel.

When word had reached the Technion that I was bringing the gown, General Dori's secretary postponed her wedding until my arrival in order to be the first to wear it. She looked magnificent in that gorgeous dress--ivory slipper satin with a long train, lace sleeves and yoke, and a generous veil with simulated orange blossoms. Mr. Held had even included a pearl necklace and lace gloves.

Eighteen brides used that outfit. If a girl was slender, I took in the side seams to fit her; if she was plump, I let the seams out to the limit. The front hem went down for a tall girl, and up for a shorter one. I kept the dress at my home, always ready for immediate use.

Life was still so rugged in Israel that young, hard-working girls had few clothes of any kind, let alone nuptial dresses. Even though Mrs. Ben-Zvi was of the old pioneer school that did not believe in luxuries, she enjoyed hearing about how the girls stared at themselves in astonishment as they stood before my long mirror in that bridal gown.

Walter urged me to tell her about his favorite among our brides. She was a young immigrant girl from Yemen, the eldest in a large family living in a refugee camp. The family worked for Mrs. Goldman whose husband was in the Prime Minister's Office in Jerusalem. One day when a friend of mine was visiting Mrs. Goldman, Leah was scrubbing the tile floors and adding copious tears to the water as she worked. The ladies enquired why she was crying.

"I am going to be married day after tomorrow," she replied, "and I've always dreamed of being married in a white dress. I thought I could borrow one from a girl in the camp, but she promised it to someone else. I have only my Sabbath dress to wear and it's old and worn."

"Inez Lowdermilk in Haifa has a beautiful wedding dress to loan," my friend told Mrs. Goldman. They immediately got me on the telephone.

Walter had planned a trip to Jerusalem the following week, but he agreed to go with me the next day instead. We arranged to meet Leah at the home of archaeologist Philip Guy's widow, with whom we had renewed acquaintance. She arrived promptly after work, a beautiful girl of eighteen with black curly hair and big brown eyes. She was shabbily dressed and her hands were chapped and red from her work. Soon her scrubbing dress was off and she stood before Mrs. Guy's long mirror, dazzling in the white satin dress. Its train swept around her feet like a fan and her smiling face was framed by the orange blossom-trimmed veil. For a moment she seemed transfixed, then she burst out in Hebrew. Mrs. Guy translated, "Why, I look just like a Hollywood star, don't I?"

"Leah's Biblical ancestor, Ruth, could not have looked more beautiful to Boaz than this girl would look to her new husband," I commented. Mrs. Ben-Zvi laughed appreciatively.

Every time Walter and I went to the Ben-Zvi's residence, we commented that the colorful heterogeneous mixture of Israel's peoples was naturally reflected in the guests at the President's home. Besides Jews from all parts of the world, there was an indigenous population of Jews and Moslems, Samaritans, Circassians, Armenians, Ethiopians, Maronites and other kinds of Christians, and Druze. On one occasion, Rachel Ben-Zvi introduced Walter and me to Kamal Mansur, a young Druze educated at the Technion and elected to the Knesset. He cordially invited us to visit his home.

At our first opportunity, we met Kamal in the picturesque village of Isfia, on Mount Carmel above Haifa. We shortly became friends with him and his father, the mayor of Isfia. In the streets, Druze life seemed the same as Moslem life. But, inside the homes, Druze women met and talked with us easily, like women of the Western World. We began to visit frequently in each other's homes. From the

Mansurs we learned much about the life of minorities, the advantages to them from the democratic system, and the problems still to be solved.

The Druze had broken away from the main-stream of Islam ten centuries before, and were set apart by their secret religion. However, on occasion they converged publicly at the tomb of Jethro, father-in-law of Moses, near Hattin. They were fierce mountain people who constituted about one-tenth of the population of Galilee. They composed crack units in the Israeli army and were considered some of its toughest fighters. As veterans and heroes, Druze men received special assistance in building new houses for their young families which were going up all around the village of Isfia.

From the beginning the Israel government tried to be humane and practical regarding their non-Jewish citizens and attempted to try Theodore Herzl's advice to the Zionists: live peacefully with your neighbors. For instance, the Jewish marketing system was a modern, cooperative one in which the government insisted on strict quality control. But in those first years of overwhelming problems, they did not want to tamper with the historic livelihood of the small farmers. To ameliorate this problem, Jewish farmers were not allowed to sell along the roadsides but Arab farmers could do so. City dwellers who could get out to the country found colorful Arab produce stands provided an extra treat to add to the standard rations.

Life in Haifa was so full and interesting that time flew by. When Mrs. Sam Brody came from Detroit to see the new Agricultural Engineering Department (for which her husband had given the first $100,000 for a building), it was already being called the Lowdermilk School of Agricultural Engineering. We invited her to join us on a trip north to the Huleh Valley for the gala 1956 celebration of the "First Plowing" of the rich peat lands that Israel had reclaimed from a great swamp. This project would eventually provide Israel with 16,000 acres of rich land, enough to produce food for 100,000 people.

When Israel celebrated, she did it in a big way. The new roads in the Huleh were decorated with colored streamers. Out on the newly-drained lands some huge tractors awaited the signal for the "First Plowing." Notables spoke of God's gifts to man and man's duty to care for the earth. There, in the bright sun, pioneers from many countries stood joined in their love of Israel, thankful to God that they had lived to see that day.

Not long after the opening ceremony, we made another trip to the north, taking with us Mrs. Rabbani, wife of the head of the Bahai World Headquarters in Haifa. First we went along the fence separating Lebanon and Israel and we remarked how peaceful everything was. Then we went back to the Huleh so that, without the crowds, we could see the wildlife and the channels used to complete drainage of the swamp.

Walter had arranged for us to be met by a motor boat and we had a delightful ride. The tall papyrus loomed high above us; toads and turtles took to the water as we passed; and a wide variety of birds--many of which we had seen pictured in the 2,000-year-old Roman church mosaics near Tiberius-- either flew up at the sound of our motor, or paddled off across the water. Walter pointed out one area where, at the request of the members of a nearby kibbutz, he had once shot two wild boar because they were so destructive of the crops.

Entering the section to be preserved undisturbed as a wildlife sanctuary, we suddenly saw a speedboat racing toward us. It stopped alongside momentarily while its driver said something in Hebrew to ours, then sped away. At once our boatman swung our boat around and returned at full speed to the small dock. The outing was abruptly over. We had no explanation other than that the boatman was "called away."

We drove leisurely back to Haifa. All the way to the city everything was quiet--too quiet. As we arrived at our house and unlocked the door we heard the phone ringing. It was Mary Rose, Dr. Albert Black's wife, calling from Tel Aviv.

"Israel is at war with Egypt," she announced, "The wives and children of United Nations personnel are being evacuated.

You are to be at the airport at five-thirty tomorrow morning."

"But Mary Rose, I refuse to go," I told her emphatically. "I have been in plenty of wars in China and I certainly am not afraid here. I know the Israelis will fight hard and win. You are not leaving, are you?"

No, she admitted, "but it is my husband's duty to see that you have the instructions."

Just then someone knocked at the door and handed Walter a special delivery letter from the U.S. Ambassador ordering all American citizens out, men and women. The embassy would keep only a skeleton staff.

After the first planes left, most American women were to leave by ship. The next day a number were assembled at our home to await transport to the harbor where a ship would take them to Greece. Each was allowed just one suitcase and some few toys for the children. The American Government was behaving as though a catastrophe might overtake Israel.

That night we heard Cairo Radio blaring in Hebrew and in English that the guns of Egypt's largest destroyer had set fire to Haifa. We went up onto the flat roof to see, and witnessed a short sea battle between Israel's new little navy and the destroyer. We saw its shells fall harmlessly into the country-side while Israeli sailors captured the destroyer almost intact, complete with its crew. The next morning we watched from our balcony as it was hurriedly put back into commission as part of Israel's navy.

Israel made it plain from the outset that the Sinai campaign was not intended for conquest, but for simple survival. It was her response to the enemy's border viola-tions, which had become intolerable, and to Egypt's plan for annihilating her small neighbor with Soviet help. At the same time, the French and British tried to retrieve the Suez Canal which Nasser had seized in July.

When Israeli forces were clearly on their way to Suez, the United States suddenly ordered Israel to withdraw. U.S. Secretary of State John Foster Dulles threatened to cut off all help--financial, technical, and sale of surplus food--if she did not comply. He even urged West Germany to threaten to stop reparation payments to the victims of the Holocaust! (Germany refused.)

Israel won the battles and the world knew it; but President Eisenhower's order deprived her of political victory and enhanced Nasser's prestige with Arabs everywhere. We were dismayed at our country's shortsighted action. The Suez Canal was lost to the U.S. allies: the French and British.

Israel achieved such a sweeping victory that she simply could not deal with the enormous number of surrendering Egyptians, so she helped them cross the Sinai back to Suez, parachuting water to them as they crossed the torrid sands. Only 5,000 enlisted men and 200 officers were interned and these were exchanged for two officers, the only Israelis captured by Egypt.

To counteract Egyptian propaganda, Israelis gave captured Egyptian officers bus tours of whatever they wanted to see. Israeli homes and settlements were opened to them, and many Technion families entertained them for dinner or tea. Some friends of ours were driving some Egyptian officers to their house when a tire blew out. The officers could have walked off, but they repaired the tire and all drove on.

On the Independence Day following the Sinai Campaign, half a million people collected along the line of parade, on rooftops, balconies and lamp posts to honor the men and women who had kept the nation safe. The military part of the parade was modest and austere. The young people of the armed services marched with open-necked shirts under the hot sun. They were prepared to defend borders practically in their backyards. Women had not been used in combat since the 1948 War of Independence, but they had an important backup role and they looked ready to die for the country, if necessary, alongside the men.

At one point the loudspeakers announced: "The following represents a part of Nasser's contribution to Israel's defense." Then came ten long trailers carrying captured Soviet-made tanks, with the sand of the Sinai still on them. Next came captured Russian field guns, mortars, anti-aircraft guns, armored cars and troop carriers, followed by thirty marching sailors representing the group which had taken the Egyptian destroyer. The Israelis in the grandstand prayed aloud that now the terrorism on her borders would cease and there would be peace.

The Sinai Campaign created serious problems for many persons, including our adopted family, the Cohens. They had managed to obtain a small house in Holon, a brand-new city on the sand dunes near Tel Aviv. Albert, or Avram as he is now called, added a room so that they could all be together on festive occasions. Then the older children were called to army service and had to leave their jobs. The war had lasted only a few days but the army was kept mobilized for some time afterward. The family was unable to meet the house payments with some of the children in the army.

It seemed as though the Cohens might lose the first and only home they had ever owned. Walter went to our bank in Haifa and exchanged sufficient dollars to cover the purchase. That way, if anything happened to us or the family encountered further problems, their home, at least, would be secure.

Mrs. Cohen deserved it. She had married at fourteen, raised eight children of her own and one of her sister's, and was now a widow. She could boast of being the only one in her neighborhood with a debt-free home.

All that Walter and I wanted to give that young country did not equal the rewards Israel constantly offered to us. One example I especially remember is the day we took some guests for a drive around the Sea of Galilee. On our way down to Tiberius we saw a group of school children with their teacher on the road ahead. They had gathered bunches of wildflowers (one of the rare luxuries in a land of hardship) and were dancing and singing as young folk in Israel so often do. It was a lovely sight, and Walter just had to catch it on film.

While the children were posing for him I asked the teacher, "Do you know who is taking the pictures?"

"No," he answered.

"It is Professor Lowdermilk," I said.

The teacher turned and spoke to the children in Hebrew. Instantly and with one accord, they all rushed to my husband and thrust their flowers into his arms, calling greetings and thanks in Hebrew. Walter was deeply touched by this spontaneous gesture.

CHAPTER 21
RETIRING ——— AGAIN? (1957)

By July, 1957, Walter had reached his sixty-ninth birthday. After years of strenuous overseas work, he was finally retiring. We were sad to leave our "eagle's nest" on Mount Carmel but, as Walter had often said, the young Israelis were so keen they "worked him out of a job." Now his task was complete. The men he had trained to take over the School of Agricultural Engineering were competent. The money had been raised for the new building and a superb administrator selected. The new Dean would be Dr. Nathan Buras, the Tel Aviv sabra of whom Walter was so proud, the school's first graduate student and Ph.D. There was no doubt in Walter's mind that all would go well.

There were many farewell parties. After the last one, Walter and I walked out onto our balcony still feeling the glow of pleasure that comes from being with good friends. Standing under the stars, we talked of all the places we had been during our forty years together.

"What experience has been most rewarding to you, Walter?" I asked him.

"Israel," he said without hesitation. I agreed. Hand-in-hand we went back inside for our last night in the house where we had been so happy.

A large group of friends saw us off at the Lydda Airport. As the plane lifted us above the Holy Land, the tiny struggling young democracy of Israel lay like a map beneath us, still beset by problems, but vibrant.

We flew to Rome. Walter delivered his report to FAO headquarters and we made final preparations to return home to California for good.

While at the hotel, we received a phone call. Dr. de Vajda, Chief of FAO's Division of Waters for Irrigation, told Walter he was just the man for a project in Yugoslavia which would coordinate the work being done on the Cetina River. They wanted him to establish a "Little TVA" in the limestone region of the Dalmation Coast. The task would embrace the fields of forestry, soils science, grazing, and hydrology, including drainage, irrigation and control of storm waters and erosion. In Yugoslavia, no one had attempted to consolidate all these in one conservation project. Dr. de Vajda said the task called for several men, but if Walter agreed to undertake it, he would only need to send one man--Walter.

Walter was excited by this unusual challenge. Besides, we had never been behind the Iron Curtain. Once again, the idea of retirement flew out of his mind.

We left for Belgrade so that Walter could be briefed by government officials before proceeding to the Cetina river basin. There we were given a suite in a fine hotel where we met Mr. Gurman, an American official who had the job of distributing $1 billion worth of American foodstuffs in Yugoslavia. "I stayed in the same suite as yours," he told us, "and I was sure that it was bugged, but I could never discover how or where."

That season was the hottest weather on record and we spent a great deal of time in our room, always wondering just how we were being overheard. For fun we interspersed our conversations with Chinese sentences, just to give Big Brother's translator a bad time. When we checked out of the hotel to move to the town of Split, I remembered I had left an earring on the bathroom window sill. I dashed back, opened the door, and there, on a ladder, was a startled workman with the ceiling light fixture off and the nice little "bug" in his hand. He climbed down the ladder and sped down the hall as though being chased by a wild animal. We had many a good laugh afterward thinking of the translator trying to decipher our Chinese.

We traveled through the heartland of Yugoslavia and saw its farm families at work. In Israel we'd come to know the young people as the singingest, dancingest, whistlingest young people we'd ever known, even under conditions of hardship. In Yugoslavia we rarely saw anyone even smiling. People did not stop and talk to one another on the street. They walked briskly, alone on their way. No one was actually ragged, but clothes were patched, and sometimes the patches were patched. We were told that rents, movies and plays were cheap and government subsidized, as was transportation, but everything else was expensive.

About three percent of the people were members of the Communist Party. They had the power of life and death over the other 97 percent. All businesses employing three or more people were government-run. Cash, bank accounts, buildings and homes had been confiscated and owners given back one to three rooms to live in, according to the size of the family. No one dared complain.

"Walter," I observed one day, "we can easily tell whether people belong to the three percent or the ninety-seven percent by the way they act. The latter look both ways before answering questions to see if anyone nearby can hear."

We did obtain a lot of political information from Yugoslavian citizens, but it came only when we were out in the field, often sitting on a stone wall overlooking the area, where no eyes could see and no ears could hear.

In 1957, Yugoslavia as a whole had a literacy rate of more than eighty percent, yet the average yearly income was only $294. "It is sad to see such fine people caught up in the net of poverty," Walter remarked. "They are courageous, proud and hospitable and they work hard from dawn to dark for an annual income that would bring feelings of lethargy and hopelessness to most other peoples." This surely accounted, in part, for their somber demeanor.

Here again, we were grieved to read in the landscape the tragic story of man's abuse and misuse of natural resources. The mountain slopes were overpopulated and the lands grossly overgrazed. Most of the soils had been washed away, leaving the glaring limestone rocks of the karst landscape exposed. During the winter rains the lowlands became swampy and produced only sedge grasses of little nutritional value for the herds. We saw neither farm mechanization nor rural electrification and almost no irrigation. Farm families (65 percent of the population) were very poor.

Walter's first job was to make both officials and farmers aware that it was possible to stop a certain amount of erosion and that some sections could be restored by reforestation. He would work with various Government departments three days a week in Split, and on other days would drive twenty miles over the mountains to Sinj from where he would work forty miles up and down the Cetina River. He made a tremendous hit with the farmers in this valley. Besides being clearly competent, he openly recognized that farmers are a country's number one asset, and he treated them with respect.

In his first general discussions with the Government groups together, Walter discovered that the Cetina River project was not to produce electricity for the Yugoslavians of the area as he had assumed, but was intended as a profitable export to Italy.

"What!" Walter exclaimed in alarm. "Do you mean to say that you plan to sell the electricity to Italy and deprive your own farm population of the benefits of their own resources? Think what it would mean to your farm women to have washing machines and electric irons and lights for night reading and sewing. And for the men to increase their production using machinery. Don't deny your own farm families a better way of life while you make money from their own river!"

Walter's persuasiveness won over the government, and I rejoiced that his efforts would bring about an easier life for the Yugoslavians who were struggling in a way that

Americans had not since Colonial days nearly 200 years before.

Meantime, in Split, I was very busy keeping Walter's letters and notes up to date and preparing his final report. There was scarcely time to enjoy our Park Hotel near the beach. I had a good test of what it was like without social contacts. Although we had found English-speaking people everywhere else we had been, here the language barrier was complete. I could not understand the radio, newspapers, menus or ordinary conversation. Once in awhile, though, we received some 'communication' in an indirect way. One thing I learned was that people talked about Walter and me as "that loving old American couple." On our evening stroll we always walked arm-in-arm or hand-in-hand along the cobblestone streets.

When the Cetina River plan was completed, Walter called in officials from all the involved government departments and invited some of the farmers from the river valley to hear his report and to discuss the plan he proposed. It was quite an experience; in Yugoslavia the official view was that farmers were too ignorant to be included in the conferences. But Walter made no secret of respecting the farmer's experience and knowledge; he asked their opinions and included them in discussion of the details. Everybody was given the opportunity to say something. Walter's water and landuse plan was accepted unanimously and the government immediately began to implement it.

Before leaving for America, we went to Sinj for the annual celebration of the historic Serbian victory over the Turks 400 years ago. The people dressed in national costume, banners and streamers were flying, and the young men raced their finest horses, carrying long pole-like spears. Sitting with the officials in the grandstand, we enjoyed seeing the generally somber people being carefree and happy--for this day, anyway.

The next morning we were due to leave by ship for Dubrovnik at 6:30. We arrived at the dock at 5:30 am and were surprised to find a number of officials with whom

Walter had worked. They and their wives were waiting alongside the ship in the dawn light to bid us goodbye. One woman gave me an heirloom that had been in her family for 400 years--a large pistol, inlaid with silver, that had actually been used against the Turkish invaders. Naturally I protested, but she and her husband insisted that we have it. Even more touching, the wives told me how their husbands had said that Walter Lowdermilk had been the most democratic, understanding consultant who had ever come to them.

The day after our arrival in New York we bought a new car to drive west. It was the first time we had traveled across America alone together, not rushing to keep a schedule. Our son and daughter were both raising families of their own and we were, at last, starting out on the adventure of retirement--a beautiful prospect at ages 69 and 67.

"I feel young and carefree again," I told Walter as we drove homeward. He felt the same.

As we put the Berkeley house in order, we enjoyed the view of the San Francisco Bay as I'd dreamed we would. But Walter seemed increasingly susceptible to flu and pneumonia in the winter months of 1957, so we went to our desert place in Southern California. Morongo Valley was only a twenty minute drive from Palm Springs. In the exhilarating air and amid the views of Mount San Jacinto and Mount San Gorgonio, we thrived, appreciating the peace and the many forms of desert fauna and flora. Walter sought the quiet to write many of the articles and book chapters which he had promised to do. My days were filled with typing for him, with homemaking, with growing flowers in the desert, and involvement in community affairs. Also, I was not ready to retire and liked the challenge of building more than one home at Morongo Valley on the family's adjoining homesteads. One house we sold later to Al and Mary Rose Black, so they could be near us.

After a while, we realized that our peaceful valley was not as peaceful as we had thought. There were problems that needed solving and some of the residents did not get along together. To foster united action on issues important to community progress, Walter spearheaded the formation of a Property Owners' Association. He was promptly elected chairman while some people were still asking, "Who's Lowdermilk?"

Before long we had more than 400 members in the Association. People came forward to offer their talents. Most of the settlers lived on small pensions, so we did what we could for each other. Life had something of a pioneer flavor. New land was constantly being opened up for development, and we had many local celebrations like the community gatherings of pioneer days.

The Morongo Valley Chamber of Commerce voted to have Walter work out its charter and by-laws. In the desert, one problem was water. At our end of the valley water had to be hauled in trucks to our homes and stored in tanks to service our modern appliances and us.

Knowing that Walter was a hydrologist, the Association members said to my husband one day, "Since you have done so much for water development in other countries, how about locating water for us?"

Walter then went about the job of finding water for upper Morongo Valley. He spent hours sitting atop a small hill near the mouth of Little Morongo Canyon at the edge of its outwash fan, studying the geology! The canyon extends up Mount Gorgonio to an altitude of 8,000 feet. During winter rains or melting snows, flood waters pour down the stream bed to the west of the hill as they have for centuries and disgorge great boulders. The east side of the hill was covered by an alluvial fan from another canyon, and Walter found no visible evidence that there had ever been a streambed there. But he studied further and after several weeks he had some answers. We called in our neighbors and he gave them the report:

"Over the centuries, that alluvial fan has grown and pushed the surface stream bed over to its present location on the west side of the hill. Morongo Canyon's ancient stream bed and drainage lie underground to the east of that hill. If my geology is correct, they lie under a corner of our land.

We can dig into the ancient stream bed and catch the canyon's underground water."

The neighbors were fascinated. Soon the whole valley
was excited. However, it became obvious that there would be
no other source of money for the job but our own. So we
decided to put our life-savings on the line and Walter hired a
well-digger. Calculating from levels at the lower end of the
valley, he and Walter estimated that they would find water at
185 feet and made the contract for 250 feet. But at 250 feet
there was still no water and the well-digger wanted to quit.

Our savings were gone and if we were to go on drilling we
would have to borrow money to do so. Walter left the
decision up to me. Some friends from outside thought we
were fools for risking so much money on our own, but I
refused to accept the possibility of having spent so much
without finding water. There was still an option open to us.

"Let's sell our Telephone stock and a few other things,
and borrow," I said. "There's too much at stake to stop now."

We did, and people kept coming by to see the progress.
Some people obviously felt sorry for us. The suspense was
agonizing. Walter would scarcely come in for a meal. The
loud jarring noises of the drill continued day after day. At
275 feet, then 300 feet, there were still only dry boulders. It
took ten days of racking pounding for the rig to pound its way
through just one fourteen-foot-thick rock, at a cost of over
$67 a day. We had been digging for four months!

Suddenly one afternoon the drill burst through the rock
and artesian water gushed twenty feet up into the well. That
was Walter's ancient underground stream bed. After another
thirty feet they hit the aquifer, and the water shot out into
the air. I thought of the words of Isaiah.

> I will open rivers in high places, and fountains in
> the midst of the valleys; I will make the
> wilderness a pool of water, and the dry land
> springs of water.
>
> Isaiah 41:18

Our jubilation was tempered by the necessity of borrowing more money for the 20-horsepower pump necessary to test the well. Once this was installed, however, tests proved that the well would supply good water for the needs of 900 people at a rate of 150 gallons per person per day!

As Walter and I lay talking together one night, with the winter moonlight coming through our windows, we realized we hadn't considered how to share this wonderful resource fully with our neighbors. Then, by putting bits and pieces of people's remarks together we concluded that the reason no one else had offered to help us was that they thought we were drilling a well for profit!

Next morning we invited everyone to the first of numerous meetings of property owners to organize a water cooperative. We donated the land on which the well was located. Then others came forward; a lawyer gave his legal services. We got a low-interest Federal Housing Administration loan of $40,000 as a nonagricultural rural community. As a result, people at our end of the valley got 5,000 gallons of water per month for just four dollars. Anything above this cost only fifty cents per thousand gallons. Everyone was assessed five dollars a month toward repayment of the FHA loan. Eventually we were reimbursed for most of our expenses. The organization of the co-op and the ongoing administration brought the valley people together in a way that had not happened before. The next time I went down to our little Community Church for women's meetings, I was received much more warmly.

Our Community Church had no bell and it was unlikely that a congregation like ours would ever be able to afford one. Then I learned during a trip to the Seattle World's Fair with my sisters that the church built by my grandfather in eastern Washington had been torn down and my cousin had its beautiful 600-pound bell. At my request he gave it to our Morongo church. Walter and I paid the cost of transportation and saw to it that a steel spire was erected to hold the bell. Once again, others were inspired to join in by contributing some of the labor.

The bell was rung for the first time on Easter morning. Walter went down to the church very early and began ringing it so that its peals could be heard in the cool, clear spring air, far and wide, even as far as our mountainside at the upper end of the valley, to celebrate the message of Easter.

After four winters in the south, we decided to return to Berkeley permanently. Leaving the vast grandeur of the desert, we settled once again for year 'round living among the tall trees, green hills, and magnificent views of San Francisco Bay. The University of California Geography Department made Walter an honorary Associate Professor, which made us part of the campus "family." I joined the faculty wives Writers' Club, for my daughter was urging me to write up my Chinese experiences for the grandchildren. We renewed contacts in the University, Forest Service, Soil Conservation Service, and Trinity Church.

My husband, an early riser, always enjoyed getting his own breakfast, then inspecting the garden. At about eight o' clock each morning he appeared at my bedside with a cup of coffee and a rose, or a "little dancing girl" as he called the double ruffled fuschias. They looked like ballet dancers with stamens forming spindly legs. "For my precious girl," he would say. Now we were living "the last of life for which the first was made." Contentment and happiness were ours.

At this time quite unexpectedly, Walter returned to his first love, forestry. Two old friends, Ralph Chaney and Newton Drury of the Save the Redwoods League, came to see him with a tragic story. They told him that more than 500 of the giant redwood trees in the Bull Creek Rockefeller Forest of Northern California--many of them a thousand or more years old--had been lost in the flood of 1956. They asked him to devise preventive measures against such losses in the future.

Walter was alarmed for this national treasure and wanted to help, but he frankly doubted that the young engineers would listen to an old man in his 70's. However, he agreed to try. As was usual, he examined the site of the damage, then looked for the cause. Directly above the forest was a sickening sight: lumber companies had clear-cut the mountainsides so that not a tree remained to hold the soil. There were only black stumps to show man's mindless squandering of a precious resource.

Heavy rains poured off the naked slopes, carrying a burden of rock and forest debris, and rampaged through the peaceful redwood forests below, undercutting the curved river banks. "How are the mighty fallen," Walter said, quoting King David 2 Samuel 1:27 when he saw how the giant trees with their shallow root systems had been toppled.

The young engineers admired Walter's ability and eagerly followed his leadership in straightening and rebuilding the river banks. They used steel nets to hold reinforcement boulders in place which also made the banks look natural. Walter also suggested that the Save the Redwood League buy out the little town of Bull Creek Flats above their redwood forest. Walter felt sure it would be smashed in the next flood by a river of gravel disgorged from Cuni Creek. This was done. The inhabitants were grateful to have a buyer and were doubly grateful when the next flood came the following year and almost buried the former town. There was no loss of life or property and only minimal damage to the forest.

It was a wonderful time to be alive and to exchange views with the neighbors and visitors from abroad who came frequently now that we were settled back in Berkeley. We commonly gathered around our dining room table where I always served a "high tea" with all my most beautiful dishes and flowers and plenty of good things to nibble on, and where I could hear people best. From the host's chair, Walter would stimulate our guests to share their experiences and observations.

Some visitors helped bring back the past. Especially rewarding were the ones that re-enforced our belief in the value of helping the people, especially young people. Among these was Yukap, son of Clarence Hahn, the young Korean student I met on the ship from China in 1921 and brought home to my family. Clarence had returned to Korea with a Ph.D. in the mid-1920's and became a democratic influence by teaching at a Methodist-supported college, founding his country's first public library, translating important Western literature into Korean, and running an educational radio program. We had corresponded for years, until we suddenly lost contact after 1950.

Then Clarence's son Yukap, (whom he had wanted to follow in his footsteps), wrote us a letter explaining that his father had been killed in 1951. He pleaded with us to help him get to this country. We were just leaving for Israel and Walter said, "No, we have already sponsored two people. We just can't take on another right now." Later Yukap wrote me again, this time while I was on a trip to California. He told me that he had tried writing everywhere for help to get to the United States. I was his only hope to get an American education.

This was the one and only time I would ever disobey Walter; but thinking of how helping Yukap's father, Clarence, had led to his doing so much good for his country, I wrote and told Yukap to come. I helped him, as I had with his father, to apply for scholarships and a job. He did brilliantly and eventually became a professor at Yale University. In 1964, he brought his wife and family to visit us. At last we heard the details of what had happened to his father, Clarence.

"First, Father's democratic ideas brought him into conflict with Korea's Japanese rulers," Yukap told us. "He was arrested on trumped-up charges and tortured. Fortunately the liberation of Korea at the end of World War II saved his life."

"Father returned home," Yukap continued, "and resumed his role as educator. He became a leading exponent of democracy. Then the communists infiltrated South Korea and friends found out that he was targeted for annihilation, so they helped him escape to the countryside. One night he had such a longing to see his family that he disguised himself as a common laborer and slipped back into our home, not realizing that our gateman was a communist informer. When he left my mother about 3:00 am he was captured. We never heard from him again." There was silence at the table as Yukap concluded.

In addition to old friends, we were making new friends in Berkeley among the young as well. A "Chicano" youth named Edel Alejandre, born in the United States of Mexican parents, came to work for us weekends in the garden. One day his father, in broken English and with tears in his eyes, came to me. Edel had dropped out of school and had taken a job at the Marine base.

"I left Mexico and worked hard to give my son a better life than I had," he said. "Will you please try to get my boy back in school?"

All summer I pounded away at Edel on the theme that if he threw away his chance at an education he would always be known as "just a Mexican laborer," but, if he went on through school, the sky was the limit for him.

That fall, Edel went back and made up his work in school. Wanting to lift his ego and give him prestige before the other students, I had him take to his history class some of my choicest Chinese things, most of which are now in a museum. Edel had seen me showing them to guests from time to time and felt he could give a lecture on Chinese arts to his class. (I wish I could have heard it!) I was overjoyed when he decided to go on to college and become a teacher and later when he was chosen "teacher of the year" in the county.

Walter and I both treated him like a son and encouraged his participation in our activities. Edel began to take an interest in poor Mexican families, and I often drove with him to take the food and clothing he had collected to the destitute. Just before Christmas he discovered that the family of one of his Mexican students was living in a shack by a swamp. They had nothing but two blankets for four people and they slept on the floor. Edel at once went to work telephoning his friends until he was able to drag from their attics and storerooms, mattresses, bedsteads, bedding, furniture, clothing and toys--even a small Christmas tree--for the family. All these he delivered to the astonished family Christmas Eve. Then, exhausted, he stopped by to see us and flung himself into a big chair.

"This has been the happiest Christmas of my life," he said. Edel had true compassion, and his willingness to act on behalf of others in need made us proud.

About that time, two graduate students from Greece appeared at our door asking whether we could possibly make room for them in our home. They somehow appealed to us. We agreed and so began another mutually rewarding series of relationships.   We started taking in college students as roomers--students of many nationalities. We found them to be not only congenial young people, but intelligent, respectful, and helpful as we were beginning to be faced with the problems of old age. And we, in turn, helped them all we could.   One roomer in particular, a forestry student named David Whitman, has been special to me. After two years in the Peace Corps, David found it impossible to find a job in his field with Forest Service budget reductions. With my help he learned what prayer and faith can accomplish; he has become Concert Coordinator at the University of California in Berkeley, and is a close friend.

Every now and then a delightful change altered the rhythm of our days. By 1959, the Israelis had developed their agriculture to the point where they felt ready to share what they had learned with other countries, particularly those of the Third World. Israel was solving for itself many of the problems and handicaps faced by other nations in Asia and Africa. When Israel organized the world's first International Farmers' Convention, and Walter was invited to come and was asked to lead the United States Delegation.

It was touching to see the pride the Israelis showed in their country's progress, and the warmth with which they welcomed the delegates to their farms and their homes. The developing nations seemed to reach out toward Israel as to a big brother.

Later, when the Convention meetings were over and we were sightseeing with delegates in Nazareth, Walter said suddenly, "I feel miserable. I'll go into this cafe and drink some hot tea. You go on with the others. Enjoy yourselves. I'll join you later at the bus."

It was later than planned when our bus arrived at the hotel in Haifa. Because there was not enough room for everybody at the delegates' main hotel, Walter gave up our room to others. With some friends, we continued south to a Tel Aviv hotel. When we arrived, Walter still did not feel well enough to join us for dinner, so he went straight to our cottage. It was Friday night, shabbat eve, and we were reluctant to disturb a doctor.

When I awakened the next morning, I saw how flushed Walter looked and I took his temperature. It was 104. Startled, I called a doctor, who immediately ordered an ambulance.

"We are fourteen hours too late," the doctor told me gravely. "Dr. Lowdermilk has pneumonia."

News of Walter's illness spread rapidly. President Ben-Zvi was deeply concerned and phoned the hospital. The head nurse said that the President told them: "You cannot, you must not let that man die."

Israeli radio issued frequent reports on Walter's condition. I knew that prayers for his recovery were coming from every part of the nation. As I left the hospital the second night the doctors told me that Walter's heart was failing. Distraught with fear and grief, I returned to our hotel cottage. Sometime in the night, I awakened from a restless sleep and saw the door open. In the doorway there appeared the white-clad figure of a hospital attendant. He spoke to me quite clearly:

"I have come to tell you that you can go to sleep now, for the Lord has taken over and your husband will recover."

"Oh," I answered him. "I'm so relieved. If the Lord has taken over then I know my husband will get well."

Then the figure quietly shut the door and I fell into a deep sleep. The next morning I awoke, relieved and thankful, and hurried to the hospital. Walter still looked weak and sick, but he was alive and with each hour he became stronger. We were finally allowed to transfer him to the home of our friend, Rifka Aaronsohn, where he recovered very rapidly.

The Bible tells how Jehovah, the God of Israel, often sent special messengers to deliver messages to certain people. I believe God does; I feel He sent a divine messenger with a divine message for me that night in Tel Aviv.

Five years later--in 1964--we came to Israel again. Then, the water works to irrigate the Negev desert region (which were developed from Walter's plan of 1939) were ready to go into operation. The Israelis called Walter the "Father of the Israel Master Water Plan," and they invited us to be present for the inauguration. The waters of the upper Jordan were to be held in the Sea of Galilee--700 feet below sea level--as a natural reservoir, then pumped into an artificial holding basin by siphoning across a steep canyon and pumping up to an altitude which would give enough pressure to send the water southward through a grid of pipes and canals. Downstream dams would hold water for late spring irrigation.

We were taken deep inside the mountain to see the water pipes, which were nine feet in diameter. Walter was allowed to see the engineers turn on the great pumps to start the flow of water. The prophecy of making the desert bloom would soon become a reality. The thrill of the entire population was in the air, as they realized that after 2,000 years their state was not only a political reality, but could become self-sustaining.

A few days later came the groundbreaking ceremony for the Lowdermilk School of Agricultural Engineering at the Technion in Haifa. There, on the slope of Mount Carmel, with his white hair blowing in the breeze, Walter broke the first ground by pulling an electric switch which sent a cloud of red earth and rocks high into the air. The crowd cheered.

"It is wonderful to dream dreams," he said to the Israelis, "to work hard and then to see them come true. Your country now has the most complete inventory of lands of any nation. You know how many acres you have for food-growing, how many can be irrigated, how many reseeded to the nutritious ancient grasses now raised in your grass nurseries. You have put in thousands of miles of broad-based terraces. You have de-stoned and put into cultivation countless dunams of land. You have installed many water-saving devices and water-spreading dams for watering stock and erosion control. Flood waters are now being poured back into wells which were overpumped. You have re-forested many of the rocky hills."

"The projects I suggested in 1939 have nearly all been implemented." He paused momentarily and I knew he was thinking of the unfinished part of the plan--dropping Mediterranean Sea water into the Dead Sea for power. He understood this plan was not "politically feasible." How sad it was, he said, that the poor Arab farmers of Jordan would not share the benefits of such a project because their leaders refused to participate.

Then he smiled and told the audience, "I feel that my own biography is written in the lands and waters of Israel."

After this momentous month in Israel, we once again headed for home, happy at the prospect of seeing our children and grandchildren. Skip was rising in the U.S. Foreign Service, specializing in communications. He and Ina now had two little daughters--Sharon, born in Israel, and Karen, born in Thailand. They were stationed in Bangkok, but would all be on home leave in Washington D.C. by the time we got there.

Westher, besides being a wife and mother to three lively, promising youngsters--Walter, Alison and Carl--was maintaining an active interest in environmental matters and in the work of her husband, Wilmot (Bill) Hess, a leader in the National Aeronautics and Space Administration. Before he was forty, Bill received the 1963 Arthur S. Fleming Award of the U.S. Junior Chamber of Commerce as one of 10 outstanding young men in Government. They lived in Silver Spring, Maryland.

CHAPTER 22
WALTER (1969-74)

For years Walter had wanted to write his memoirs, but life had been too full for him to give the time it required. Fortunately, the Oral History Department of the Bancroft Library at the University of California decided to record for future researchers Walter's 50 years of experience in forestry and soil and water conservation. The project, funded by the Water Resources Center of the University of California, was to be done at our home. Walter said he felt that this was one of the finest things that had ever happened to him.

However, what I heard through the partly-opened door was dismaying. It was obvious that no matter how capable the interviewer, she could not know what questions to ask about Walter's work. So I typed sixty pages of questions about his work in one country, and submitted them to Willa Baum, head of the Oral History Department. She was delighted and asked me to continue for the entire project, which I did. I tried to anticipate the questions researchers might ask 100 years from now. Thus, the interviewer had the background, in advance, about Walter's activities in each country.

When the taping was finished, Walter's memoirs were published in an 800 page, two-volume set. Copies were made for research libraries in the U.S. (including Roosevelt's Hyde Park Library), the U.S. Soil Conservation Service in

Washington, D.C., and the Lowdermilk School of Agricultural Engineering in Israel. When it was finished, Walter carried one of the volumes around the house with him. "This would never have been done if it had not been for you," he said, and he kissed me. I felt adequately thanked for whatever was my part and returned the kiss, for he had made my life a joyous one.

To celebrate the publication of the memoirs, the Bancroft Library and the Berkeley Hadassah planned a big reception at the Magnes Museum in Berkeley. It was the summer of 1969, close to Walter's 81st birthday. A few days before the event he suffered a small brain hemorrhage. He seemed very tired and I wanted to cancel the affair, but Walter insisted he was able to go. That day, his smile with the twinkling eyes was the same, but his speech had been slightly confused. Yet he seemed physically strong enough to stand in a receiving line, smile and shake hands, so we went. He was pleased and honored by the affection and respect lavished on him.

Three weeks later, though, he was hospitalized. Additional strokes left Walter mentally impaired. The Berkeley hospital, unable to care for him, gave me a deadline for transferring him elsewhere.

Westher, who had come out to help, and I phoned every nursing and convalescent home in the Bay Area, but all of them refused to accept his type of case. The only exceptions were places either unaffordable, or so bad that it would be unthinkable to have Walter there. After each visit or call I would hang up the phone, sobbing, and then try again. "How could no one want this wonderful man?" I asked myself.

I prayed for a miracle. Then, the day before I was required to remove Walter from the hospital, a friend phoned me and in conversation asked if Walter was a veteran. When I answered, "Yes, and in very high standing," he said, "The Veterans Hospital in Palo Alto is closing some wards and dismissing patients, but with some real pull you might get your husband accepted."

I phoned our friend, Dr. Rogers of Palo Alto, who immediately contacted the hospital director. "Tell Mrs. Lowdermilk to bring her husband here tomorrow morning," he was told. My gratitude knew no bounds. I knew now that Walter would have the best of care for the remainder of his life. The following day we drove to Palo Alto. After going through the red tape of admission, we entered the geriatric ward dining hall where the nurses and patients were having their afternoon tea.

"Oh look, Walter," I said. "They are giving you a reception."

He stepped into the room graciously and accepted the punch and a cookie with such charm he might have been at the White House. He began to talk about the land problems in Africa, and I could see by the hostess' kind expression that she understood.

The psychiatrist in charge of the ward was Dr. Burian, a Viennese Jewish refugee. If Walter had been his own father, he could not have been treated with more love and respect. Even so, it was hard for me to leave Walter alone in a strange place, even a good place. Fortunately I could cry, and cry I did. I sobbed all the way to the freeway entrance and then prayed to be able to drive safely back to Berkeley.

Knowing that Walter was now in safe hands, I finally was able to listen to what my own body was telling me. Almost immediately I had an attack of severe diverticulitis and was hospitalized for major surgery. Mary Rose came home from Israel to look after me and Walter, and for several weeks she made the weekly trip to Palo Alto to see him and report to me and the family until I was well enough to go again myself. Westher was driving across the country to move to a new home and job in Colorado with her husband but she came to California to help me home from the convalescent hospital.

Then, each week, for almost five years, I drove the 125-mile round trip to Palo Alto. Walter's appetite was good, so I always took a picnic lunch with everything he loved, from soup to nuts. Sometimes a friend would help me take him to Foothill Park or to a nearby Chinese restaurant where they knew Walter and treated him with typical Chinese respect for the elderly.

Week in and week out, friends and family shared with me in visiting my beloved. My prayers for Walter's easy passing to his reward went unanswered, but he did not suffer. He would walk, and talk some, and he seemed to know me.

Meanwhile, there was much to do. Eighty-five cartons of soil samples, books, papers and thousands of photographs were stored at home. Walter never could bear to part with them. Now I faced the job of sorting it all alone. Knowing the material was valuable and should be shared, I made up ten two-volume sets of collateral material for his memoirs and shipped them to the libraries and institutions which housed them. By sending scientific books to the Lowdermilk School at the Technion in Israel, I felt we were continuing his work.

During the Yom Kippur War in 1973 I told Walter that Egypt and Israel were again at war. His response was so typical of him: "Oh, let's go out to Israel at once and volunteer our services." Fortunately, Israel didn't need Walter and me.

Years before, we had intended to spend our fiftieth wedding anniversary in Israel. Now it wasn't possible to go together, but I received a gift of a trip from our dear friend Samuel Lepkovsky. In 1972, Westher, Bill and their three teenagers joined me and we met with the new president, Zalman Shazar. He knew that Bill Hess had been NASA's chief scientist in the Apollo project landing the first man on the moon. Shazar pointed to a piece of moon rock on his desk sent to him by the President of the United States.

"Did you send us such a small piece of the moon because we are such a small country?" he wanted to know, smiling.

"No, Mr. President," Bill assured him. "To tell you the truth, there was one big rock that happened to fall down and get smashed into many pieces, all about the same size as yours, and a similar piece was sent to each country in the world."

I thought of how Walter would have chuckled at this little incident and was overcome momentarily with sadness to be without him on this trip. He would have been thrilled to see all the progress made by the Israelis, and to teach his grandchildren to "read the landscape."

How he would have enjoyed Jerusalem, reunited in 1967. What a transformation! In the Six-Day War, Israeli soldiers had meticulously avoided destruction of any holy place. Construction was going on at a fast rate as the government made the Old City a healthy place for its inhabitants by installing sewers, running water, electricity, and other modern facilities. The Old City walls were clean and surrounded by gardens. The ancient Jewish Quarter, leveled by Jordan after the truce of 1948, was being lovingly recreated. Everything was being done with consideration for both the historical and spiritual atmosphere.

What an indescribable thrill to see Jerusalem, the capital of Israel for a thousand years, united and restored by the People of the Book. We mingled there with visitors from the world over, even from Moslem countries, still self-declared enemies of Israel.

Back home I resumed my weekly visits to Walter. He enjoyed hearing about the trip, but his comprehension was dwindling and he was in a wheelchair now. Although instinctively polite and always appreciative, I could see he was slipping further away. His voice became very low at times. With my poor hearing and no hearing aid, it was hardly possible for me to understand what he said. He no longer seemed to know I was his wife.

Now I always visited him alone. After spending most of the day with Walter it hurt me to see him locked back in his ward. To comfort myself during the ride back to Berkeley, I would begin singing hymns. I devised a list of 50 titles I wrote on cardboard to hold near the steering wheel. Those inspiring words, familiar from childhood, made the trip bearable.

Toward the end of April, 1974, the doctor called to tell me that Walter would soon be gone, that only a few days were left to him. I prepared to drive down to be with him during those last precious moments. I was startled to see that a yucca plant in our front yard that had been about the same size for well over 40 years had shot up a stalk four feet tall. It was one of three yucca plants Walter had rescued from a bulldozer at the San Dimas Hydrologic Experiment Station in 1932 and brought home to plant in our Berkeley desert garden. Within two years a pair of them had sent up ten-foot stalks and bloomed magnificently and died, but the third never grew at all.

Then, from the time of the doctor's call, it grew at least a foot a day. On May 6, when Walter went peacefully to heaven, the plant's stalk was about fifteen feet tall and dripping with thousands of beautiful, creamy, bell-like flowers. I accepted this as Walter's going away present to me. The flowers lasted the entire month, until the day I took Walter's ashes to the family niche in the Pasadena mausoleum. Then the blossoms faded almost overnight.

After our fifty-two years together, Walter was gone, but his presence surrounded me. His spirit was no longer confined to a fragile body, but was free at last to soar to new heights. Often I went into the library, looked at his picture, and wept. Then I would feel his presence and I seemed to hear his voice saying to me, "Oh, Ina May, do not grieve. I am so happy. Heaven is wonderful." Then I would breathe a prayer of thankfulness.

The world quickly learned of Walter's death. Notices were published in the overseas editions of Time and Newsweek magazines, as well as newspapers and magazines throughout the United States. A long article appeared in the New York Times. Telegrams, cables and cards arrived in great numbers. The California Christian Committee for Israel undertook to sponsor the planting of a Memorial forest of 10,000 trees in Israel. Jews and Christians from across America joined in this tribute.

Before long, a beautiful letter came from President Katzir of Israel saying that his nation wanted to give national recognition to Walter's death with a commemorative service in the new President's Residence in Jerusalem. He invited me to come.

Westher and Mary Rose accompanied me to Israel. It was a warm, friendly affair, crowded with old friends and officials with whom Walter had worked. Among the speakers who recalled Walter's contribution was Eliahu Elath, Israel's first Ambassador to the United States. He told us that when the partition of Palestine was to come before the United Nations in 1947, he and Chaim Weizmann, later Israel's first President, went to see President Truman on behalf of an independent Jewish state.

"We knew that Britain's Prime Minister, Ernest Bevin, was determined to deny Israel the Negev desert," he said, "but we realized the region was crucial to the new state for settling the overwhelming numbers of refugees expected to pour in. So we explained to President Truman, Dr. Lowdermilk's plan to irrigate the Negev desert with waters from the north that had always evaporated in the Dead Sea and did no one any good. President Truman listened carefully, then assured us that he would see to it that Israel got the northern Negev. He kept his promise." Ambassador Elath said "Walter Lowdermilk will go down in Jewish history for his many contributions to the development of the State of Israel."

Two years later, in 1976, funds had been raised to complete the Lowdermilk Memorial Forest. I went to Israel once more, this time with an Inter-faith Friendship tour of Californians to dedicate the forest. Mrs. Golda Meir met me, Westher and Mary Rose, at the airport reception room with her arms full of flowers. She clasped me in a warm, spontaneous hug. We also had a delightful dinner together where she autographed her autobiography for each of us.

The dedication ceremony was held above the forest site in the Hills of Galilee. The government provided buses to bring friends from as far away as the Negev. The forest site overlooks a portion of the canal bringing water from the north toward the thirsty southland, in accordance with the Lowdermilk Plan. The forest's 10,000 trees will turn the rocky hillside into a green emerald. My family had given an extra $3,500 to provide a beautiful picnic area on the corner by the highway.

Raindrops began to fall as the ceremony drew to a close, and I smiled to myself, remembering how people said that Walter always seemed to bring rain to see erosion in action. I felt he was very close to me as we dedicated his forest.

Why had our hearts been so at home in Israel? For centuries we knew Jews were among those who contributed most to mankind in the arts, sciences and in medicine. But I could not help but share Walter's special gratitude to the Jewish people for restoring the good earth of the Holy Land, especially at a time when a blueprint was so badly needed for the two-thirds of mankind who were emerging from a primitive agriculture to the twentieth century. Israelis were, as Walter called them, "good stewards of the land."

CHAPTER 23
LIFE MOVES ON

It has been fascinating for me to live through these years--the last decade of the nineteenth century and more than eight decades of the twentieth--to observe and to have been a part of these stirring times. The events of this period...mankind's grandest achievements and also greatest problems...shaped the path that Walter and I traveled together.

We shared a long and rich life that included, of course, some tragic times. After all, there is no gain without pain. There were moments, especially in later life, that seemed to be more than I could bear--failing eyesight, curtailed hearing, loneliness for Walter. While we were together, he and I always sought and received divine guidance in our major life decisions. When I was alone, I continued to seek that guidance and I also acted according to a long-engrained family tradition: putting my best foot forward so no one would know the depths of my sorrow or how often I repeated King David's prayer, "Cast me not off in the time of old age. Forsake me not when my strength faileth" (Psalms 71:9).

My two beloved sisters, Winifred and Beatrice, retired to the Episcopal Home in Alhambra, California, dying there at ages 96 and 95. The night after Winifred's death, I suffered a particularly severe attack of heart fibrillation, which had bothered me for so long. I do not know what privileges

Heaven gives to new arrivals, but I do believe that Winifred looked down upon me and asked God to free me from this curse. Never once since then have I had another attack. I am sure that those who leave us demonstrate from Heaven their love and care for us. Winifred comforted me in my illness just as Walter had comforted me in my sorrow.

After each heavy moment, my life has become full again because of the inspiration and joys of my life with young people. With all the laughter and sharing in my life I have no time to grow old, even at ninety-five, and there is no way to measure the rewards of friendship with promising young people. In such I can see Walter's hopes for a better world, and hear another voice:

> For I know the plans I have for you
> They are plans for good and not for evil.
> To give you a future and a hope
> Then shall you call on me and
> I will answer you.

                                                    Jeremiah 29:11

Walter felt his biography was written on the face of the earth--in water, forest and soil conservation. I feel that my biography is etched on people, through personal relationships--helping Walter, teaching children, and caring deeply for family, friends and people across the world, old and young. I treasure the joy of watching the triumphs and successes of those we have been in contact, such as Nathan Buras, the Cohen family in Israel and the U.S., David Whitman, Edel Alejandre and so many others. Over the years we were grateful to be reminded, in various ways, that our work was worthwhile, that the world is a little better place because we passed through.

I began my adult life with Chinese girls and lived ten years in China. Now I am having my last years with mature Chinese women teachers. They are on a cultural exchange program from the Peoples Republic of China, and can tell me about developments there since I left fifty-seven years ago. It pleases me to know that Chinese women have been freed from the curse of footbinding and that they have equality today.

Walter and I often wondered whether his conservation work actually had lasting results in the years that followed our departure with all the changes in China. How thrilling it was, last year, to find in the mail a letter from China, from one of Walter's former colleagues during the Nanking days, Dr. C. C. Chang.

The letter reviews Walter's 1943 lecture and visit to the staff of China's first soil conservation experiment station at Tien Shui, Kansu. Chang asked Walter, upon his return to Washington, to send some drought-resistant American grasses. As usual, Walter did more than was required of him. In addition to grass, he speculated that honeydew melon might do very well in the Lanchow, Kansu, area of China. He thus included some melon seeds along with the grasses to be delivered by Henry Wallace, then Vice-President of the U.S., who was going to China.

Walter was right. Dr. Chang reported that the honeydews proved to be exceptionally popular and became a famous and profitable fruit with "flesh that really tasted like honey and dew."

At the celebration of the experiment station's 40th anniversary in August 1982, a staff member presented "Some Reminiscences of the World Ecologist, Dr. Walter C. Lowdermilk." Chang wrote: "we want to show that the Chinese people of the Loess highlands will long remember what he had done for them and for our soil conservation."

With Walter gone, our dream home with its ever changing views of San Francisco Bay means more to me than ever. I often look out at the redwood tree which I planted as a sapling when we built our Berkeley home more than fifty years ago. Today it is straight and more than 100 feet tall. It has great beauty and strength because it has triumphed over the smog and storms of its life and reached always for the sun. My life, too, found a goal to strive for.

As I look out over the Bay, intervening years seem to evaporate and I see a young couple standing on a mountain overlooking the Pacific Ocean. Walter, the young forester, proposing marriage to the girl who would "never amount to a hill of beans." Surely my cup runneth over.